European Integration Revisited

Progress, Prospects, and U.S. Interests

Michael Calingaert

WestviewPress

A Division of HarperCollins*Publishers*

Copyright © 1996 by Westview Press, Inc., A Division of HarperCollins Publishers, Inc.

Published in 1996 in the United States of America by Westview Press, Inc., 5500 Central Avenue, Boulder, Colorado 80301-2877, and in the United Kingdom by Westview Press, 12 Hid's Copse Road, Cumnor Hill, Oxford OX2 9JJ

A CIP catalog record for this book is available from the Library of Congress.
ISBN 0-8133-2953-1 (hc) — ISBN 0-8133-2954-X (pbk)

The paper used in this publication meets the requirements of the American National Standard for Permanence of Paper for Printed Library Materials Z39.48-1984.

10   9   8   7   6   5   4   3   2   1

European Integration
Revisited

*Published in cooperation with
the National Planning Association's
Global Economic Council,
Washington, D.C.*

Contents

Preface

This book was written at the request and on behalf of the National Planning Association's Global Economic Council (GEC), which deemed it relevant at the midpoint of the 1990s, a decade of radical change and underlying uncertainty, to assess the progress and implications of European integration. The timing is particularly appropriate as the European Union (EU) has entered into a public debate over what has been accomplished and what directions it should take in the future—a debate that will set the stage for the negotiations at the Intergovernmental Conference, beginning in 1996, where the fifteen EU member states will consider possible changes to the structure and operation of the Union. The GEC, whose members are senior business, labor, agricultural, and academic leaders, believes this study will contribute to an understanding not only of recent and prospective developments in Europe but also of their implications for US interests.

The focus of this book is European integration: the successes and failures of efforts in what is now the EU to achieve greater economic and political integration; the prospects for the future; and the implications of present and prospective developments for the United States.

"Integration" is, of course, subject to many different definitions, interpretations, and theories.[1] I have used integration in the general sense of referring to actions, policies, programs, and other activities that the EU member states undertake in a common manner rather than individually. In other words, integration is the process whereby the EU member states operate on a collective, rather than an individual, basis—either as the result of intergovernmental agreement or submission to supranational authority, decision making, or influence exercised by or through the EU institutions.

An enormous amount of published material is now available on developments in the EU, unlike the situation when I wrote my earlier book.[2] However, this book is not based on an exhaustive examination of existing literature. Rather, it draws on official documentation; selected studies and commentaries; personal opinions (based on more than 100 interviews) of a wide variety of participants in and observers of different aspects of the EU's activities and the US-EU relationship; and my own perceptions and opinions, drawn from my observations and experiences during the past six years in Brussels as well as in various circumstances, professional and personal, over much of my adult life.

I should note that I chose not to carry out a detailed survey of the views and experiences of the private sector on the single market program and other aspects of economic integration. To have done so would have extended the research and writing time considerably, rendering it impossible to complete the book at an appropriate time for taking stock of the process of European integration and compounding the problem of keeping up with a moving target. Accordingly, I have used a more selective sampling of the private sector and anecdotal evidence.

A final word. While other books cover specific topics or aspects of European integration in great depth, I have sought to provide an overview, focusing on what I consider to be the most important recent developments and areas of prospective change in integration. For that reason, I have dealt with agriculture in somewhat cursory fashion. Along with the elimination of member states customs duties, the Common Agricultural Policy (CAP) was the base on which European economic integration was built, and it remains an important element of EU economic policy. In addition, the CAP constitutes a central feature of the critically important Franco-German relationship, and agriculture has consistently been a major source of conflict between the United States and the EU. However, agriculture has not been a component of the overall post–1985 integration effort, and no significant developments regarding integration in the agricultural sector have taken place during the 1990s (CAP reform being a separate issue). In any event, European agricultural policy and the US-EU battles over agriculture merit a book in itself, and that I will leave to others.

I have excluded consumer policy as being not directly germaine to integration as well as the EU's research and development programs because they affect the integration process only marginally. I have mentioned regional policy only as an instrument, albeit an important one, for facilitating integration rather than as an element in the integration process. And I have described only in passing the so-called third pillar issues—cooperation among member states on judicial matters and internal affairs. Although this area of activity may develop into a significant component of European integration, it is at the initial stage and, in any case, conceptually and organizationally separable from the other issues treated in this book.

For these and any other lacunae, I apologize.

Finally, a word about nomenclature. Although, as explained in the

"Introduction," the European Community continues to exist as a component of the European Union, it has become commonplace since the Treaty on European Union (the "Maastricht Treaty") came into effect in 1993 to replace all references to the EC with EU. In accordance with that practice, I have used, albeit reluctantly, EU except when referring to events that clearly and exclusively predated the treaty.

Michael Calingaert

Notes

1. For an examination, with extensive references, of the development of integration theory as it relates to the EU, see James A. Caporaso and John T. S. Keeler, "The European Union and Regional Integration Theory," in Carolyn Rhodes and Sonia Mazey, eds., *The State of the European Union*, Vol. 3 (Boulder: Lynne Rienner Publishers/Longman, 1993).

2. Michael Calingaert, *The 1992 Challenge from Europe: Development of the European Community's Internal Market* (Washington: National Planning Association, 1988).

Acknowledgments

I would like to thank the National Planning Association's Global Economic Council—and in particular Richard S. Belous—for having asked me to undertake a study on Europe, thereby forcing me to think about the wide range of developments in the European Union (EU) comprehensively rather than as separate pieces of a puzzle and to draw conclusions about where the process of European integration may be heading.

I am indebted to a vast number of people on both sides of the Atlantic who shared with me their knowledge, experience, and opinions about the EU and the US-EU relationship. This includes officials at the EU institutions (Commission, Council, and Parliament), US government agencies in Washington, US diplomatic missions in Europe (in particular the staff of the US Mission to the European Union) who were most indulgent with an ex-colleague, the private sector (companies and representative organizations), media, and academics. That I do not list them individually—having promised anonymity—does not detract from my gratitude.

I am particularly grateful to those who read and provided many useful comments (and corrections) on my manuscript: Richard Belous, Daniel Calingaert, Michael Ely, Charles Grant, and Riccardo Perissich. Desmond Dinan not only offered a detailed critique of the manuscript, but also provided invaluable advice and assistance throughout the process of writing and made available the facilities of the library of the Center for European Integration Studies at George Mason University. In addition, a number of people reviewed individual sections of the manuscript, identifying errors of fact and interpretation, and to them I offer my sincere thanks. Needless to say, I did not always accept these views, and I alone bear responsibility for the final text.

Finally, I owe a special debt to my wife, Efrem, who encouraged me to undertake this study, urged me to persevere on those frequent occasions when my efforts flagged, and accommodated to the many inconveniences my work entailed with patience and understanding.

Michael Calingaert

Introduction

The underlying theme of Western European history since the end of World War II has been the efforts to bring the nation states closer together economically and politically. The motivating force behind integration attempts has varied over time. The original rationale was to prevent the countries of Western Europe from going to war with each other. The peoples of Western Europe came increasingly to believe that they could better achieve their aspirations by merging some of their national prerogatives into collective forms of activity. While joint security concerns were centered in the North Atlantic Treaty Organization (NATO), economic and political cooperation was the focus of the European Community (EC), which was formed in 1958 with six members and progressively expanded to twelve by the mid–1980s and to fifteen in 1995.[1]

The history of the EC has been characterized alternatively by forward movement and by retrogression, as the member states have dealt with changing economic and political situations and with changing views regarding the desired structure and content of their cooperative efforts.[2] However, the secular trend has moved in the direction of further integration, a process punctuated by a number of important milestones.

One recent milestone was the conclusion of the "EC 1992" program, an ambitious undertaking aimed at "completing the single market" by removing the remaining barriers to the free movement of goods, services, capital, and people among the member states. This effort, launched in 1985, consisted of approximately 300 legislative proposals that were to be drafted and adopted before the end of 1992, thereby achieving an unfulfilled objective of the EC's founding fathers in the 1957 Treaty of Rome.[3]

Although the EC 1992 program constituted the centerpiece of the undertaking to achieve a single market, a number of other elements played important roles. Competition policy, carried out under the provisions of the Treaty of Rome, contributed to the discipline of removing barriers; decisions by the European Court of Justice reinforced and extended the scope of the single market; an effort was undertaken to harmonize labor and social legislation in the member states to reduce interstate market distortions and to provide workers with a more directly visible stake in the single market; and, finally, a process was begun toward the establishment of an economic and monetary union (EMU) with a single currency.

The other recent milestone was the Treaty on European Union, which entered into force in November 1993, usually referred to as the Maastricht Treaty because negotiations were concluded in that city in December 1991. The treaty that emerged from complex and protracted negotiations contained significant changes to the competences and structure of the European Community.[4]

Previously, three separate "communities" existed: Atomic Energy; Coal and Steel; and Economic. Together they constituted the European Communities, although the term European Community was usually used to refer either to the European Economic Community or to all three communities jointly. The Maastricht Treaty modified and expanded the European Community into a European Union comprising three "pillars":

- the three existing communities, with the European Economic Community now formally renamed the European Community;
- a structure for the development of cooperation in foreign policy and security policy, the Common Foreign and Security Policy (CFSP); and
- Cooperation in the Spheres of Justice and Home Affairs, referred to simply as the "third pillar," on matters falling within the responsibility of the ministries of justice and internal affairs, such as immigration and asylum policy, police cooperation in combating drug trafficking and terrorism (and other serious forms of international crime), judicial cooperation in civil and criminal matters, and customs cooperation.

The interrelationship among the three pillars is complicated and confusing. As the term pillars implies, the structures and processes are parallel but separate. The legal status of the European Union (EU) is indistinct, and unlike the European Community, the Union does not have a legal personality.[5] However, the pillars are "joined" in an ambiguous way through the treaty, which provides that "The Union shall be served by a single institutional framework."[6] In other words, the three main decision-making institutions remain in existence—the European Commission (executive body); the Council of Ministers (ministers of member states representing their governments), including when it meets as the European Council (heads of government); and the European Parliament—but the decision making procedures vary under each pillar.[7] Although these institutions interact in decisions taken by the European Union, the CFSP is determined by the European Council and the Council of Ministers, with a subsidiary role given to the Commission and none to the Parliament (or to the European Court of Justice). A similar constellation, firmly controlled by the member states, exists for the third pillar. For all three pillars the highest decision-making body is the European Council.

The Maastricht Treaty contains a number of important changes in the decision-making procedures under the first pillar. While maintaining the primacy of the Council of Ministers and the exclusive legislative initiative of the Commission, the treaty significantly increases the powers of the Parliament. It is given the right to negotiate as an equal with the Council of Ministers, and ultimately to veto, certain categories of legislative proposals through the introduction of a "co-decision" procedure. It is also given the power to confirm in office the new Commission that is appointed every five years.

The other main component of the Maastricht Treaty is agreement on the establishment of an economic and monetary union. Following a lengthy period of consultation and discussion, the member states worked out a three-stage process, which is scheduled to culminate in a single monetary policy and currency no sooner than 1997 and no later than 1999 for member states that meet the requisite criteria.

It might have been expected that once the countries of Europe and the institutions they have developed had passed these two important milestones—formal "completion" of the single market program and entry into force of the Maastricht Treaty—they would be embarked on a well-plotted route toward greater integration. However, that has not been the case. Rather, Europe must address a number of critical and complex issues at a time when fundamental questions are being raised about the basic purpose and direction of the EU. Specifically, the EU must deal with three overlapping sets of issues, each with major implications for the future of the Union:

- Establishment of EMU, for at least some of the member states. EMU's importance is symbolic, economic, and political. It is the next milestone in the integration process. It will bind the economies of the participating countries much closer together, but it will establish a sharply defined two-tiered EU, separating the participating from the nonparticipating member states.
- Inevitable substantial extension of EU membership, particularly to countries formerly controlled by or part of the Soviet Union. This will broaden the range of interests represented inside the EU and extend the economic disparities among the member states, thereby increasing the difficulty of arriving at decisions.
- Pressures for changes in the EU's institutional structure, decision-making procedures, and scope of competence. Although all three

subjects are open for discussion and there is substantial agreement that some changes are necessary, the diversity and intensity of views among the member states and interested groups makes an extended period of debate and uncertainty the likely outcome.

The locus for discussion of these and other issues will be the Intergovernmental Conference (IGC), which must be convened, as provided for in the Maastricht Treaty, during 1996.[8] Its decisions will be taken in the context of the vast changes that have occurred during the past few years in Europe as well as elsewhere in the world. Clearly, the Europe of 1995 is far different from that of 1985, when the single market program was launched. In addition—in part as a result—public enthusiasm for integration has diminished, and Europe is now in a period of "Euro-Pause," groping to find a consensus on its future direction.

With these considerations in mind, this book examines the state of European integration in the mid–1990s and looks to the year 2000 and beyond. It seeks to provide answers to three sets of questions:

- To what extent and in what ways has economic and political integration taken place in the European Union? What have been the successes and failures, and what has been their significance?
- With the EU now engaged in a period of reflection (to put it positively) or confusion (the negative interpretation), triggered by the unexpected and sharp opposition aroused in many member states to the Maastricht Treaty, what factors will determine the future course of integration efforts, and what are the likely outcomes?
- Based on developments to date and changes forecast for the coming years, what are the implications for US interests, both regarding public policy and the private sector? How are they affected, and how will they be affected? What should be the response of the US government and the business community?

The latter set of questions is included because developments in Europe continue to be crucially important for the United States. Although the basic economic and political factors accounting for this have remained unchanged, the public mood in the United States has shifted in recent years. As the EC 1992 program got under way, the interest of the US public was aroused, with an insatiable appetite for information about the rejuvenated European Community, tinged with concerns over the potential for a "Fortress Europe." Within a few years, however, the focus had shifted. By the beginning of the 1990s, post–Cold War, recession-bound Europe had been written off by many as "yesterday's continent," while the economically dynamic areas of the world, particularly Asia but also

Latin America, came to be looked upon as the lands of economic growth and opportunity where America's future lay.

It is undeniable that much of Asia and Latin America are areas of economic dynamism, whose prospects for substantial and sustained growth are bright. Accordingly, the United States has an intense interest in developments—and in remaining actively engaged—in those parts of the world. At the same time, Europe suffered from a severe recession in the first half of the 1990s, and prospects for growth in the coming years are relatively modest. Furthermore, the momentum behind European integration, with its expected economic payoff, has abated.

However, it is unproductive and misleading to debate the relative importance of Asia and Europe to the United States. In an ever-shrinking world, it would be a critical error for the United States to lose interest in an area of the globe with which it carries on such an intense economic relationship and with which it shares common political goals and objectives and the potential for achieving them by working together.

The economic relationship is obvious. Two-way trade exceeds $200 billion annually, with the balance fluctuating within a fairly narrow range. Including trade in services and income flows as well as merchandise trade doubles the total. US firms have invested over $200 billion in Western Europe, which represents 40 percent of total US overseas investment, and investment by firms of EU member states in the United States is slightly higher and accounts for over half of all foreign investment in the United States.[9] The importance of these investments is reflected in the sales figures of overseas companies: annual sales by American companies in Europe (employing three million people) amount to $850 billion, while those of European-owned companies in the United States (also with three million employees) have registered $650 billion.[10] In both quantitative and qualitative terms, the relationship is enormously important to US interests, and under any conceivable circumstances it will remain so.[11]

Although the political relationship between the United States and Europe cannot be quantified, it is no less important. Its basis is a shared attachment to representative democratic government, the significant contribution of European culture and tradition to the American political system, a similar optic of the world and its problems, and similar foreign policy objectives. In other words, with the possible exception of Canada, the member states of the EU are the most "like minded" of America's allies and collaborators in the world.

With this, then, as prologue, Chapter 1 catalogs the major changes that have taken place in Western Europe since the second half of the 1980s and that have affected the context in which efforts at integration have proceeded. Chapters 2 and 3 describe the actions taken thus far to promote economic integration—first the single market program and then the many other parallel policies and actions—and assess their significance. Chapter 4 is a parallel description of political integration, covering foreign policy, security, and decision making. In Part Two, Chapter 5 describes the inherent internal conflicts in the EU that will affect the future course of integration, while Chapter 6 considers the factors that will contribute to determining the outcome of further integration efforts, and Chapter 7 provides a forecast of likely outcomes. Turning in Part Three to the future of US-EU relations, Chapter 8 analyzes the implications of present and prospective integration in the EU for US business and US-EU economic relations. Chapter 9 considers the respective international roles of the United States and the EU in the economic, political, and security areas, and Chapter 10 assesses US policy toward the EU, describes potential areas for conflict and for cooperation, and offers recommendations for actions and strategies by the US government and private sector.

The study concludes that considerable progress has been made in the recent past in Europe's economic integration. On the political and security side, a number of significant developments have taken place; however, the level of integration is far less advanced.

Although many scenarios for the future are plausible, the key factor is that the pendulum is swinging from the "integrationists" to the "intergovernmentalists" who seek to preserve the primacy of member state power. The new realities of an increasingly large and diverse EU membership, the myriad of conflicting pressures and interests among and within the member states, and the difficult trade-offs that will be necessary to reach agreement on the key outstanding issues—all in the context of weak political leadership and increasing public discomfort with the concept of further integration—point to the probability that Europe will have to be content in the coming years with a more modest vision than what many proponents and promoters of integration have sought. In fact, when what will undoubtedly be a lengthy process of debate and negotiation has been concluded, the "new" EU that will emerge is likely to contain a considerably higher degree of diversity of participation by its member states in its activities and structures. As such it will reflect the new realities.

Notes

1. The founding members were Belgium, France, Germany, Italy, Luxembourg, and the Netherlands; they were joined between 1973 and 1986 by Denmark, Greece, Ireland, Portugal, Spain, and the United Kingdom and in 1995 by Austria, Finland, and Sweden.

2. For a comprehensive recent history, see Desmond Dinan, *Ever Closer Union? An Introduction to the European Community* (Boulder: Lynne Rienner Publishers, 1994).

3. The treaty, signed in 1957, provided for the EC to come into existence at the beginning of 1958.

4. For a comprehensive, yet comprehensible, description of the Treaty on European Union, see Belmont European Policy Centre, *The New Treaty on European Union* (Brussels, 1992).

5. Ibid., p. 41.

6. Maastricht Treaty (Treaty on European Union), Article C.

7. For a post-Maastricht description of the EU's institutions and competences, see Dick Leonard, *Guide to the European Union* (London: The Economist Books and Hamish Hamilton, 1995).

8. Maastricht Treaty, Final Provisions, Article N.2.

9. US Mission to the European Union, "US-EU Facts and Figures," report, Brussels, April 1995.

10. Jeffrey E. Garten, "The United States and Europe: New Opportunities, New Strategies," speech to US Chamber of Commerce, Brussels, April 25, 1995.

11. Robin Gaster and Clyde V. Prestowitz, Jr., "Shrinking the Atlantic: Europe and the American Economy" (Washington: North Atlantic Research Inc. and Economic Strategy Institute, 1994), report, makes a strong case for the importance of this relationship to the United States, particularly in comparison with US interests in Asia.

PART ONE

Maastricht and Beyond:
Consolidating the EU

1

The Changing Scene

The Europe of the mid–1990s is much different from the Europe of the mid–1980s that saw the launch of the European Community's 1992 program. Fundamental changes in the economic and political landscape of Western Europe have altered the setting in which integration efforts have been undertaken, thereby affecting the process of and prospects for European integration. For that reason it is important to describe those changes before assessing of the various programs and actions designed to promote integration in the European Union. The changes—in many respects shocks to the system that prevailed in the mid and late 1980s—fall into two categories: those that were external to the EU and those that were internal.

External Shocks

The End of the Cold War

The seminal event of the post–World War II era was the end of the Cold War, with the collapse of the Soviet empire and the resultant unification of Germany. Following the efforts of Gorbachev to reform and liberalize the Soviet Union, a combination of remarkably rapid events culminated first in the elimination of Soviet control over the "satellite" countries of Central and Eastern Europe—symbolized by the destruction of the Berlin Wall in November 1989—and then in the fragmentation of the Soviet Union—symbolized by the lowering of the Soviet flag over the Kremlin in December 1991. Within only a few years, the overwhelming power of and perceived threat from the Soviet Union disappeared. In its place appeared a politically and economically weakened Russia, still posing concerns and challenges to the West but of a far different nature than before. Concurrently, the unification of the hitherto divided Germany took place, essentially through a takeover of the East by the West, and the slow process of national integration began.

Significance. First, although pre-unification Germany was the most powerful EU member economically, Germany was placed on an equal footing with France, Italy, and the United Kingdom in terms of formal powers, and as a general rule, it acted accordingly. However, with unification, Germany has clearly become the predominant power in the EU, and that will have economic and political consequences over time. Second, the termination of the Cold War, although primarily important for its security implications, also removed one rationale for European integration—the perceived need to build a strong economy in Western Europe as part of the effort to counter the hostile Soviet bloc.

EU Enlargement

As a result of the changing map of Europe, the nature of the relationship between the EU and the other countries of the European continent changed dramatically. Historically, the EC's non-Communist neighbors (i.e., the members of the European Free Trade Association, EFTA), boasting a long tradition of democratic representative government and highly developed market economies, had followed a policy of tightening their economic bonds with the EC but without seeking membership. That policy culminated in the formation at the beginning of 1994 of the European Economic Area (EEA), which in effect expanded the EU's internal market to include Austria, Finland, Iceland, Norway, and Sweden,[1] although these countries did not thereby join the EU or undertake to participate in all its programs and activities.

However, well before the negotiations for EEA had been concluded, the governments of most of these countries had determined that their interests would be best served by membership in the EU rather than through a form of association. Thus, four of the six members of the EFTA that joined the EEA (the exceptions being Iceland and Liechtenstein) entered into negotiations for accession. These were successfully concluded in early 1994, and following positive referendum results, Austria, Finland, and Sweden entered the EU at the beginning of 1995, though without Norway whose voters rejected membership, as they had in 1972.

Significance: Unlike the case of the previous three entrants—Greece (1981), Portugal (1986), and Spain (1986)—these countries joined the EU as economic and political equals. Hence, relatively few adjustments were required. However, although their accession increased the size and strength of the EU only modestly (6 percent by population and 7 percent by gross domestic product, GDP),[2] it increased the EU's land mass by over one-third, gave the EU a long common border with Russia, added to the urgency for institutional changes, particularly regarding decision-making procedures, and increased the weight of the "northern tier," generally liberal (economically and politically) countries within the Union (see Chapter 5).

The Emergence of Central and Eastern Europe

Even more directly affected in their relationship with the EU by the collapse of the Soviet Union were the former satellite countries of Central and Eastern Europe. These had been controlled until the late 1980s by authoritarian Communist Party regimes, they were largely subservient to the Soviet Union, and they were saddled with highly inefficient, centrally planned economies tied to a system operated by and for the benefit of the Soviet Union. Once they had achieved their independence, these countries instinctively turned to the West for support and assistance, as they began their long and difficult transformation to democratic government and a market economy.

From the outset, the EU clearly recognized that it had a direct interest, if not obligation, in the success of the efforts of the Central and Eastern European countries to transform their political systems and economies. As a result, a substantial aid program was undertaken, and a framework of economic and political cooperation was developed through a series of bilateral agreements, culminating in so-called Europe Agreements with Bulgaria, Czech Republic, Hungary, Poland, Romania, and Slovakia. However, these countries' goal was membership (to take place sooner rather than later), a development they deemed essential for making the transition to a Western-style democratic and market economic system and for obtaining and maintaining the support of and sacrifices from their citizens for that transition. Thus, in mid–1993 the EU accepted the principle of eventual membership by the countries of Central and Eastern Europe, and by the end of 1994 Hungary and Poland had formally applied to join the EU, followed in 1995 by Bulgaria, Romania, and Slovakia, while the Czech Republic was expected to follow suit soon thereafter.

Significance. The countries of Central and Eastern Europe, which had hitherto figured only marginally in the activities and policies of the EU, have become a major object of EU attention and concern. These countries are being progressively drawn into the EU orbit—through aid, trade concessions, political cooperation, and, more generally, prospective membership. Many of these countries will join the EU in the coming years, with the result that the geographical balance of the EU will change, and the EU will be forced to deal with a number of fundamental structural and policy issues (see Chapter 6).

The Balkan War

Another external shock was the civil war in ex-Yugoslavia, which engulfed part of the European continent in bloody warfare for the first time since 1945. The breakup of what had been Yugoslavia challenged the EU to develop and carry out a coordinated foreign policy. Although the EU played a prominent role in the early stages in seeking to negotiate a cease-fire and settlement, it proved unable—as did the West as a whole—to halt ex-Yugoslavia's slide from dismantlement of the federation of republics into brutal fratricidal war.

Significance. The EU's inability to contribute to settlement of a conflict in its own backyard, and the subordinate role of the Common Foreign and Security Policy (CFSP) structure to that of the major EU powers operating as members of the "contact group" (see Chapter 4), sharply damaged the EU's credibility as a present or potential international political player. This situation provides a prime argument for forces favoring a strengthening of the CFSP, and at the same time puts into question the ability of the member states to move farther in that direction.

The Clinton Administration

In 1993, a new US administration came to power with a significantly different focus from that of its predecessors. Responding to the demands of the electorate, the Clinton administration consciously and publicly placed domestic, particularly economic, issues at the top of its agenda. Not only did the administration give lower priority to foreign affairs, but its attention internationally was directed more toward Asia and Latin America than Western Europe. Although this was partly due to the paucity of specific outstanding issues between the United States and the EU, the Clinton administration gave the impression during its first year or two that it attached less importance than the preceding Bush administration to developments in the EU and to the US-EU relationship.

Significance. Although the actual situation is less stark than it might appear, the perceived lessened interest and involvement by the United States has tended to support a European view that the EU should seek to assume a stronger global leadership role, particularly politically, and that implies a strengthened CFSP. The perceived US focus has also led some Americans and particularly Europeans to suggest various ways to "improve" or "deepen" the US-EU relationship (see Chapter 10).

NAFTA and the Uruguay Round

Two events brought significant changes to the world trading system: conclusion of the North American Free Trade Agreement (NAFTA) in

1992 and of the Uruguay Round of world trade negotiations in early 1994. NAFTA established a free trade area comprising Canada, Mexico, and the United States that covered a population of 370 million with a combined GDP of more than $7 trillion. Building on the Canada-US Free Trade Agreement of 1988 but going beyond it in many respects, NAFTA represents a major step in the reconfiguration of the world trading system—the establishment of a wider and deeper market, to use a European term, though liberal in outlook. In many respects, it also provides a North American free trade parallel to the customs union of the EU, whose population and GDP is roughly equivalent.

At least as significant was the agreement reached by the members of the General Agreement on Tariffs and Trade (GATT) in the Uruguay Round, which sharply expanded coverage of the rules of the international trading system (adding trade in services, the trade effects of investment policy, and intellectual property protection); contained the first significant agreement on agricultural trade in the history of GATT rounds; established a new international institution, upgrading the GATT into the World Trade Organization (WTO); and introduced a new, more effective dispute settlement mechanism.

Significance. Although these events do not directly impinge on integration in the EU, they represent important changes in the world trade scene: resolution of a number of outstanding issues; establishment of the WTO, which offers at least the prospect for less contentious trading relations; and further development of trading blocs within the multilateral system.

The Telecommunications and Information Technology Revolution

A final shock, although a secular trend rather than a time-specific development, was the telecommunications and information technology revolution, primarily due to stunning progress in microelectronics and digitalization. This revolution, which progressively accelerated and facilitated the transmission and exchange of information, is, according to the experts, still in its early stages. As a result, the world has seen an increase in economic globalization, in which information and transaction barriers have been progressively lowered and the ability of an individual country or region to isolate itself from economic developments, and competition, elsewhere in the world has been sharply reduced. As the pace of globalization has accelerated, companies have increasingly felt the competitive need to develop global structures.

Significance. The competitive pressures generated by these developments constitute a strong force for continuing the process of European integration because of the recognized contribution of integration to enhancing the competitiveness of European firms.

Internal Shocks

Recession and Unemployment

Inside the European Union the major development of recent years was the sharp economic downturn of the early 1990s, in which Europe experienced one of its most severe recessions since the end of the World War II. An important adjunct of the recession has been the high level of unemployment, which rose steadily in the 12 member states from an already high 8.8 percent in 1991 to 9.6 percent and 10.9 percent in the two succeeding years, to 10.8 percent in 1994, and to 10.6 percent in the second half of 1995.[3] The number of unemployed in the EU during 1994—more than 17 million—roughly equaled the combined population of three member states: Belgium, Denmark, and Ireland. These totals mask substantial differences among the member states, in particular the extremely high unemployment in Ireland and Spain (both over 18 percent), as well as the high incidence of long-term and youth unemployment: 48 percent of the European unemployed have been out of work for over a year, one-third have never been employed, and youth unemployment remains over 20 percent.[4]

A worrisome feature of the EU's unemployment situation is the virtual unanimity among forecasts that the level of unemployment will not fall substantially before the late 1990s, even with a healthy economic recovery.[5] Accordingly, the view is increasingly expressed that European unemployment is a more serious, and more intractable, problem than in the past, requiring a more targeted response than simply awaiting the benevolent effects of economic growth.

Significance. It has long been evident that public receptivity to economic integration, and thus progress toward that objective, has been greatest during periods of economic prosperity. Indeed, the Commission's optimistic estimates of the effects of the EC 1992 program were predicated, at least implicitly, on an assumption of continued economic growth (see Chapter 2).[6] However, the downturn in the economic cycle inevitably put a damper on member states' willingness and ability to move forward as rapidly and comprehensively as had been envisaged. Although that situation changed with the economic recovery beginning in 1994, the persistent problem of unemployment continues to temper enthusiasm for the further removal of economic barriers.

The Collapse of the ERM

While the economic situation in the EU reflects in part the economic effects of developments elsewhere in the world, the collapse of the exchange rate mechanism (ERM) was essentially an internal event. The centerpiece of the European Monetary System, established in 1979, the ERM consists of a grid of exchange rates among the participating currencies (the major EU currencies with the exception, until 1990, of the British pound) and intervention rules designed to maintain the currencies within the established margins of fluctuation. By the early 1990s the ERM was viewed as a great success, a source of monetary stability and a contributor to the general lowering of inflation in Europe, since the currencies of the participating member states had remained within the established bands with few, and increasingly rare, realignments.

All the greater the shock, then, when speculation against the lira and the pound resulted in the withdrawal of these two currencies from the ERM in September 1992. This event was followed in August 1993, by a second crisis that was resolved only by a widening of the bands of permitted exchange rate fluctuation. Thus, the ERM, the stepping stone on which economic and monetary union (EMU), with a single currency, was to have been built, was eviscerated by the upheaval in foreign exchange markets.

Significance. The collapse of the ERM represented a material and psychological blow to the prospects for EMU, a key feature of the process of economic integration (see Chapter 3).

The Maastricht Ratification Fight

Finally, the unexpected and bitter fight in most of the member states over ratification of the Maastricht Treaty was a shock to the system. The key event was the rejection of the treaty, by the slimmest of margins, by the Danish voters in June 1992. Prior to that vote it had generally been assumed that the member states' electorates—whether through referenda or other means—would accept the agreements reached at Maastricht without major objections. However, that was not the case. The Danish rejection revealed a substantial gap between the largely "pro-European" political classes and the ordinary citizens, who turned out to be far less convinced of the advantages, and relevance to their concerns, of European integration. That vote triggered a vigorous, often passionate debate in most member states. At the end of the process, all twelve member states, including Denmark (having held a second referendum), ratified the treaty, but not before fundamental issues had been raised concerning the direction and objectives of the Union.

Significance. The Danish referendum and its aftermath shifted the momentum in the EU from a consensus in favor of continuing the integration process, at least on the economic side, to widespread questioning of the purpose and direction of the Union (see Chapter 5).

Notes

1. Switzerland's electorate embarrassingly repudiated Swiss participation, which its government had negotiated. Although Liechtenstein, the other EFTA member, ratified the EEA, its entry was delayed until mid–1995 because of the complications caused by its customs union with Switzerland.

2. Eurostat news release, No. 60/94; December 13, 1994.

3. Statistical Office of the European Communities, Eurostatistics, 12/94; and Eurostat figures quoted in "Mild decline in December jobless figures in EU," *European Report*, No. 2015, February 11, 1995, p. II/3, and in "EU Jobless Rate Stays at 10.5% for Three Months," *European Report*, No. 2083, November 11, 1995, p. II/5.

4. European Commission, "Employment in Europe 1995," COM(95) 396, July 26, 1995, pp. 72 and 77; and "Europe and the Underclass," *The Economist*, July 30, 1994.

5. European Commission, *European Economy*, Supplement A, November–December 1994, estimates 10.4 percent unemployment in 1995, and 9.8 percent in 1996.

6. Paolo Cecchini, *The European Challenge 1992* (Aldershot [U.K.]: Wildwood House, 1988).

2

Movement Toward Economic Integration: The Single Market Program

Ever since the establishment of the European Community, greater efforts have been devoted to achieving economic integration than to securing political integration. This reflects a far broader consensus—varying, of course, over time and among specific issues—for economic than political integration. It also reflects the recognition from the outset by the proponents of political integration that their objective could be achieved only if it were preceded by a high degree of economic integration and of benefits visible therefrom to the peoples of Europe. Thus, a review of the recent history of integration efforts necessarily begins with the economic side, where the focal point—but by no means only element—since 1985 has been the EC 1992 program.

As mentioned in the "Introduction," the EC 1992 program, proposed by the European Commission and approved by the European Council (heads of government) in 1985, consisted of a set of legislative proposals designed to eliminate the remaining barriers to the free movement of goods, services, capital, and people. This compilation took the form of a schedule that specified, for each of the 300-odd proposals, dates by which the Commission was to present its draft legislation, the Council of Ministers (member state representatives) was to adopt the legislation, and the member states were to transpose it into national law or regulation.[1] The deadline for completion of legislative action on all measures was December 31, 1992; hence, the popular name given it of the "EC 1992 program," or simply "EC 1992."

Although characterization of the program in a single sentence bears some risks, it should nonetheless be noted that a key element was deregulation. As stated by the Commission, "Community legislation completing the single market is by nature a deregulation exercise, since it is aimed at eliminating national measures that create barriers to trade."[2] This was coupled with mutual recognition of the laws and regulations among the member states. In other words, the general intention was not to extend the scope of regulation, but rather to reduce it where possible. Broad areas of activity were to remain subject to the laws and regulations of the individual member states—albeit under a general framework established by the European Union—which would accept the regulatory regime of the other member states for goods and services originating in other jurisdictions.

The set of proposals was divided into three categories of barriers to be overcome:

- physical barriers, i.e., control of goods and of individuals;
- technical barriers, i.e., movement of goods (including standards and sectoral policies), public procurement, movement of labor and professions, services, movement of capital, company law and taxation, intellectual property, and competition policy, and state aid; and
- fiscal barriers, i.e., value-added tax (VAT) and excise tax.[3]

Quantitative Assessment

How much has been achieved? Any assessment of the EC 1992 program must take into account the four-step process from conception to reality:

- approval of the requisite legislation by the EU institutions, i.e., adoption of a directive or regulation by the Council;
- transposition (usually, but somewhat imprecisely, referred to as implementation) of this legislation into appropriate legal form in each of the member states, except in those cases (roughly 15–20 percent) where the EU legislation becomes legally binding without further action by the member states (i.e., when it is a regulation rather than a directive);
- application of the legislation in the member states, i.e., the actual effects, as opposed to the legal formalities; and
- the response by individuals and organizations inside the EU.

The first step can easily be measured statistically. After a certain amount of adjustment, the EC 1992 program consisted of 271 legislative proposals. At the EU level the record is impressive. By early 1995, 259 measures had been adopted, accounting for more than 95 percent of the total.[4]

Transposition of EU legislation contains an element of ambiguity in that directives usually set the parameters within which member states must take action to put them into effect, but the precise legal form and content will vary in accordance with different national conditions and administrative structures, thus leaving room for some flexibility in response. Once transposition has taken place, the member states are required to notify the Commission of the action they have taken.

The rate of member state transposition of EU legislation has improved substantially over the past couple of years. By late 1995, the member states had completed 93 percent of the necessary transpositions.[5] However, because of inaction by one or more member states a considerably lower share of the measures had been fully transposed throughout the EU (60 percent as of early 1995).[6]

Not surprisingly, there are considerable differences in the rates of transposition among member states and among types of legislation. While the rank-order of performance among the member states has tended to vary over time, the best record has consistently been held by Denmark, followed, as of late 1995, by the Netherlands, France, Luxembourg and Portugal, with Finland, Germany, Greece, and Austria at the bottom of the scale. It should be noted, however, that the range of compliance between the first and last on the list is relatively small—88 to 96 percent, if the figure for Denmark is excluded—and that only three member states fall below the 90 percent mark. The Commission ascribes the delays in transposition primarily to procedural difficulties in member states' national decision-making processes (this is the case with Germany because of the competence of the *Laender*) and the technical complexity of the required measures. The Commission notes that the delays are concentrated in a limited number of areas—notably public procurement, but also intellectual property, insurance, and movement of people.[7]

An independent account of implementation of the single market program, compiled by the US International Trade Commission (ITC), came to similar conclusions regarding member state performance.[8] Covering an earlier period (up to September 1993) and a considerably broader range of measures, the ITC identified Denmark and the United Kingdom as having achieved the highest level of transposition, with Germany and Greece as the least active. The ITC ascribed the delays in implementation to: administrative reasons, which were most frequent; technical reasons, most often in the case of transposition of standards (which account for 70 percent of the measures assessed); and, albeit rarely, political reasons. And it agreed that delays have been most frequent in the areas of public procurement and intellectual property, to which it added social legislation (although the latter is not part of the single market program).

In evaluating the degree of success in carrying out the EC 1992 program, it should be noted that most EU legislation takes effect at a date subsequent to its adoption. This is the case with some regulations and all directives. In the latter case, member states must make the necessary transposition within a specified period of time, usually a year after adoption of the measure. However, frequently the period between adoption and entry into force is longer: (a) because of the preparations or adjustments deemed necessary (e.g., the regulation establishing a medicines evaluation agency took effect a year and a half after adoption because new structures and procedures had to be established); or (b) because the legislation in question was controversial and part of the compromise was to give the member states more time to come to terms with the adjustments they would have to make (e.g., the investor services directive, adopted in May 1993, provided for entry into effect only at the beginning of 1996). In addition, many measures include a variable timetable for phasing in, with a later deadline for the less economically advanced member states (typically Greece, Ireland, Portugal, and Spain).

As regards the final two stages of the process from conception to reality of the single market program, mentioned above—actions by the member states affecting developments in the market and responses by individuals and organizations to the measures taken—it is premature to draw conclusions, whether general or specific. More relevant to an understanding of the situation is a sector-by-sector balance sheet, necessarily preliminary and subject to periodic updating, subdivided according to the stage reached of "completing" the single market, as set out in the EC 1992 program.[9] The list, which admittedly contains an element of oversimplification and a strong dose of subjectivity, is discussed in the next section.

Qualitative Assessment

Success (Intended Action Largely Completed)

1. Controls have been removed on the physical movement of goods at EU internal borders. Customs checks have largely disappeared, and custom forms are no longer required for border crossing, eliminating 60 million forms annually.[10] This has not only psychological importance, as a visible manifestation of the single market, but has resulted in a significant reduction of transit time and costs.

2. Capital movements have been liberalized. All controls on the movement of capital have been eliminated,[11] and, significantly, none was reimposed during the 1992 and 1993 crises in the European Monetary System. Thus, a key element of the single market has been achieved.

Nevertheless, differences among the member states in their tax treatment of savings and the corresponding lack of harmonization of withholding taxes have distorted the flow of investment funds. In particular, the absence of a tax on savings in Luxembourg has attracted a massive inflow of funds, especially from Germany. Efforts by Germany and other member states to harmonize savings and withholding taxes have been blocked by Luxembourg and the United Kingdom, which object both as a matter of principle and out of concern that funds presently invested in their countries would simply be transferred out of the EU.

Moving in the Right Direction
(It Is Likely that EC 1992 Goals Will Be Met)

1. The basic legislation in the field of financial services to remove the barriers to establishment and operation has been adopted. It is based on three principles: (a) the harmonization of essential laws and practices, i.e., a common legal framework aimed at ensuring that the firm is financially sound; (b) home country control, i.e., the member state where the firm has its head office is responsible for supervision of the firm; and (c) mutual recognition of the license granted in the country of origin, i.e., a firm needs to be licensed in only one member state to be permitted to conduct business throughout the EU. This legislation represents a radical departure for the EU: it offers financial services firms the possibility of operating virtually unimpeded across national borders, replacing a patchwork of national regimes, many of them highly regulated.

The first such legislation, which entered into force in 1993, covered the banking sector. A similar regime for nonlife and life insurance, put in place through a series of directives, entered into force the following year. As of mid–1995 most member state transposition had been satisfactorily completed.[12] However, insurance companies have complained of cases of inappropriate transposition and the erection of other barriers to impede transborder operations by some member states.

A 1987 directive provided for the mutual recognition of company prospectuses, thus enabling companies to list their stock on exchanges around the EU on the basis of a single prospectus. However, no legislation has been proposed to regulate the stock exchanges in the various member states. On the other hand, a major piece of legislation was the investor services directive, which is intended to facilitate the crossborder activities of intermediaries (e.g., banks, brokers, portfolio managers, and underwriters). The adoption of the directive was delayed for three years—it was adopted in 1993 and enters into effect in 1996—by a heated debate over the appropriate degree of transparency, at issue because of two conflicting concepts of market organization: order-driven (e.g., France) and quote-driven (e.g., United Kingdom).[13] The result was a compromise, criticized by some observers as insufficiently bridging the gap between the two systems.

Passage of legislation in the financial services sector will not, of course, automatically guarantee change. That will take time, as the financial community, consumers, and regulatory authorities adapt to mandated changes and new opportunities. In addition, one area, important both financially and in terms of popular perceptions about the single market, where little progress has been registered is the high cost of cross-border payments (and the delays involved), particularly for small transactions.

2. Although air transportation has been the scene of a bitter struggle between the forces of deregulation and member state protection for their carriers and markets, the major battles have been won by the former (largely the result of strong pressure from the Commission, supported by a minority of national airlines). Three "packages" of EU legislation have been adopted: the first in 1987, the second in 1990, with the last and most important entering into force in 1993. The legislation provided for a single operating license valid throughout the EU, eliminated most government price-setting restrictions, authorized unilateral increases in services on existing intra-EU routes, and expanded airlines' rights to carry passengers beyond the initial stop in another member state. Under the latter, airlines were permitted to continue a flight to a third member state, to provide service between two other member states, and with restrictions until 1997, to continue a flight to a second point in another member state. Indications of progress include British Airways' introduction of service from Brussels to Nice and Rome and the French authorities' opening, under duress, of Paris' Orly Airport to non-French carriers on intra-EU routes.

However, this deregulation program is being carried out over a number of years, some issues have not yet been addressed (e.g., the allocation of landing rights), and resistance in several member states remains strong. The situation is also clouded by a number of bailouts by member states of their national carrier, actions that have been approved by the Commission, albeit reluctantly (see Chapter 3). Nonetheless, the direction of liberalization has been firmly established. Capacity-sharing arrangements between carriers have been virtually eliminated, and airlines have begun to take advantage of the new "beyond" rights.[14] Over time, the result should be a substantial increase in competition and a lowering of the cost to consumers.

3. Greater progress has been made in removing the intra-EU barriers on road transportation: the stage is set for full liberalization. The severe limitation by member states of the right of carriers from another member state to transport goods between two points outside the borders of their

member state resulted in great inefficiencies and higher shipment costs (an estimated one-third of all trucks returned empty after delivering their cargo). Differences in road charge systems and social legislation, hence of transportation costs, made some governments reluctant to agree to the introduction of deregulation, as did political pressure (especially in Germany) by carriers facing the prospect of competition from other member states.

However, by the mid–1990s, restrictions had been removed on road transportation between any two member states (whether or not one is the state of registry), and the only remaining restriction was applied to cabotage operations (the carrying of goods between two points in another member state). Legislation adopted in 1993 provided for a phaseout of this restriction, to be completed in 1998. That measure was coupled with agreement on minimum rates of vehicle taxation and on the introduction of a joint motorway tax system by five member states in 1995. The liberalization process, present and prospective, will significantly reduce transportation costs in the EU.

4. A "new approach" has been adopted for the harmonization of technical standards, under which EU legislation establishes "essential requirements" in a number of specified categories, including electromagnetic compatibility, gas appliances, medical devices, machinery, simple pressure vehicles, and toys. Coordinated by the European standards organizations—the European Standards Committee (known by its French acronym, CEN), the European Electrotechnical Standards Committee (CENELEC), and the European Telecommunications Standards Institute—the private sector develops harmonized European product standards to meet these requirements. Each member state must adopt such standards in place of previously existing national standards. The standards-setting procedures thus established are potentially significant elements in the creation of a single market, and a heavy volume of work has been undertaken by the relevant bodies.[15] Nonetheless, progress in drawing up standards in the European standards organizations has been slow.

The "old approach" to harmonization remains in a number of important sectors—such as automobiles, chemicals, food products, and pharmaceuticals—basically because the member states wanted to maintain control over the process. Under this approach, harmonization, where it exists, results from sector-specific legislation, which includes detailed requirements. The EU has made reasonably good progress in this area (see sectoral descriptions in Chapter 8).

Finally, many product areas are not covered by any EU-wide harmonizing legislation of standards, such as analog telecommunications equipment and sports equipment. In these sectors, mutual recognition, as enforced by the European Court of Justice, is intended to prevail. However, reports are widespread of member states not recognizing the standards of others.[16]

5. Although long one of the most contentious areas, the legislative program for harmonizing veterinary and plant health controls has been largely completed and put into effect. However, by its very nature the significance of this sector in the single market is limited.

6. Efforts to ensure that a person duly qualified to practice a profession in one member state can practice in other member states without requalifying predate the single market program. After the Commission failed in its efforts to obtain the agreement of the academic communities in the member states to recognize each others' degrees, it shifted to drafting legislation on a profession-by-profession basis. A number of directives, providing for mutual recognition of professional qualifications based on a few common requirements regarding training, were adopted, primarily among health care professionals. However, because this proved extremely time-consuming, the Commission moved to a generic approach, which was ultimately accepted by the Council.

Under two directives that entered into effect in 1991 and 1994, respectively—one covering professions for which at least three years' post-secondary school education is required, and the other requiring less than three years—the principle is established that a person with the requisite educational training and certification in one member state has the automatic right to work in all member states. A member state that considers the qualifications required by another member state not to be equivalent to its own must prove that assertion, in which case it can require additional qualifications. Although the number of people affected by mutual recognition of professional qualifications is small, the issue is important, particularly for multinational companies, both regarding their own personnel and the development of support for their operations (e.g., lawyers and accountants). Although this system is working reasonably well, a parallel regime for determining the comparability of vocational qualifications has not been completed.

7. After a slow start, the EU has made considerable progress in harmonizing measures protecting intellectual property. Agreement was finally reached at the end of 1993 to establish an EU trademark and a European Trademark Office after the proposal had been held hostage for several years to controversy over the site of the EU's new trademark office and the selection of the working languages to be used.[17]

A number of measures have been adopted in the copyright field, notably the harmonization of the term of protection, legal protection of computer programs, topography of semiconductors, and broadcasting by cable and satellite. An anticounterfeit regulation was adopted in 1994, which broadened the scope of enforcement at the EU's external borders, adding copyrights to the existing coverage for trademarks, transit goods, exports, and imports. Patent protection for pharmaceutical products was extended in 1992 in partial offset for the lengthy period required for the development of new products and the approval process, and a similar measure was subsequently proposed for plant protection products.

However, as of mid–1995, some important legislation remained pending: proposals on the legal protection of databases and the legal protection of industrial designs (consisting of harmonization of national legislation and the establishment of an EU system of design). And legislation covering the legal protection of biotechnology products—the subject of a lengthy, heated conflict between the Parliament, on the one hand, and the Commission and the Council on the other over the scope of protection to be accorded—was definitively rejected by the Parliament in early 1995.

Unlike most of the other component sectors of the single market program, intellectual property rights in the EU are significantly affected by intergovernmental agreements and international agreements. The prime example of the former is the European Patent Convention (the so-called Munich Convention), whose membership is Europe-wide rather than EU-wide and which predates the EC 1992 program. Because the European Patent Office operates effectively, there has been little support for proceeding with the establishment of a specific EU patent regime. Among international agreements, the most recent is the Agreement on Trade-Related Aspects of Intellectual Property Rights (TRIPS) section of the Uruguay Round concluded in 1994, which placed obligations on the member states, in some instances requiring changes in national legislation (e.g., limiting signatories' ability to grant compulsory licenses).

Although intellectual property issues have not figured prominently in discussions of the internal barriers in the EU, presumably because companies have been able to cope with the disparate national regulations, the long-term beneficial effects of the harmonizing measures described above could be considerable.

More Needs to Be Done (Some Action Has Been Taken, but It Is Premature to Forecast Whether the EC 1992 Goals Will Be Met)

1. Work on the second stage of standards policy, i.e., mutual recognition of testing and certification of products, is proceeding more slowly. Generally, products subject to the new approach are supposed to receive a "CE" mark (French acronym for "European Community or "European conformity") once a European standard has been established. In the absence of such standards or when required, tests are conducted by "notified bodies" (i.e., bodies meeting specified standards and certified by

member state authorities), whose findings are recognized throughout the EU, to determine conformity with the new approach directives. However, as of the mid–1990s, little more than half of the directives establishing CE marks for particular products had been fully transposed, and most of them will not become mandatory until late in the decade.

In the case of unregulated products, work is less advanced. The European Organization for Testing and Certification (EOTC) was established in 1990 to work out harmonization procedures among the member states for testing and certification in the unregulated sectors and to train and upgrade the competence of officials in this area. Although EOTC is making considerable progress in harmonizing test procedures, methods, accreditations, and inspections, it has not succeeded in replacing national certification schemes with a unified EU voluntary certification system. At the same time, however, some harmonization is being effected by the increasing insistence by purchasers of equipment that products conform to the ISO 9000 International Standards Organization.

Clearly, teething problems are being experienced with these various procedures. Industry groups report that duplication of testing and certification continues to be widespread, in part reflecting the fear of national authorities that mutual recognition will reduce their work-load and employment,[18] and concerns relating to the level of competence of bodies in other member states. This view is reflected in a 1994 study of barriers in the single market carried out by the EU's Economic and Social Committee.[19] According to observers, much work needs to be done on developing uniform competence of professional testing and inspection companies throughout Europe to guarantee that a test applied in the producing member state can be reproduced in the consuming country. The Commission has undertaken a number of programs with that objective. A further area of ambiguity is differences in the interpretation of laws and standards, a problem being addressed by the Commission, member states, and notified bodies in different sectors through published guidelines and interpretations.

2. Comprehensive legislation has been adopted in the field of public procurement, requiring transparency and nondiscriminatory treatment and providing remedies including financial compensation to aggrieved parties. This legislation covers the activities of government bodies and agencies throughout the EU (estimated by the Commission to number about 400,000) as well as of private bodies operating on the basis of special or exclusive rights granted by governments.

Although the necessary legislation is in place—and it represents a sharp reversal of previously existing protection afforded domestic companies by member state authorities[20]—change is taking place only slowly. That is not surprising because it runs counter to entrenched local and national interests, and the economic stakes are enormous (the Commission estimates that public purchases account for about 15 percent of gross domestic product, GDP). As mentioned above, member state transposition of the legislation has proceeded slowly. Many firms are not geared to selling to public bodies; many are hesitant to file complaints against government bodies, which are often their actual or potential customers; and most important, the task of monitoring and enforcing hundreds of thousands of purchases annually is far beyond the capabilities of the EU authorities, and probably those of the member states as well.

However, the process has clearly begun. The number of public tenders published in the EU's *Official Journal* has increased exponentially (more than doubling between 1992 and 1995, by which time they were running at about 500 per day). The Commission had concluded that by 1995 major benefits could be identified, though less through crossborder purchasing than by suppliers expanding their supply networks across borders. The Commission also notes that the Government Procurement Agreement, concluded as part of the Uruguay Round, offers a significant, new advantage to non-EU signatories (including the United States) by giving them legal rights to contest the decisions of public authorities.

Nonetheless, it should be recognized that controversies are bound to arise in this area, pitting important member state interests against each another. The first such instance involved the tender for construction of a new airport in Athens, where France (the loser) sought unsuccessfully to persuade the Commission to force the winning bid (German) to be reconsidered.[21] As will undoubtedly happen in the future, what appeared to be legitimate grounds to question the award had to be balanced against important political realities, a situation not dissimilar from that often prevailing in competition cases (see Chapter 3).

3. The record on the free movement of people across the EU's internal borders has been mixed, although a major step forward was taken in 1995. In a basic sense, free movement has been achieved in that the right to work in another member state was first established, and then in 1992, students, retired people, and other members of the non-working population were given the right to reside anywhere in the EU. In addition, procedures are in place for interchange among national social security systems.

The remaining barriers relate largely to the physical movement of people—as distinguished from people changing residence—between member states. The obstacles to the elimination of these barriers have been: (a) the physical separation of some countries from other parts of the EU (primarily the islands of Ireland and the United Kingdom); (b) divergent systems of keeping track of the identity of people inside member states (again, primarily a problem for the United Kingdom, which does not issue identity cards, but instead imposes its controls at the border); (c) concern over the sharply increased volume of economic "refugees" and other asylum seekers from non-EU countries, including concern that many of these people will "seep" into their country via another less rigorously controlled member state (e.g., into France from Italy or Spain)[22]; and (d) the time and expense of reconfiguring airports to separate the flow of passengers arriving on intra-EU flights from those originating outside the EU.

The barriers that exist relate largely to air and sea travel. Controls have been abolished at many road borders in continental Europe or have been replaced by the "wave through" of citizens of member states, and immigration controls on trains have been reduced or eliminated between certain countries. However, these measures have evolved in part autonomously by the member states in question (essentially France, Germany, and the Benelux countries) and largely through a process not formally part of the EC-EU framework, the Schengen Agreement.

Signed in 1990 by the five above-mentioned member states, with the addition of Greece, Italy, Portugal, and Spain in 1992, and Austria in 1995, the Schengen Agreement provides for the complete elimination of border controls on people. However, it did not formally enter into operation until 1995. The main stumbling block, which assumed increasing importance as concerns rose over immigration from third countries, was the delays—resulting from technical (and political) difficulties in obtaining the requisite computer software[23]—in putting in place the Schengen Information System, a data bank of records on people denied entry to individual member states, to be shared among the participating countries.

When the Schengen Agreement went into operation in early 1995, only seven member states participated in the new system; Greece and Italy were not yet able to police their long, exposed external borders, a key requirement in the Schengen process, and Austria, which joined a few months later, had not completed the necessary arrangements. Furthermore, the agreement does not include Denmark (which, however, participates as an observer, as presumably will Finland and Sweden), Ireland, or the United Kingdom. Nonparticipation by Denmark, Finland and Sweden results from their membership in the Nordic Union, under which the free movement of people is guaranteed. Since Norway is a member of the Nordic Union but not of the EU, Denmark's participation in the Schengen Agreement would automatically extend the EU's free movement of people to it, thus making it a de facto EU member.[24] Even among the seven participants, practical problems of implementation arose at the outset, particularly France's delay in eliminating border controls, because of concern over the inflow of drugs (especially from the Netherlands) and lack of reciprocity in returning asylum seekers, and the malfunction of the system at the Amsterdam airport for separating passengers from EU and non-EU flights.

In terms of the other nonparticipants among the twelve pre–1995 EU member countries, the United Kingdom vociferously denies its obligation to open its frontiers to travelers from other member states, and Ireland is obliged to remain outside the Schengen Agreement because participation would require it to close its border with Northern Ireland. The United Kingdom bases its position on a declaration in the 1985 Single European Act (which amended the Treaty of Rome) that reaffirmed the right of member states to take measures to control third-country immigration and combat crime, terrorism, and drug trafficking. However, that declaration lacks the force of a treaty obligation; furthermore, the United Kingdom weakened its case when it signed the Maastricht Treaty because the treaty reaffirms the right of movement. This remains a point of sharp controversy.

Three other obstacles impede the free movement of people. Ratification of the External Frontiers Convention establishing a single external border for the EU has been blocked by continuing controversy between Spain and the United Kingdom over the status of Gibraltar, which Spain does not recognize as a part of the United Kingdom. Similarly, the Dublin Convention of 1990, which regulates the right of asylum and provides that the first member state entered by a nonnational will examine an asylum request, has not been ratified by all members. Finally, agreement on standardizing a visa policy throughout the EU for third-country nationals was not reached until 1995 because of divergent national policies and interests. Even then, ambiguities remained. Although a list of 101 countries whose nationals will require a visa to enter the EU was agreed upon, it was not to take effect until 1996; member states retained the right to require a visa from countries not included on the list;[25] and separate visas were still required for each member state to be visited (because the External Frontiers Convention had not been ratified). Nonetheless, there has been general agreement on a common visa format and on nonbinding principles on immigration and asylum.

4. The EC 1992 program called for an agreed narrow range of value-added tax rates throughout the EU to eliminate trade distortions resulting from the rather substantial variations in rates among the member states.[26] However, it was not possible to obtain the required unanimous approval by the member states for such an ambitious measure. Some member states were concerned over the loss of tax revenue; others considered a uniform schedule unnecessary since market forces would bring about an approximation of rates. Accordingly, it was decided instead to set minimum VAT rates as of January 1, 1993: a standard minimum of 15 percent (requiring small increases by Germany and Spain), a reduced rate

of 5 percent for a specified list of goods and services, and a derogation for the United Kingdom and Ireland to continue to exempt a limited number of categories from VAT. The rationale for setting minima was that member states would not be able to sustain considerably higher rates because of the arbitrage opportunities that would be provided, and that is what happened.[27]

However, the main problem lay in obtaining agreement on a "definitive" VAT system based on payment of the tax in the country of origin rather than, as at present, the country of final purchase. The latter system runs counter to the concept of a single market without internal borders because it requires traders to differentiate between sales in the same member state and those in other member states. An origin-based system would require a clearing arrangement among the member states to prevent the substantial redistribution of tax revenue that would otherwise result from the differences in VAT rates and the different levels of member state exports. Although they were unable to agree on such a definitive system, the member states committed themselves to adopt an origin-based system by 1997. Pending agreement on this regime, they put into effect an interim regime at the beginning of 1993, whose main feature is that companies are required to submit reports on their transactions in lieu of documentation previously required when goods physically cross internal borders.

The interim regime has received mixed reviews from the business community. Some companies consider it to have worked reasonably well, while others complain about the added burden on their accounting departments. In addition, a number of problems with the system have been identified, in part because of different interpretations of the regime by the member states.[28] Furthermore, the prospect of further alteration in the system (i.e., introduction of the "definitive" regime) is unsettling to business.

Limited Progress

1. The single market program provided for legislative action on a number of issues of company law and taxation designed to facilitate crossborder operations by enterprises. Some progress has been made, including provision for the establishment of European economic interest groups (a form of joint venture for small-scale, specific projects, particularly of interest to small and medium-sized enterprises), the establishment of single-proprietor private limited liability companies, disclosure requirements for branches, relaxation of certain accounting rules for small and medium-sized enterprises, and a number of measures regarding a common tax system for mergers and acquisitions and for parent-subsidiary relations.

However, several major legislative proposals remain blocked, mainly because of controversy over proposed provisions that would require large companies to permit workers to participate in the firm's decision-making process, either directly as board members or indirectly outside the board. The most important proposal would create a new legal entity called a European company, enabling companies to operate throughout the EU under a uniform legal regime. Another proposal, blocked over the same issue, is a directive on corporate governance (i.e., setting rules for the internal organization of companies), and a third would establish rules for mergers of firms of different nationalities. In all three cases, the unwillingness of some member states to agree to the provision for worker participation has blocked action. Other important legislative proposals that have remained blocked on other grounds include those relating to consolidation of losses and takeovers (the latter aimed at harmonizing member state laws).

A related, but separate issue relating to workers' rights was the proposal for the establishment of works councils for the consultation of employees of companies having establishments in different member states (see Chapter 3). After many years of controversy, agreement was reached in 1994 on this proposal, albeit with an opt-out for the United Kingdom, which had tenaciously opposed it. Despite the conceptual affinity between works councils and worker participation, it is unlikely that agreement on the first will lead to agreement on the second, unless the proponents of worker participation are willing to lower their sights.

Although these changes in company law would facilitate crossborder activity and reduce company costs, the business community in Europe has not accorded them high priority, preferring to concentrate its efforts on blocking the workers consultation and participation provisions.

2. Excise taxes fall into the "limited progress" category because of lowered expectations. The substantial differences in member states' rates and the economic and political problems that would result from harmonization caused the EU eventually to opt for a more modest arrangement. Legislation established minimum rates for tobacco products, alcoholic beverages, and mineral and fuel oils at the beginning of 1993 (when payments at the border were abolished); maintained the principle of payment in the country of purchase; and provided for an EU-wide duty-suspension system based on authorized warehouses. The economic effects of the legislation have been minor, although one consequence of the combination of the elimination of border controls and the differences in excise taxes has been the rise of some cross-border trade from high-tax member states, notably British purchases of alcoholic beverages across the Channel in France.[29] Nonetheless, the excise tax regime is only a marginally important element of the single market.

Measurement of Results

In attempting to assess the degree to which the single market program has achieved its objectives, it is important to bear in mind that "1 January 1993 marked neither the beginning nor the end of efforts to construct a single market."[30] It is a continuing process with no specific or recognizable end point, and developments vary considerably among sectors. Thus, it would be misleading to pin either a "success" or "failure" label on the EC 1992 program. Although success stories can be matched by accounts of failure, the balance is clearly weighted on the side of success. The EU has made a substantial, and in many respects remarkable, beginning to an ambitious and complex undertaking, even though much remains to be done, especially in the member states.

Despite these caveats, some measurement can be and has been made. The first effort to measure the effects of the EC 1992 program was the so-called Cecchini Report, a multi-volume sectoral study conducted by the Commission in 1988, which was also issued in a readable, single-volume version.[31] The study was necessarily prospective and therefore conjectural. Its optimistic macroeconomic forecasts were given wide publicity; indeed, the purpose of the study was to develop support for the single market program. However, the report overestimated the extent to which accompanying internal policies would be carried out and did not foresee some of the economic and political developments of the intervening years (see Chapter 1). In any event, the economic trends in the EU moved, at least in the early years of the 1992 program, in the opposite direction from those predicted in the report. For that reason, the study has been dismissed by some critics as a public relations exercise. However, even if its relevance is now limited, it was a serious effort to forecast in detail the changes and benefits that would derive from adoption of the program.

Although one can now begin to look retrospectively, two factors extend the time period before which relevant conclusions can be made: the time lag in the publication of statistics and the phasing in over a period of time of much of the single market legislation. However, a more important limiting factor than timing is the difficulty of pointing to specific evidence of changes resulting from the single market program—or economic integration in the broader sense. There are inherent difficulties in attempting to distinguish single market phenomena from other factors in explaining economic developments, macroeconomic as well as sectoral. In terms of the most general economic indicator, changes in GDP, developments in the EU in the early 1990s reflected the deep recession, a factor not directly related to the single market. And as Europe emerged from the recession by the mid–1990s, the resulting increases in GDP were as difficult to relate to the single market and economic integration as when GDP was moving in the other direction. In any case, the causal link between integration and macroeconomic indicators is tenuous at best.

Nonetheless, a number of studies have been written on the single market, which examine both macro and micro (sectoral and factor mobility) factors.[32] However, for the most part the conclusions of these studies are narrowly focused, and it is difficult to draw generalizations from them. In the first effort by an EU institution to review progress on the single market program, the Economic and Social Committee investigated obstacles to the freedom of movement of goods, services, capital, and people. However, that study was based largely on submissions by representative groups and did not include an overall analysis or assessment.[33]

At most, one can analyze some broad macroeconomic trends, which provide a general indication of the effects of the single market. The first is direct inward investment, which doubled between 1980–86 and 1987–92.[34] At least part of that increase can be ascribed to market expectations of gains to be derived from the single market. The same implication can be drawn from merger and acquisition (M&A) activity. As the EC 1992 program was being formulated, M&As increased sharply. After a measured increase in 1986 and 1987, M&As tripled in 1989. M&As involving companies of the same member state peaked in 1989 (at twice the 1986–88 level), while intra-EU M&As and those including a non-EU partner reached their peak in 1990, with about 4.5 times as many M&As registered as in the mid–1980s.[35]

Since then there has been a modest decline in M&As among EU firms, although such activity has remained significantly higher than in the mid–1980s. M&As involving a non-EU partner have remained near their historic highs. The decline has taken place largely in the manufacturing sector (presumably because companies, on the whole, moved faster in making their adjustments to the single market), while M&As have remained high for services. Interestingly, according to the Commission, the rationale for M&As shifted from being defensive (rationalization and synergies) in 1985–86 to offensive (reinforcing market position and expansion) in 1991–92. The most active acquiring countries have been France and United Kingdom, while Germany has led the list of those whose companies have been acquired, in part reflecting activity in former East Germany. Not surprisingly, the United States is the most prominent among non-EU countries whose companies have made acquisitions.

Finally, trade flows can provide indications of the effects of integration. According to one study,[36] the EC 1992 program and German unification had a powerful impact in reorienting EU external trade toward European markets. Of forty sectors where intra-EU trade had been limited (especially in the high-technology and public procurement sectors), thirty-eight experienced large increases in intra-EU exports, considerably more than exports outside the EU.

However, these data merely give a general indication of the response of the private sector to the acceleration in economic integration; they provide little specific connection between the single market program and the expected economic benefits. Whatever the connections are, the effects of integration will become apparent only after considerable time has elapsed. The first major effort to reach some conclusions will be contained in a study by the Commission—mandated by the Council in 1992 for publication in 1996—to assess the effectiveness and impact of the single market legislation. The report, which will encompass about fifty sectoral and cross-sectoral studies, will assess the effect of the EC 1992 program on the range of single market objectives, including economic growth, high employment, and economic and social cohesion among the member states (see Chapter 8), and an improved competitive position of European business. However, even though this study will contain interesting and useful information, its conclusions will necessarily be tentative.

Notes

1. European Commission, "Completing the Internal Market," White Paper from the Commission to the European Council, COM(85) 310, June 14, 1985.

2. European Commission, "The Single Market in 1994," COM(95) 238, June 15, 1995, p. 20.

3. For a description of the genesis and contents of the EC 1992 program, see Michael Calingaert, *The 1992 Challenge from Europe: Development of the European Community's Internal Market* (Washington: National Planning Association, 1988). The contents of the program are summarized in Appendix E.

4. Pierre Buigues and John Sheehy, "The Internal Market Programme: The Impact on European Integration," European Commission, Document II/133/95, pp. 8–9.

5. European Commission, "Commissioner Monti to Outline Single Market Priorities to 23 November Council," Memo (95) 154, November 22, 1995.

6. Buigues and Sheehy, "The Internal Market Programme," p. 9.

7. European Commission, "Commissioner Monti to Outline Single Market Priorities to 23 November Council," Memo (95) 154, November 22, 1995.

8. *Implementing the European Community Single Market: Sixth Followup Report* (Washington: United States International Trade Commission, January 1994), USITC Publication 2723.

9. The Commission's balance sheet, which is less qualitative, although it does describe specific problems, can be consulted as well in its annual report on the single market. The most recent report is European Commission, "The Single Market in 1994."

10. Riccardo Perissich, "1 January, 1993: one day in the life of the internal market," *European Business Journal*, Vol. 5, Issue 1, January 1, 1993, p. 12.

11. Complete capital liberalization dates from 1994, when the final (Greek) restrictions were lifted.

12. European Commission, "Liberalization of Insurance in the Single Market—An Update," MEMO (95) 130, October 4, 1995.

13. In an order-driven market, price and volume data are published rapidly, whereas in a quote-driven market, little data is published on executed trade.

14. For details, see "Bleak Performance in the First Year of Deregulation," *European Report*, No. 1957, June 11, 1994, pp. III/4–5.

15. According to the European Commission "The Single Market in 1994," p. 45, over 300 technical committees are working on 10,000 standardization projects. Of these, 3,000 are required by legislation, while the remainder are being undertaken at industry initiative.

16. For a comprehensive discussion of standards, testing and certification, see Stephen Cooney, *American Industry and the New European Union* (Washington: National Association of Manufacturers, 1994), pp. 69–96.

17. Spain had blocked agreement in its effort, ultimately successful, to host the new agency. It had also pressed, equally successfully, for Spanish to be a working language. The legislation provides that any of five working languages can be used—English, French, German, Italian, and Spanish—although in the case of a dispute between parties, they must agree on a common language, which the Commission hopes will be English or French. Although it has received little publicity, the official designation of five working languages is possibly the only legislative language provision that does not give equal status to all official EU languages (numbering eleven as of 1995).

18. According to one source, there are 12,000 testing employees in the *Land* of North-Rhine Westfalia alone.

19. Economic and Social Committee, "Opinion on the [Commission's] annual report on the functioning of the internal market," CES 999/94, September 14, 1994.

20. The usually cited figure is that prior to the launch of the EC 1992 program only 2 percent of public procurement took place outside the member state in question. However, the Commission questions the accuracy of this figure since "domestic firms" include nonnational ones that supply the products or services from elsewhere. Its rough estimate is between 12 and 20 percent.

21. However, technically the tender did not fall under the new directives, which did not yet apply to Greece.

22. According to "Refugees find doors bolted," *Financial Times*, February 10, 1994, asylum requests in European countries rose from 65,000 in 1982 to 680,000 in 1992, of which about 70 percent were in Germany. However, the numbers have decreased significantly since then. According to a study by the European Consultation on Refugees and Exiles, quoted in "Europe tries to shut the floodgates," *Financial Times*, June 3, 1993, at least 80 percent of asylum seekers remain, by one means or another, in the country they have entered.

23. For details, see "What lies behind the collective failure of the Schengen Agreements?," *European Report*, No. 1924, February 9, 1994, pp. IV/8–9.

24. In 1995, the countries participating in the Schengen Agreement, desirous of extending the free movement arrangement to Scandinavia, agreed in principle that Iceland and Norway could join the agreement. However, the establishment of a free movement zone cutting across the EU's external borders could create constitutional and practical problems.

25. The corollary, of course, is that for some countries whose nationals previously could enter an EU member state freely, a visa would now be required, e.g., Romanians entering Germany.

26. It should be noted that the single market program does not directly address the issue of differences in direct taxation regimes. See Calingaert, *The 1992 Challenge from Europe*, p. 21. The Commission has focussed its attention on a number of areas—the elimination of double taxation income and gains, the introduction of a more neutral system of taxing savings, the establishment of a neutral system of taxing insurance services, the taxation of citizens living in one member state but earning income in another, and the improvement of the fiscal environment of small and medium-sized enterprises—but, by its own admission, with little success. See European Commission, "The Single Market in 1994."

27. According to "Much closer convergence between VAT rates, says Commission," *European Report*, No. 2002, December 17, 1994, p. II/6, the spread between rates declined from 26 percentage points in 1992 to 10 points in 1993.

28. According to the Union of Industrial and Employers' Confederations of Europe (UNICE) statement, "VAT Definitive System," June 17, 1994, the main problems relate to the need for multiple registrations, the diverse rights and obligations of fiscal representatives, and the difficulties involved in the calculation of VAT on chain transactions, triangular transactions, and distance selling.

29. According to one estimate, such purchases have reached ECU 1 billion ($1.25 billion) annually. (The ECU-dollar exchange rate has, of course, fluctuated over the years. For consistency's sake, the rate of ECU = $1.25, the approximate rate for August 1995, has been used throughout the text.) See Sandra Smith, "Flood of cross-border shoppers drains home markets," *The European*, June 16, 1995.

30. Riccardo Perissich, "1 January 1993," p. 8.

31. Paolo Cecchini, *The European Challenge 1992* (Aldershot [U.K.]: Wildwood House, 1988).

32. See Peter Hoeller and Marie-Odile Louppe, *The EC's Internal Market: Implementation, Economic Consequences, Unfinished Business*, (Paris: Organization for Economic Cooperation and Development [OECD], Economics Department, 1994), Working Papers No. 147, pp. 16–25.

33. Economic and Social Committee, "Opinion on functioning of the internal market."

34. Hoeller and Louppe, "The EC's Internal Market," p. 45.

35. All figures are contained in European Commission, *European Economy,* Supplement A (Recent Economic Trends), No. 2, February 1994. See also "Competition and integration: Community merger control policy," *European Economy,* No. 57, 1994.

36. Buigues and Sheehy, "The Internal Market Programme," pp. 22–25.

3

Other Aspects of Economic Integration

Although the main focus of efforts to bring about economic integration—and certainly the most visible one—has been the EC 1992 program, many developments have taken place in the European Union that, while not a part of the formal program, are nonetheless highly relevant to the integration effort. These developments fall into three categories:

- economic sectors—economic and monetary union (EMU), telecommunications, environment and energy—in which (with one exception, energy) a significant degree of integration is taking place;
- policy sectors—social policy and structural policy—where "flanking policies" directly affect integration; and
- EU enforcement mechanisms—the Commission, EU competition policy, and the European Court of Justice.

Before turning to the four economic sectors, mention should be made of the EU's Common Agricultural Policy (CAP). Dating from the beginning of the 1960s, the CAP, along with the customs union, was the earliest component of European economic integration. It guaranteed a minimum price to producers for certain key commodities, and it protected that price level by a system of variable levies on imported products, counterbalanced by export subsidies to make the products of European producers competitive on world markets. Although this system provided substantial benefits to the European Community's agricultural sector, the end of the fixed exchange rate system in the 1970s brought distortions to the EC's agricultural market. Because the level of payments was denominated in the EC's notional single currency, producers in member states whose currency was devalued obtained proportionally greater returns, while their exports became increasingly competitive in the other member states. Accordingly, a currency adjustment mechanism (using so-called monetary compensation amounts) was established to offset the effects of the currency fluctuation, thereby erecting a barrier in a nominally "single market" program.

In response to the increasingly unsustainable growth in stocks and costs to the EU budget, an important reform of the CAP was instituted in 1994 that reduced and changed the structure of support to producers. However, the reform was neither part of the EC 1992 program nor the general effort to achieve economic integration. On the other hand, the elimination of the monetary compensation amounts in 1993 was tied to implementation of the single market; however, its effects were offset by the adoption of other mechanisms to shield producers from currency fluctuations and changes.

Economic Sectors

Economic and Monetary Union

In many respects EMU represents the culmination of economic integration. It is widely viewed as the next crucial step in the integration process, important symbolically and economically. For those reasons, EMU is the focal point of discussion on the future of the economic integration of the EU.

EMU, long the subject of debate, moved to center stage in the late 1980s, as a consensus emerged that a genuine single market could not exist as long as member states pursued separate monetary policies and, more generally, economic policies. What was needed, it was asserted, was economic and monetary union, meaning: (a) a single monetary policy and currency, with a European Central Bank; (b) coordination of economic policy (as opposed to a common policy), but without a central institution; and (c) fiscal policy remaining within the purview of the member states, whose freedom of action, however, would be limited because of the single monetary policy.

As the single market program accelerated, increasing attention was given to the concept, and then the specifics, of EMU. Various reports and discussions led the European Council to accept at the end of 1989 a recommendation by a committee of central bankers and economic experts, chaired by European Commission President Jacques Delors, to begin a three-stage process leading to EMU. It was then decided to convene an intergovernmental conference to negotiate a formal agreement and procedures for EMU; the results of that conference formed a major portion of the Treaty on European Union (the Maastricht Treaty). The treaty confirmed stage one, already initiated in 1990, in which monetary cooperation among the member states was to increase and those member states that had not joined the exchange rate mechanism (ERM) of the European Monetary System (see Chapter 1) were to do so. In stage two, which came into effect at the beginning of 1994, there was to be intensified cooperation on economic policy making and the establishment of a European Monetary Institute to make the technical preparations for stage three, in effect serving as the precursor of a European Central Bank.

The process was to culminate in a third stage, when a European Central Bank would be established and a single currency put into circulation. To participate in EMU, a member state would have to meet specified criteria of "economic convergence": "price stability" (measured by comparative rates of inflation); the "sustainability" of the government's financial position (deemed to have been achieved if the budgetary deficit was not "excessive"); the observance of "normal" currency fluctuation (measured by adherence to ERM margins); and the "durability" of convergence (measured by long-term interest rates).[1] These criteria were further refined in protocols attached to the Maastricht Treaty, which made the following definitions:[2]

- "price stability" means an average rate of inflation not exceeding 1.5 percent of the average rate of the three member states with the lowest inflation rate;
- "excessive" deficit means a ratio of government budgetary deficit to gross domestic product exceeding 3 percent and/or a ratio of government debt to GDP exceeding 60 percent;
- "normal" currency fluctuation means having remained within the margins of the ERM during the two previous years and not devaluing against another member state's currency;
- "durability" of convergence means average long-term interest rates during the past year not exceeding by more than 2 percent the average rate of the three member states with the lowest rates.

Stage three would begin under one of two circumstances: either (a) a qualified majority[3] of member states would determine by the end of 1996 that a majority of member states met the necessary conditions and then would set a date for entry into force; or (b) a qualified majority would decide which member states could join the EMU, which in any case would begin in 1999.

Unfortunately, the events that transpired did not fit the mold set by the negotiators. First, despite the relatively non-contentious nature of the public discussion of EMU (to the extent it took place) in the period leading to the final negotiations, loud alarms were raised in Germany over the perceived threat to German monetary policy and the sanctity of the deutsche mark almost as soon as the Maastricht Treaty had been concluded. Fanned by the popular press, concerns were raised that the Bundesbank, which had achieved considerable success over the years in its anti-inflation policy, would no longer be able to carry out German monetary policy independently. Rather, it was feared that despite the treaty's provisions that the "primary objective of the European System of Central Banks [the European Central Bank plus those of the member states] shall be to maintain price stability" and the prohibition on the European Central Bank or the national central banks' taking instructions from any EU institutions or national governments,[4] the political pressure on other member states' central banks and their national biases would result in a more inflationary monetary policy for the EU. By the same token, some other member states feared the opposite. Finally, the notion that national currencies would be replaced by a single European currency was viewed with horror, particularly in Germany and the United Kingdom.

Second, the much-vaunted exchange rate mechanism imploded. A growing imbalance between some of the weak currencies and the mark, for which no adjustment was made (i.e., neither revaluation of the mark nor devaluation of the weak currencies), resulted in irresistible pressures on the lira and the UK pound, both of which withdrew from the ERM in September 1992 and were left to float outside. In the following August, a second round of pressures, directed primarily against the French franc, effectively cut the heart out of the ERM. The bands of fluctuation were widened from 2.25 percent (and 6 percent in the case of the Portugese escudo and Spanish peseta) on either side to 15 percent. Thus, the European currencies had effectively reverted to the free float that had characterized the situation before the introduction of the ERM in 1979, although the ERM continued to define the central parities, to institutionalize monetary cooperation, and to provide a short-term financing facility.

Finally, it became increasingly clear that many member states would have difficulty meeting the convergence criteria laid down in the Maastricht Treaty. Although it had been recognized from the beginning of the negotiations that the less economically advanced member states would not be able to participate in EMU initially, it was generally assumed that a hard core would constitute the founder members. These would consist of the six EC original members with the probable exception of Italy, plus Denmark and the United Kingdom, if they so desired (since both had obtained an opt-out of the treaty provisions on EMU, i.e., the right to decide not to join). However, it soon became apparent that virtually all member states found it difficult to meet the convergence criteria. Indeed, by 1993, only Luxembourg had fulfilled all the conditions; in 1994, Germany was added to the list; and only a few other member states came close (see Chapter 7). The biggest obstacles were the criteria on budgetary deficit, particularly government debt.

Remarkably, however, these body blows to the cause of EMU did not result in its hasty burial. Despite the widening of the ERM fluctuation bands, within a short period of time the spread between the currencies remaining in the ERM[5] returned largely to within their previous exchange rate margins, the result both of government policy (e.g., the French and Belgian monetary authorities pegging a "hard" franc to the mark) and of the inability of speculators to force adjustments of the exchange rate grid (because of the wide bands of permissible fluctuation before monetary authorities are required to defend their currency).

While these developments were taking place, the view gained favor that introduction of EMU should proceed on schedule on the grounds that the urgency of, and potential benefits from, such economic and monetary union remained at least as strong as before, and it took into account the return of stability to the EU's foreign exchange markets. In any event, no change in the EMU timetable can be made (acceleration or deceleration) unless the Maastricht Treaty is amended. Thus, by 1994, attention had again focused on the timing and modalities for introducing EMU (see Chapter 7).

Telecommunications

By its very nature, the telecommunications sector occupies an important place in the EU economy. The turnover of telecommunications services accounts for about 3 percent of GDP, with growth increasing, despite the recession, at a steady 7 percent annually during the first half of the 1990s.[6] As described in Chapter 1, this sector is characterized by rapid and extensive change, which has revolutionized global communications in general and the way business is conducted in particular. These changes have placed immense pressure on the system of monopoly control and heavy government regulations in the EU member states. As a result, the telecommunications sector has been the focal point of considerable attention by EU institutions and sharp debate among the many interested parties.

Although telecommunications was not included in the EC 1992 program, the European Commission began efforts to liberalize the sector across the Community more or less concurrently with the launch of its efforts to establish the single market. The motivating force behind the Commission's deregulation campaign was its recognition that the member states' tight regulation had resulted in a sector characterized by high costs, inflexibility, and a resistance to innovation, thereby undermining the competitive position of European firms.

The Commission's opening salvo was the publication in 1987 of a "green paper" (discussion document),[7] calling for broad deregulation of the EC's telecommunications sector. The Commission's proposals directly challenged the system prevailing throughout the Community of national monopoly operators, except in the United Kingdom where liberalization had already begun under the Conservative government. Not surprisingly, these proposals met with considerable resistance in the member states, though with varying degrees of intensity.

The principal argument was that unless government agencies maintained monopoly control, they would not be financially able to ensure the "universal" provision of essential public services, particularly voice telephony, which represented about 90 percent of the telecommunications business. Major elements in the resistance to deregulation included concerns of the large number of often politically powerful employees in state telecommunications agencies about potential staff reductions; concerns of governments over the decline in revenue that would result from competition; and concerns of the management in some, but by no means all, member states over losing the advantages offered by monopoly operations.

Nonetheless, the situation has changed drastically as a result of the Commission's aggressive pursuit of deregulation and of the pressure of market forces, i.e., the actions of telecommunications users and technological change. By the mid–1990s, liberalization of the telecommunications sector was either under way or on the schedule in every member state.

The Commission's first significant step was its 1988 directive mandating the right to connect terminals to the networks and abolishing the monopoly of national telecommunications authorities over the sale of terminal equipment—giving freedom of choice in purchases (as long as the equipment meets the relevant standards). Unlike the normal procedure under which legislation is adopted by the Council of Ministers, with the Parliament's input, the Commission used the authority given it under Article 90 of the Treaty of Rome to ensure that public undertakings do not violate the treaty's rules on competition. Despite strong objections from certain member states (ostensibly over the procedure, though undoubtedly containing an element of substantive objection), the European Court of Justice upheld the Commission's action.

Subsequent legislation established a competitive market for value-added services for data transmission (mostly communication between computers using leased lines) in 1990, established a framework for open network provision (the right of and conditions for interconnection and access to telecommunications networks) also in 1990, and provided for mutual recognition of terminal equipment conformity in 1991. Equally important, the member states' telecommunications authorities were required to separate their regulatory functions from their operating role.

A renewed push was given to telecommunications liberalization by a Commission communication, in which it reviewed the situation in the telecommunications sector and described its intended timetable for future legislation. The Council approved the timetable in mid–1993, and, most important, called on the Commission to draw up the necessary legislation so that public voice telephony services could be liberalized by January 1, 1998. This date has since been challenged by proponents of an earlier deadline, who argue that the delay will adversely affect European competitiveness in world markets, adding that in any case technological developments may force the date to be moved forward.

The important role of telecommunications in the Union's economy was also recognized by the European Council at its meeting in December 1993, when it set up a committee chaired by Commissioner Martin Bangemann to recommend "specific measures ... for the infrastructure in the sphere of information" in the context of its deliberations over promoting economic growth, employment, and competitiveness in the EU. The committee, which included a number of leaders from the telecommunications industry, gave a resounding call for further liberalization of the telecommunications infrastructure and services that remained under monopoly. Its recommendations[8] were given broad support by the European Council at its mid–1994 meeting, and Bangemann has continued to take an active interest in this development of the "information society," as part of the EU's efforts to enhance European competitiveness.

In 1994 and 1995, the Commission issued green papers on the liberalization of telecommunications infrastructure. The first proposed general principles (notably ensuring free choice of infrastructure for the provision of liberalized services) and a timetable for the liberalization of infrastructure, while the second set forth procedures for liberalizing infrastructure. Subsequent to wide consultation among interested groups, which revealed broad support for the directions outlined, the Commission laid out a program of legislation covering the period up to 1998, designed to ensure full liberalization of telecommunications infrastructure and services by the time restrictions are lifted on voice telephony. As part of that program, the Commission adopted a directive in 1995, under its Article 90 authority, lifting restrictions on cable television networks, so that they can be used for all liberalized communications services as of 1996.

A recent object of Commission attention has been the rapidly expanding and economically important cellular telephony sector. The Commission has required that at least two cellular operators be licensed in each member state to ensure a competitive environment. In addition, because cellular telephones must use the public network, the Commission has sought to prevent telecommunications authorities from restricting the development of this sector. In fact, in 1995, it took steps toward forcing the complete liberalization of the cellular sector by the following year (although with delays of implementation in five countries).

A vast number of changes have taken place in the EU telecommunications sector, and much progress has been attained in removing barriers and increasing efficiencies. However, the situation varies among the member states. On the whole, more has been accomplished in the northern member states than in the southern tier. The 1994–95 green papers move in the right direction, as do the decision on the liberalization of voice telephony and the activities of the Bangemann committee. Nonetheless, the key requirement for success will probably be guaranteeing freedom of choice in the use of infrastructure.

Environment

The EC 1992 program did not contain a section on environmental issues, although a few environmental proposals were included.[9] However, the EU's involvement with environmental issues dates from the early 1970s, when it adopted the first of a series of environmental action programs. Since then, as the public's concern over environmental issues has grown—a concern translated into political pressure—environmental protection has become an increasingly prominent component of the EU's policy agenda. The resulting legislation must thus be considered an element of the EU's economic integration program.

Environment was first mentioned in an EC treaty when the 1987 Single European Act included a separate title on environment (albeit consisting of only one article) and determined that legislative proposals concerning environment "will take as a base a high level of protection."[10] The Maastricht Treaty went further, including among the Community's objectives the promotion of "sustainable and non-inflationary growth respecting the environment" and among the activities of the Community "a policy in the sphere of the environment."[11] In addition, whereas the Single European Act introduced the possibility of Council decisions on the basis of a qualified majority (instead of unanimity), the Maastricht Treaty extends the scope of qualified majority voting, albeit under a set of complicated rules.

The rationale for taking action at EC level has been two-fold:

- Many environmental problems require transborder solutions, since the elements do not respect national boundaries (e.g., air and water pollution) and the effects of one country's policies can directly affect another (e.g., transportation of waste products).

- Differing national regulations and requirements add costs to the private sector, which would benefit from a uniform, EU-wide regime (even if not one it considers ideal).

However, the Commission's motivation in many of its legislative proposals has been the desire to increase the level of environmental protection in the EU rather than—or at least more than—to bring about benefits from harmonizing member state policies. One example was 1993 legislation that tightened the previously existing limits on levels of emission of pollutants from motor vehicles (such legislation goes back to the 1970s), with effect from 1996 and 1997, and providing for subsequent legislation to reduce the levels further by 2000, based on technological advances occurring in the interim. Another example was the highly controversial proposal to tax sources of energy, starting at $3 per oil barrel equivalent and rising to $10 by 2000, to combat the growth of "greenhouse gasses" (the other objective, at least as given at the outset, was to promote energy efficiency). This so-called CO_2 tax was bitterly opposed by European industry, for competitive and other reasons, and by the United Kingdom, which objected in principle to an EU levy; by the end of 1993, the proposal was effectively dead (the European Council reaffirmed the objectives, but left appropriate action up to the individual member states).

On the other hand, the rationale for the directive on packaging and packaging waste was the growing disparity of national legislation, with attendant cost and confusion. The lengthy and vigorous debate over this proposal reflected not only the range of affected economic interests, but also the differences among member state concerns. Typically, Denmark, Germany, and the Netherlands support an activist environmental protection policy, almost invariably pushing for the most stringent policies, whereas the economically less developed member states tend to support less far-reaching solutions out of concern over the costs of such policies.

The ability of the EU to arrive at harmonized policies is also limited by the flexibility given the "high-protection" countries in the Single European Act. Article 100a(4) permits a member state to impose tighter restrictions if these are deemed necessary for "protection of the environment" (unless the Commission determines they are trade restrictions in disguise). While this may be justifiable objectively, it clearly undercuts the potential for harmonization. That will presumably be the case with the packaging and packaging waste directive adopted in 1994, because the three above-named member states issued a joint declaration during the debate on the legislative proposal in which they reserved their rights under Article 100a(4).[12]

In recent years there has been a broadening in the approach of EU environmental policy. For example, the emphasis in legislation has shifted from regulatory measures to economic and fiscal measures such as taxes, incentives, and subsidies.[13] This approach was reflected in the adoption in 1992 and 1993, respectively, of regulations on eco-labeling and eco-auditing, although less so regarding recent legislation on waste. The broader approach is spelled out in the fifth environmental action program, which is based on the concept that environment considerations should be integrated into other policy areas.[14] Whereas the first four action programs were essentially legislative programs, the fifth, covering the period from 1993 to 2000, looked to other areas for action. In addition, the fifth action program was accorded greater weight than its predecessors; rather than being "noted" by the Council, it was specifically "adopted" by the Council and the Parliament and thus can be considered an EU, rather than a Commission, strategy. The Commission's interim assessment of the success of its program was one of "cautious optimism."[15]

A possible force for future harmonization of environmental policies in the EU will be the European Environment Agency. Although the requisite legislation was adopted in 1990, the agency's operation was delayed by a protracted debate over the site. Finally, in October 1993, as part of a package agreement on the sites of several EU institutions, Copenhagen was selected. The agency's main task will be to coordinate the development of a European network providing environmental statistics and information to the EU and the member states—on a comparable basis, not previously available—with a view to enabling the latter to develop appropriate policies. Although the agency has no operational functions (which had been desired by some member countries), the legislation calls on the Council of Ministers to consider a possible broadening of the agency's activities within two years of its coming into operation.

Energy

Despite restrictions in virtually all member states on production, importation, and distribution, energy was not included in the single market program. Until recently, all these activities were carried out by organizations in the member states endowed with monopoly powers, justified mainly by the generally accepted requirement for governments to fulfill their public service obligation of ensuring supplies. Thus, the Commission's efforts to open the energy sector to competition within and among member states has been sharply opposed by most national governments and utility companies, though not by the United Kingdom (the only country where extensive deregulation and privatization have taken place) or by major industrial consumers who would be the main beneficiaries.

Legislation having been passed in the 1980s on access between national systems, the Commission has focused its efforts on introducing competition into the transmission and distribution of gas and electricity through third-party access (according to one estimate, the integration of the EU's gas and electricity markets would result in a 15 percent reduction in energy bills).[16] This means that the monopolies would open up their grid networks to competing suppliers (including those from other member states) to give a choice, and presumably lower prices, to consumers. Since the Commission's original proposal that such access be automatic ran into sharp opposition, it was redrafted to require regulated access, in which the access is negotiated. An alternative method of regulating access is the single purchaser system, whereby a body independent of the power-generating authority sells the gas or electricity. Needless to say, negotiated access in whatever form represents less than full access or free competition.

In any event, as of the mid–1990s, agreement had not been reached in the Council on the Commission's proposed third-party access legislation or on legislation prohibiting discrimination in the granting of prospecting and drilling licenses. However, in 1994, the Commission took five member states[17] to the European Court of Justice over the continued existence of their energy monopolies.

Despite the standoff, there has been some liberalization in the member states. Whereas five years ago there were no independent grid networks in member states, by mid–1994 there were five.[18] Another indication that member states may be less resistant to integration in the energy sector was their agreement to include energy in the Maastricht Treaty's list of issues to be reviewed at the Intergovernmental Conference with a view to possible expansion of EU competence.

Policy Sectors

Social Agenda

From the early days of the EC 1992 program, strong political support was given to the view that labor and social policy should be covered in a parallel manner to the single market program; in other words that some form of basic working conditions and social rights should be established and harmonized EU-wide. The most prominent proponent of this view was Commission President Delors. The rationale for EU activity in this area was two-fold: (a) to gain the political support of wage earners for the single market program by making them feel they had as direct a stake in its success as did the European business community; and (b) to prevent "social dumping," i.e., a country using a lower level of labor and social welfare to attract investment and thus gain an "unfair" advantage against its competitors in the EU.

With the political support of the member states, the Commission drafted a "Community Charter of the Fundamental Social Rights of Workers" that was adopted by the heads of government at a European Council meeting in 1989 (though it was not signed by UK's Prime Minister Margaret Thatcher). This Social Charter took the form of a declaration, without legal force, that consisted of a framework of principles, listing fundamental social rights of workers, ranging from the rights of employment and social protection to freedom of association and health protection and safety at the workplace.

To put these principles in tangible form, the charter provided that the Commission would draft a legislative program in areas where there was EC competence. The result was a social action program or social agenda, also issued in 1989, consisting of 47 proposals. However, only 17 of those measures were new; the other 30 were already on the table. Furthermore, only somewhat over half involved legislation at the EC level; the rest would take the form of recommendations and other nonbinding actions. By 1995, most had been adopted. Among the most important were directives requiring employers to inform employees of the terms of their contracts, setting minimum requirements for safety and health protection at the workplace, mandating maternity leave rights, and establishing working times (such as maximum hours per week and minimum rest).

However, three major legislative proposals met stiff opposition. One, dating back to 1990, proposed the regulation of employment conditions for part-time workers, workers with fixed-term contracts and temporary workers, requiring that they be given rights similar to those enjoyed by full-time workers. Despite efforts at compromise, the United Kingdom vetoed its adoption in late 1994; accordingly, the other member states undertook to reconsider the issue under the Maastricht Treaty provisions for the British opt-out (see below). A second proposal provided that workers posted temporarily from one member state to another enjoy the same basic employment rights, most important of which is the minimum wage, as workers in the host country. Although some member states supported the proposal as a means of protecting themselves against cheap imported labor, others opposed it either on principle or to benefit from the advantages they derived from the status quo. The result was continuing deadlock.

However, the central issue of controversy for at least 15 years (the so-called Vredeling proposal was made in 1980) was the effort to establish EU-wide information and consultation rights (concerning company activities) for workers in multinational companies. In effect, the proposal would extend throughout the EU the system that has operated—successfully in the opinion of most participants—in Germany and in various forms in some other continental countries. However, it was bitterly opposed by most of the business community and its representative organizations as impinging on companies' prerogatives and injecting unnecessary inflexibility and regimentation to processes they believed could best be handled in accordance with local and national conditions and traditions.

To that it must added that employers were concerned about the increased power and prestige that the measure would give to unions, particularly at a time of declining union strength, and they feared that over time it would add pressure for what they assume is the long-term goal of European unions—EU-wide collective bargaining. In part for these very reasons, the proposal enjoyed strong union support (the head of the European Trade Union Confederation asserted that the directive "constitutes the keystone of European social policy").[19]

The works councils directive was finally adopted in September 1994; its provisions will apply as of September 1996. It requires that multinational enterprises with 1,000 employees or more, of which at least 150 are employed in two member states, enter into negotiations with employer representatives to set up a council or other form of information and consultation forum. If negotiations do not succeed within three years, a "European Committee" or "Works Council" (defined in the directive) must be established. It is estimated that about 1,200 firms will have to comply with those provisions.[20]

Agreement was finally reached on the works councils directive mainly because the United Kingdom did not participate in the Council vote, nor is it covered by the provisions of the directive.[21] The background to that circumstance is the sharp philosophical divide—and the resulting major controversy—between most of continental Europe and the United Kingdom that has existed since the Conservatives came to power in 1979 over the EU's labor and social policy. The mainstream continental traditions of social welfare and role of the state are at stark variance with British government policy. Indeed, the British government believes that much of the EU's social program constitutes an intrusion into member state prerogatives and furthermore that it threatens to overturn Conservatives' policies that, the government believes, have contributed significantly to the favorable performance and increased competitiveness of the British economy.

The British were able to block or delay much of the proposed legislation because of the requirement that it be passed unanimously. However, under the 1987 Single European Act, qualified majority voting was introduced for measures relating to the "health and safety of workers," and that unblocked some legislation. Not surprisingly, the Commission, in introducing legislation, has taken a broad interpretation of this phrase to improve the chances of member state approval, which occasionally has given rise to British objections, as in the case of the working time directive.

However, the most important development was the British opt-out of the Social Protocol attached to the Maastricht Treaty, whose most immediate result was the adoption, described above, of the works councils directive. During the negotiations leading to the Maastricht Treaty, a major effort was made by some member states to expand the scope of EU involvement in social policy and to extend the use of qualified majority voting. When attempts to obtain British support by progressively weakening the proposed texts proved unsuccessful, the other eleven member states decided to proceed on their own. Although this is referred to as the British opt-out, in a formal sense it was the opposite. While the preexisting social provisions of the treaty remain unchanged and apply to all EU members, the social chapter was contained in a separate protocol that applies only to members other than the United Kingdom. In fact, however, the social chapter will operate as if it were part of the basic treaty, making normal use of the existing institutions and decision-making procedures of the EU, except that it will do so in the anomalous and somewhat confusing circumstance of involving fourteen of the fifteen member states.

Apart from a revision of the agreed policy objectives of social policy, the social protocol contains three main provisions. First, it extends the range of issues over which agreement will be reached by a qualified majority (i.e., of the participating member states—eleven at the time the treaty was signed, but now fourteen), rather than unanimity, such as working conditions, information and consultation of workers, and equality of treatment between men and women. Second, it provides for unanimous voting on proposals relating to social security, termination of employment, and the condition of employment of third-country nationals. Finally, it institutionalizes consultations on social policy matters between the "social partners," i.e., workers' and employees' representatives, a consultation and advisory process begun at EC level in 1985, and it opens up the possibility for Europe-wide employers' and trade union organizations to enter into collective agreements that substitute for EU legislation.

Following conclusion of the Maastricht Treaty, the Commission turned its attention to the next phase of social policy for the EU. In late 1993, it issued a green paper, in which it offered its view of the achievements of social policy, the challenges facing Europe, and possible responses.[22] Taking into account the problem of rising unemployment, the Commission gave as its premise that economic and social progress must go hand in hand, asserting that "[s]ocial progress is possible only through economic success but equally high social standards are a vital part of building a competitive economy."[23]

Following consultations, the Commission issued a white paper (general statement of proposals) in mid–1994, intended to form the basis for its social action plan for the coming year.[24] The Commission offered its diagnosis of the situation facing Europe, recognized the limited ability of the EU to resolve the problems, and stressed the role that member states will have to play. Thus, the white paper contained no broad program for legislative action, concentrating instead on offering advice. It set forth a number of proposed activities in what it considered to be the six priority areas: jobs; building a "world class labor force"; high labor standards; building a European labor market; equality of opportunity between men and women; and maintaining and adapting the European model of the welfare state.

These themes were reflected in the Commission's social action program, issued in follow-up to the white paper in early 1995, setting out its plan for the coming three years.[25] Identifying competitiveness and job creation as the top priorities, the Commission emphasized the need for discussion and close cooperation at all levels rather than regulation and additional legislation, and it stressed the need to consolidate (rather than expand) the legislative agenda.

Structural Policy

At the time of the EC's creation, the differences in level of economic development among the six founding members were fairly minor (an exception was Italy, which began an upward spurt in the 1960s). However, as a result of enlargements, particularly those in the 1980s, the disparity between the better-off and less well-off member states widened,[26] including significant disparities among regions of the richer member states. With it came pressures for the EC to undertake measures to help raise the economic level of the less developed member states to that of the others. Accordingly, a program of "structural funds" to address the intra-EC regional imbalances was instituted.

This effort was formalized by recognition of the concept of "economic and social cohesion" in a section in the Single European Act, in which the EC committed itself to "aim at reducing disparities between the various regions and the backwardness of the least-favored regions" and mandated that the Council agree on a reform of the program of structural funds within one year.[27] Concurrently, as the EC was developing its single market program, a consensus developed that a substantial increase in the structural funds should be a key component of the EC 1992 effort. That view was based on two calculations: an economic one that the market liberalization resulting from EC 1992 would cause an exacerbation of regional imbalances; and a related political one that a tangible, monetary indication of the EC's concern would be a prerequisite to obtaining the support of the less advanced member states for the program.

The resulting program for 1989–93 provided for the expenditure of European Currency Units (ECU) 63 billion ($79 billion),[28] roughly doubling the previous program. The funds were to be divided among areas and projects in the member states on the basis of five priorities: assisting backward regions (alone accounting for about two-thirds of the total); promoting economic conversion and modernization in declining industrial areas; combating long-term unemployment; integrating youth into the workforce; and developing rural areas. The main beneficiaries were Greece, Ireland, Portugal, and Spain, the four member states that are typically treated differently (they are often referred to as the "cohesion states") not only because they have the lowest per capita GDP but also because they are deemed to require more time to adapt to EU legislation.

The issue of cohesion arose again in connection with the negotiations between the EU and members of the European Free Trade Association (EFTA) to form the European Economic Area (EEA) (see Chapter 1). Concerns were expressed by the cohesion states that the EEA would produce a further shift of the balance in favor of the richer countries. As a result, the EFTA participants in the EEA agreed to a five-year ECU 2 billion ($2.5 billion) contribution that would consist of ECU 1.5 billion in interest rate subsidies on loans to the cohesion countries from the European Investment Bank and ECU 500 million in grants for development projects.

During the negotiations leading to the Maastricht Treaty, the cohesion states pressed strongly for a strengthened structural policy, and to a large extent they succeeded. Article 2 listed "a high degree of convergence of economic performance" among the Union's tasks, Article 3 included "the strengthening of economic and social cohesion" among its activities, Article 130 contained various provisions promoting such policies, and a separate protocol on economic and social cohesion further extended the scope of these provisions. Although the treaty's provisions had not yet gone into effect, they nevertheless provided the backdrop for the discussions and negotiations over the structural program for 1994–99. The package totaled ECU 141.5 billion ($177 billion)—again doubling the projected transfer of funds—and became the subject of an "undignified scramble" among the member states (including the richer ones on behalf of their poorer regions) for their share of the pie,[29] which was ultimately resolved through the diplomatic efforts of Commission President Delors.

Enforcement Mechanisms

All the legislation and good intentions in the world will not suffice to ensure that the agreed-upon integration takes place unless effective enforcement mechanisms exist. In the case of the single market and its related measures, enforcement takes three forms.

Commission Oversight

The Treaty of Rome provides that the Commission will "ensure that the provisions of th[e] Treaty and the measures taken ... pursuant thereto are applied."[30] The Commission can determine that a member state has taken an action that is not in accord with the treaty or specific legislation, or failed to take necessary action, on the basis of a complaint brought by an individual or organization, another member state, or on its own initiative. In such an instance, the Commission first sends the member state in question a "letter of formal notice," requesting an explanation of the alleged violation. If an unsatisfactory reply (or no reply) is received, the Commission then issues a "reasoned opinion" (the so-called Article 169 infringement proceedings), explaining why it considers the member state to be in violation of the treaty. If that fails to bring about remedial action, the Commission will take the offending member state to the European Court of Justice. Although the volume of infringement cases is rather substantial (approximately 1,000 letters of formal notice are issued annually), relatively few cases are referred to the Court (about 100 per year).[31] The vast majority are settled at an earlier stage, in part because deliberate noncompliance is quite rare; in most instances noncompliance results from misinterpretations or delay.

To a very considerable degree, these infringement procedures relate to the transposition of EU legislation into national laws and regulations. Each member state is required to inform the Commission of the action it has taken. Under the procedure described above, if the Commission (either on its own or on the basis of a complaint) determines that the transposition has not been appropriately carried out, it advises the member state accordingly. The member state then makes the necessary change(s) or is subject to being taken before the European Court of Justice.

This procedure does not always work smoothly. In some cases, the member states neglect to advise the Commission of the transposition they have made of EU legislation. Frequently, the Commission lacks the necessary resources and/or expertise to evaluate the measures taken at a national level. And private sector groups often consider it not in their best interests to complain about what member states have or have not done (e.g., the pharmaceutical industry has shied away from seeking action against national governments that it believes have not carried out the provisions of the pricing transparency directive because governments are the regulators and, in large part, the paymasters of the companies).

In 1994, the number of letters of formal notice dropped substantially, reflecting an improvement in member state notification of transposition measures. At the same time, the Commission adopted a tougher policy on reasoned opinions and referrals to the Court, the former increasing by 50 percent and the latter by 100 percent because "non-transposition is very prejudicial to the life of the Community."[32] The Commission also noted that despite the overall improvement in member state actions, a sharp increase in infringements in the public procurement sector had taken place (resulting in a doubling of infringement proceedings) and, to a lesser extent, with respect to value-added tax legislation. The performance of the member states varied considerably, with Denmark (no referrals to the Court since 1991) and the United Kingdom committing the fewest breaches of EU law, and Belgium, Ireland, and especially Greece accounting for the highest number of referrals.

Two other areas of Commission enforcement activities bear mention. One is its broad powers in policing the treaty's competition provisions, described below. The other—though less a question of enforcement than of protecting an EU program—concerns the promotion of European standards. Under a 1983 directive, member states are required to notify the Commission in advance of draft regulations and standards relating to technical specifications. The Commission can require the member state to suspend adoption of a standard if it determines that a harmonized EU standard is being developed.

Competition Policy

A key element in the enforcement of the single market has been the powers granted the Commission by the Treaty of Rome to combat market distortions. These cover four areas: (1) the nondiscriminatory operation of state monopolies (Articles 37 and 90); (2) the prohibition of arrangements that restrict or distort competition (Article 85) and of abuses of a dominant position (Article 86); (3) the requirement that public bodies or bodies operating under special or exclusive rights granted by member states abide by the Treaty's provisions, in particular the rules on competition (Article 90); and (4) the regulation of aid granted by member states (Articles 92–94). The treaty also leaves enforcement of these powers in the hands of the Commission without requiring confirmation of its actions by the Council (although, as in all matters relating to the treaty, recourse is open to the European Court of Justice).

Competition policy plays a crucial role in helping to ensure the effective operation of the single market, a role emphasized in the Single European Act, reiterated in subsequent Commission documents—its industrial policy statements of 1991 and 1994[33] and its white paper on growth, competitiveness, and employment of December 1993[34]—and reaffirmed in the Maastricht Treaty.[35] Starting with the appointment of Peter Sutherland as the commissioner responsible for competition in 1985, the Commission has played an activist role in carrying out the EU's competition policy and has thereby contributed significantly to the progress of the single market program. Its activities in this regard have been concentrated in three areas (a fourth, use of Article 90 powers to liberalize the telecommunications sector, was mentioned above).[36]

1. *Restrictive agreements and abuses of dominant positions.* The Commission carries a heavy load of Article 85 and 86 cases. During the first half of the decade, an annual average of almost 400 new cases were registered, and more than 800 were closed annually, thus reducing the pending cases from over 3,000 in the late 1980s to about 1,000.[37] The vast majority of cases are disposed of under informal procedures: either by administrative closure of the case or by "comfort letter," whose use has increased dramatically. Under that procedure, following negotiations in which it requires firms to accept the changes it deems necessary, the Commission informs the firm in question that it will not initiate or pursue formal proceedings against it.[38]

Despite their small number, formal decisions are a crucial component of the enforcement process. There has been a gradual increase in the number of formal decisions taken, particularly regarding restrictive agreements, which totaled 27 in the 1960s, 109 in the 1970s, and 148 in the 1980s. At first these cases overwhelmingly involved manufacturing enterprises; however, the services share has become prominent, especially since 1985, probably reflecting actions taken by firms in anticipation of the single market. On the other hand, there have been very few decisions under Article 86 (abuse of a dominant position). Only 21 such decisions were taken in the 1970s and 1980s, although the number increased in later years, including those involving services.[39] Under the two articles, an average of 23 decisions were taken annually in the 1990–1994 period, with a record 33 decisions in 1994.[40]

The Commission's penalty powers are significant—it can fine offending firms up to 10 percent of their total annual turnover—and it has used them. In 1994, it fined fourteen steel tube producers over ECU 100 million ($125 million) for price-fixing and market-sharing, and it levied a record fine of ECU 132 million ($165 million) against a nineteen-firm cartonboard cartel for price-fixing. The most celebrated recent case under

Article 86 involved Tetra-Pak's abuse of its near-monopoly of the EU market through its marketing, consumer contracts, and pricing policies, for which an ECU 75 million ($94 million) fine was levied.

2. *Mergers and acquisitions.* With the sharp increase in M&As that began in the late 1980s in anticipation of the single market, it was clear that the Commission's powers to determine whether mergers and acquisitions resulted in a "dominant position" only retrospectively were insufficient. A lengthy debate took place among the member states on the provisions of a regulation enabling the Commission to review cases prospectively, particularly regarding two issues. First, what criteria should be used in determining whether to approve a merger, the main issues being whether to view the market as the entire EC rather than one or more member states and whether mergers could be approved on the grounds that they enhanced the EC's competitive position globally. Second, what should the threshold be above which approval of mergers by the Commission would be required.

In the resulting 1989 regulation,[41] called "the cornerstone of the Community's competition policy and single market program" by one observer,[42] the first issue was resolved essentially as desired by the more free market member states, i.e., the promotion of an EC industrial policy could not be used to justify a dominant position, and the relevant market would be determined on a case-by-case basis. Regarding the second, the threshold for "concentrations with a Community dimension" was set at a worldwide turnover of ECU 5 billion ($6 billion), with a minimum ECU 250 million ($313 million) turnover in at least two member states and less than two-thirds of its EU-wide turnover in a single member state. Although it had originally been expected that the statutory review of three-years' operation of the regulation would result in a lowering of the threshold, the member states, at the instigation of the large members pressing the case for subsidiarity (see Chapter 7), opted to forgo any changes before at least 1996.

To police this new area the Commission established a merger task force in 1990, charged with making a preliminary determination of all mergers above the threshold within one month and then, for those for which an investigation was deemed necessary, a decision within four months. In such cases, the task force makes a three-step determination: the relevant product market; the relevant geographic market; and whether the merger would create or strengthen a dominant position.

Despite some initial scepticism, the task force has operated effectively. It has reviewed a substantial number of cases, acting within the specified deadlines and with considerably less controversy than many had expected. In just under the first three years of the task force's operation, 164 mergers were notified to it. Of these, eleven were determined to present a prima facie danger to competition and thus were examined in detail.[43] In only one of these cases did the task force reject the proposed merger—the purchase of De Havilland by Aerospaziale and Alenia, which was the subject of a sharp debate within the Commission over the determination of what constituted the relevant market. However, three more rejections—all in the media sector—followed over a one-year period in 1994–95: the proposed merger of a media services group involving Bertelsmann, Deutsche Telekom, and Kirch; the creation of Nordic Satellite Distribution, involving Danish, Norwegian, and Swedish interests; and a Dutch-Luxembourg venture, Holland Media Group.[44] Despite the low rejection rate, most of the cases examined in detail by the task force are approved subject to conditions, often stringent (e.g., involving some divestiture), aimed at preventing the creation of a dominant position. In addition, a number of proposed mergers have been withdrawn after informal contacts indicated the Commission would not approve them.

3. *State aid.* The Treaty of Rome recognizes the authority of member states to provide assistance to groups and individuals within their borders, but it prescribes limits to such aid. The first study of the extent of this aid, issued by the Commission in 1989, revealed they were widespread. The Commission estimated annual state aid during the 1981–1986 period as averaging ECU 82 billion ($103 billion) in the ten-member EC; this amount, it said, had a negative impact on the unity of the common market, competition, and thus completion of the internal market.[45] Subsequent reports were issued in 1990, 1992, and 1995. Although state aid declined somewhat in absolute amount, as a percentage of GDP and in ECU per person employed, the Commission termed the volume of state aid "still massive." The distribution of state aid among sectors has remained fairly constant: in 1990–92, manufacturing accounted for 41 percent of the total, compared to 29 percent for transportation, 15 percent for coal, and 15 percent for agriculture and fisheries. For the same period, annual state aid averaged ECU 94 billion ($118 billion) for the twelve member states, accounting for just under 2 percent of GDP and just over ECU 700 ($875) per person employed.[46] However, these figures mask important disparities among member states, with the highest levels relative to GDP and per person employed in the larger, more economically advanced member states: Italy, Germany (one-third of it for the coal industry), and Belgium.[47]

The Commission's activities of monitoring and challenging state aid is intended to decrease government interference in the marketplace and thereby increase competition. Interestingly, the number of cases taken up by the Commission has not increased significantly, and the share of those on which the Commission did not register an objection has risen.[48] Nonetheless, the lowering of intra-EU barriers plus the adverse effects of the recession of the early 1990s increased pressures on member state authorities to assist affected groups. To improve its oversight, as well as to keep up pressure on member states, the Commission instructed member states in 1991 to file annual reports on the financial links between the government and the public sector companies.[49]

In determining whether a particular form of state aid is compatible with EU rules, the Commission considers three questions: (1) does it address a Community objective; (2) is it an appropriate mechanism for contributing to that objective; and (3) will the beneficial effects outweigh the damage caused by the distortion of competition?[50] On a number of occasions the Commission has made a negative determination; it has then required beneficiaries of state aid to refund excess amounts to the national government, e.g., after a protracted dispute between the Commission and the British government, British Aerospace was obliged to repay the 57 million pounds (approximately $90 million) it had received from the British government as an incentive for its purchase of Rover.

However, the most publicized and politically sensitive area has been state aid to national airlines.[51] Although Article 92 of the Treaty of Rome explicitly lists the types of aid that are "compatible" with the single market, the Commission must necessarily take account of political reality in arriving at its decisions on state aid issues. In the case of the airlines it is dealing with national prestige. The Commission's decisions in this sector have usually been controversial and often questionable economically, though politically understandable. Recently, it has required that the aid be part of a restructuring plan, and in decisions approving a number of airline bailouts, it has asserted that its approval was "one time and last time" (which has not silenced the sceptics). Nonetheless, the amounts of state aid have been substantial,[52] and control exercised by the Commission has been less strict than in other areas.[53]

European Court of Justice

The Court has played an unobtrusive, but significant role in promoting the process of economic integration through its decisions and resulting legal precedents.[54] The Court's authority is based on two essential doctrines that it developed over the years: "direct effect" (the Treaty of Rome and EU legislation not requiring transposition confer rights and impose obligations without further intervention at the national or EU level) and the supremacy of EU law over national law. The Court's actions take two forms: "preliminary rulings" on interpretations of EU law, which are made at the request of a national court; and decisions on cases brought before it.

Over the years, the Court has rendered a number of key decisions enabling the EU to pursue economic integration objectives, in particular through interpretations of Article 30 of the treaty, which prohibits quantitative restrictions and measures having equivalent effect. Two landmark decisions were rendered in the 1970s. In the 1974 Dassonville case, the Court ruled that "[a]ll trading rules enacted by member states which are capable of hindering directly or indirectly, actually or potentially, intra-Community trade are to be considered as measures having an effect equivalent to quantitative restrictions," thereby establishing a legal basis for national laws to be challenged on the grounds of creating nontariff barriers.[55]

Better known is the 1979 Cassis de Dijon decision, which established the principle that a product lawfully produced in one member state cannot be barred from the market of another member state, subject to a "rule of reason" concerning national legislation based on "reasonable" policy goals, such as environment, health, and consumer protection.[56] Recent decisions have included the 1988 decision in the Vereniging Bond van Adverteerders (opening the way for the removal of barriers in the services sector), various rulings confirming the Commission's enforcement actions in the competition field, and the ruling (Francovich and Bonifaci case) that individuals could sue their government for damages resulting from the government's failure to transpose a directive within the legislatively specified period.

One significant innovation in the Maastricht Treaty was the provision that the Court can fine a member state for not complying with its judgment in a case where "it failed to fulfill its obligations under the Treaty." In such cases, the Commission can take the member state to court and declare the fine it considers appropriate. Although the Commission had not used this procedure as yet, it advised member states in by July 1994 of its concern over the continuing delays by some of them in carrying out its judgments, and it threatened to begin implementing the procedures for fines.[57]

Although the Court has not pursued an "integration agenda" as such, it has made, as indicated above, a significant contribution to economic integration in the EU. Nonetheless, as with most courts, it usually chooses to make its decisions on as narrow a legal basis as possible. Furthermore, the scope for the development of alternative views is limited by the fact that neither the voting on decisions nor the dissenting opinions are made public, reflecting judicial practice on the continent. Finally, the Court's rulings, possibly reflecting changing public attitudes, have tended in the 1990s to define more narrowly the powers of the EU institutions and to accept more readily the claims of the member states. Thus, for example, it ruled in 1991 (in the Keck case) that certain commercial restrictions on the activities of a profession did not constitute barriers to trade (and therefore fell outside the scope of the treaty), and in 1994 it denied the Commission the exclusive competence for concluding—and thus signing on behalf of the EU—the services and intellectual property agreements forming part of the Uruguay Round (in both cases, with minor exceptions, the Court ruled that these competences were shared between the Commission and the member states).[58]

Notes

1. Treaty of Rome as amended by Maastricht Treaty, Article 109j.

2. Protocol on the Excessive Deficit Procedure and Protocol on the Convergence Criteria Referred to in Article 109j.

3. A weighted voting system, specified in the treaty, with votes apportioned on the basis of population, though with a proportionally greater number of votes given to the smaller member states, requiring about 70 percent of the votes for approval (see Chapter 4).

4. Treaty of Rome as amended by Maastricht Treaty, Articles 105 and 107 respectively.

5. All except the drachma, the lira and the UK pound. Since accession, the Austrian schilling (but not the Finnish mark or the Swedish krona) has joined the ERM.

6. "Telecommunications: Commission launches debate on infrastructure deregulation," *European Report*, No. 2011, January 28, 1995.

7. "Summary Report concerning the Green Paper on the Development of the Common Market for Telecommunications Services and Equipment," XIII/197(87), May 26, 1987.

8. "Europe and the global information society," recommendations to the European Council by a group of prominent persons, May 26, 1994.

9. These relate to motor vehicle emissions and certain regulations involving the chemical industry.

10. Treaty of Rome as amended by Single European Act, Articles 130r, s, and t, and 100a(3), respectively.

11. Maastricht Treaty, Articles 2 and 3(k), respectively.

12. A somewhat analogous example is the auto emissions directive, which specifies, at Dutch instigation, that the provisions will not affect the right of a member state to include emissions in determining the level of road taxes.

13. Desmond Dinan, *Ever Closer Union? An Introduction to the European Community* (Boulder: Lynne Rienner Publishers, 1994), pp. 385–386.

14. European Commission, "Towards Sustainability: A European Community Programme of Policy and Action in relation to the Environment and Sustainable Development," COM(92) 23, March 27, 1992.

15. Commission Communication, "Interim Review of Implementation of the European Community's Programme of Policy and Action in Relation to the Environment and Sustainable Development," COM(94) 453, November 30, 1994, p. 53.

16. Riccardo Perissich, "1 January 1993—one day in the life of the internal market," *European Business Journal*, Vol. 5, Issue 1, January 1, 1993, p. 10.

17. The five members were France, Ireland, Italy, the Netherlands, and Spain.

18. "A choice of power and the power of choice," *Financial Times*, June 20, 1994.

19. Quoted in "UNICE now showing flexibility—too late?," *European Report*, No. 1920, January 26, 1994, p. III/7.

20. "Works Councils Directive Adopted," *European Report*, No. 1978, September 24, 1994, pp. IV/6–7.

21. Nonetheless, EC Commissioner Padraig Flynn noted in mid–1995 that British workers had been covered in all works councils established by non-British firms and that a number of UK companies had established works councils voluntarily. As quoted in "Works Councils: Concerns about Transposition Dispelled," *European Report*, No. 2058, July 15, 1995.

22. European Commission, "European Social Policy: Options for the Union," COM(93) 551, November 17, 1993.

23. Ibid., p. 13.

24. European Commission, "European Social Policy—A way forward for the Union," COM(94) 333, July 27, 1994.

25. European Commission, "Medium-Term Social Action Programme for the Period 1995–1997," Communication to the Council, Parliament, Economic and Social Committee, and Committee of the Regions, April 11, 1995.

26. According to European Commission, Eurostat news release, No. 60/94, December 13, 1994, per capita GDP in the four richest member states ranged from 122 to 168 on a scale with 100 representing the fifteen-member state average, while that of the four poorest countries fell between 46 and 71.

27. Treaty of Rome as amended by Single European Act, Article 130a and 130d, respectively.

28. As noted in Chapter 2, the ECU-dollar exchange rate has fluctuated over the years. For consistency's sake, the rate of ECU = $1.25, the approximate rate for August 1995, has been used throughout the text.

29. "Poorer than thou," *The Economist*, July 10, 1993.

30. Treaty of Rome, Article 155.

31. European Commission, "12th Annual Report on Monitoring the Application of European Union Law (1994)," COM(95) 500, July 6, 1995, p. 102.

32. Ibid., pp. 1e and 102.

33. European Commission, "European industrial policy for the 1990s," *Bulletin of the European Communities*, Supplement 3/91, Office for Official Publications of the European Communities, Luxembourg, 1991; and European Commission, "An industrial competitiveness policy for the European Union," *Bulletin of the European Union*, Supplement 3/94, Office for Official Publications of the European Communities, Luxembourg, 1994.

34. European Commission, "Growth, competitiveness, employment: The challenges and ways forward into the 21st century," White Paper, *Bulletin of the European Communities*, Supplement 6/93, Office for Official Publications of the European Communities, Luxembourg, 1993.

35. Treaty on European Union, Article 3(a) includes among the activities to be supported by the EU "the general economic policies in the Community, in accordance with the principle of an open market economy with free competition."

36. For a full account of the Commission's activities in the field of competition policy, see European Commission, "XXIV Report of the Commission on Competition Policy—1994," COM(95) 142, April 28, 1995.

37. Ibid., pp. 617–620.

38. The fact that comfort letters have limited legal standing has not detracted from their popularity.

39. Andre Sapir, Pierre Buigues, and Alexis Jacquemin, "European Competition Policy in Manufacturing and Services: A Two-Speed Approach?" *Oxford Review of Economic Policy,* Vol. 9, No. 2 (1993), pp. 119–120.

40. European Commission, "Report on Competition Policy—1994," pp. 617–620.

41. European Commission, COM(89) 4064, December 21, 1989.

42. Dinan, *Ever Closer Union?* p. 375.

43. "Competition and integration: Community merger control policy," *European Economy,* No. 57, 1994.

44. Although the turnover of the companies involved in the Holland Media Group did not meet the treshold established in the EU legislation for review of the merger, the case was brought to the Commission by the Netherlands because it has no merger legislation. Unlike the situation regarding the other rejected merger proposals, the Holland Media Group was given three months to modify the terms of the merger so that it would meet the conditions laid down by the Commission.

45. European Commission, "First Survey on State Aids in the European Community," Office for Official Publications of the European Communities, Luxembourg, 1989, pp. 10 and 48.

46. European Commission, "Fourth Survey on State Aids in the European Union in the Manufacturing and Certain Other Sectors," COM(95) 365, July 26, 1995.

47. The figures for Greece are excluded from this calculation because they are provisional and for Luxembourg because they include extremely large support for railways.

48. No objections were raised in 60 percent of the cases in 1987 and in 80 percent "since then." Sapir et al., "European Competition Policy," p. 123.

49. Two years later, the European Court of Justice ruled that the Commission had not followed appropriate procedures (it had used a Commission communication rather than a Commission directive) in placing its requirement on the member states. That error was subsequently rectified.

50. "Commission insistence on state aid policy," *European Report,* No. 1966, July 13, 1994, p. III/2.

51. Equally sensitive was the Commission's first decision in the banking sector, when it approved (though with conditions) state aid of French francs 45 billion (approximately $9 billion) to Credit Lyonnais in 1995, the largest amount ever authorized.

52. "Flying in the face of EU spirit," *The European*, July 29, 1994, quotes the Commission's figure of subsidies to EU carriers during 1991–94 as ECU 8.4 billion ($10.5 billion). According to one US analyst, as quoted in "Flying the flag crowds airways," *Financial Times*, July 28, 1994, the nearly $4 billion French government aid to Air France, approved by the Commission in 1994, is "enough money to create a new airline from scratch."

53. That is possibly a reflection of the fact that the commissioner responsible for transportation, not competition policy, has the lead in the Commission's consideration of state aid to airlines.

54. For an account of the theoretical basis for the Court's contribution to integration, see Anne-Marie Burley and Walter Mattli, "Europe Before the Court: A Political Theory of Legal Integration," *International Organization*, Vol. 47, No. 1, Winter 1993, pp. 41–76.

55. The Court's interpretation, according to Damian Chalmers, "Free Movement of Goods within the European Community: An Unhealthy Addiction to Scotch Whisky?," *International and Comparative Law Review*, Vol. 42, Part 2, April 1993, p. 275, "reflect[ed] a philosophy of extreme economic liberalism."

56. For a detailed account of the political aspects and implications of the Court's decision, see Karen J. Alter and Sophie Meunier-Aitsahalia, "Judicial Politics in the European Community: European Integration and the Pathbreaking *Cassis de Dijon* Decision," *Comparative Political Studies*, Vol. 26, No. 4, January 1994, pp. 535–561.

57. European Commission, "Twelfth Annual Report on Monitoring the Application of European Union Law (1994)," COM (95) 500, pp. 363–378, lists 78 cases of nonimplementation by member states of ECJ decisions. The biggest offenders were Belgium (18), Italy (15), France (10), and Spain (9). At the other end of the scale, no cases of nonimplementation were pending against Denmark or Portugal and only one against the Netherlands.

58. For a concise, readable account of rulings of the Court in 1994, see Jo Shaw, "Legal Developments," in *The European Union in 1994: Annual Review of Activities*, ed. Neill Nugent (London: Blackwell, 1995.)

4

Movement Toward Political Integration

Complete political integration—a federal union of states—was the ultimate goal of the founders of what has today become the European Union. However, they recognized from the outset that the peoples of Western Europe would not accept political union unless they had directly experienced tangible benefits from economic cooperation and acquired the habit of interacting with the citizens of the other countries. As a result both of this conceptual framework and of the boundaries of political feasibility, the history of integration efforts in the European Community, and then Union, is predominantly, if not overwhelmingly, economic.

Nevertheless, there has been an important political dimension to the integration process, which in some areas is long standing: cooperation on *foreign policy* dates from the beginning of the 1970s, and the sharing of sovereignty in *decision making* is inherent in the EC. The origins of a common *security policy* are contained in the Single European Act, and cooperation in *justice and internal affairs* (the third pillar)—included here under a broad interpretation of political integration—was added by the Maastricht Treaty. The status of efforts to achieve a measure of integration in these four areas is reviewed in this chapter.

Foreign Policy

Although the first mention in a treaty of "political cooperation" among the member states was contained in the Single European Act (1987), in fact this process was initiated as a result of a Council of Ministers decision in 1969. European Political Cooperation (EPC), as the process was called, consisted of regular and intensified interchanges among the foreign ministries of the member states. These took the form of summit meetings of the heads of government, semiannual meetings of foreign ministers (including so-called Gymnich meetings, i.e., off-the-record sessions with no fixed agenda), quadrannual meetings of a political committee (consisting of heads of foreign ministry political departments), meetings of working groups of mid-level officials on geographic and functional issues, and the establishment of telecommunications links among the foreign ministry counterparts. The results were not only organizational but political as well—a commitment to a distinct profile in international relations, consultation, and joint activities—resulting in "a regular and gradual accretion of foreign policy consultation and coordination."[1]

The Single European Act formalized the EPC system. The Act required meetings at least four times a year of the foreign ministers within the EPC framework, as well as regular meetings of the political committee and its subsidiary bodies, it provided for emergency meetings of the political committee, and it established a separate EPC secretariat. The organizational structure of EPC remained distinct from that of the other EC institutions; in other words, EPC was exclusively a matter for the member states, operating from their capitals. However, the act gave the European Commission a role that it had not had previously, of becoming "fully associated with the proceedings," it provided that the European Parliament be regularly informed of EPC activities and that its views be taken into account, and it mandated the Commission and the Council Presidency to ensure that the external policies of the EC and those agreed in EPC be consistent. The latter provision was intended to end the unnatural separation that dictated that member state foreign ministers would meet once as members of the EC's General Affairs Council and then as ministerial representatives under the EPC structure to discuss the same issues, often on the same day.

Although the task the member states set out for themselves in the area of political cooperation in the Single European Act was fairly general, it represented a significant step in the direction of integration. The member states agreed to "endeavor jointly to formulate and implement a European foreign policy."[2] They undertook to work toward "the convergence of their positions and the implementation of joint actions;" to "give due consideration to the desirability of adopting and implementing common European positions;" and to "ensure that common principles and objectives are gradually developed and defined."[3]

The Maastricht Treaty built on the provisions of the Single European Act, strengthening its objectives and mechanisms. As the second of the EU's five objectives, the treaty listed the "assert[ion of] its identity on the international scene, in particular through the implementation of a common foreign and security policy."[4] In the words of one observer, "the tentativeness of the [Single European Act] has been replaced by the firmness of Maastricht."[5] In place of EPC, the treaty established a Common Foreign and Security Policy (CFSP), which forms the second of the three pillars of the EU and thus remains an intergovernmental activity, legally separate from the first (economic) and third (justice and internal affairs) pillars.

The treaty declares without qualification that "[t]he Union and its Member States shall define and implement a common foreign and security policy ... covering all areas of foreign and security policy." It then provides that the EU will pursue its CFSP objectives by systematic cooperation and implementing joint actions.[6] Under the rubric of "systematic cooperation," it includes consultation on matters of general interest to ensure that the member states' "combined influence is exerted as effectively as possible by means of concerted and convergent action"; the definition of a common position, whenever necessary, to which the member states will ensure conformance of their national policies; and coordination of member state actions (including those in accordance with common positions) in international organizations and conferences.[7]

However, the main innovation of the treaty is the provision that joint actions will be gradually implemented in areas where the member states have "important interests in common,"[8] thereby going beyond the previously existing nonbinding machinery for foreign policy cooperation. The procedure calls for the Council to decide, on the basis of "general guidelines" established by the European Council, that a matter should be the subject of a joint action. It then decides on the scope of the action, sets its objectives, its direction (if necessary), and the means, procedures, and conditions for its implementation.[9] Decisions on joint actions are taken by unanimity; however, the Council can decide at any stage in the process which matters to decide by qualified majority, a provision intended to facilitate decisions on the implementation of a joint action.

Regarding the mechanisms for carrying out CFSP, the treaty provides that the Presidency (the member state at the time holding the presidency of the Council, which is established by rotation) will represent the Union on CFSP matters and that it can be assisted by the preceding and succeeding Presidencies (the so-called troika that has become more or less institutionalized and that, incidentally, always includes a Commission representative). The roles of the Commission and the Parliament are expanded: in addition to remaining "fully associated" with CFSP work (specifically including troika activities), the Commission can now influence the agenda through its right to raise questions and make proposals (in other words, it has acquired a shared right of initiative), while Parliament must be "consulted on broad policy directions."[10]

The history of political cooperation in the EC and then EU has been a gradual but perceptible movement toward a convergence of foreign policies and toward "speaking with one voice." This development is the result of the cumulative effects of many years of formal and informal interaction among those involved in the formulation of foreign policy, primarily but not exclusively foreign ministry officials, and recognition of the advantages of policies enunciated on behalf of the member states as a group, or at least undertaken in a coordinated manner. Even when a member state takes a position that conflicts or contrasts with that of other member states, as is often the case, it is seldom ignorant of the positions of the other EU members.

According to one observer, the international actions of the EC within the EPC framework (i.e., pre-Maastricht Treaty) could be divided into the following categories: declarations on international events; consultations with other countries; ministerial missions to areas of international tension; participation in international forums; and diplomatic sanctions.[11] Needless to say, these activities are distinct from the international activities that devolved from the EC's economic responsibilities, such as multilateral and bilateral trade negotiations and development assistance. With the possible exception of diplomatic sanctions, none of these actions represents a significant pooling of sovereign prerogatives.

Nonetheless, in recent years the EC/EU found itself increasingly drawn into the foreign policy arena, the three seminal events being the collapse of the Soviet empire, the Gulf War, and the civil war in ex-Yugoslavia.[12] The first resulted in a radical shift in policy toward Central and Eastern Europe, from marginal to intense interest and involvement (see Chapter 1). The programs and actions developed vis-à-vis that area provided a far more active and visible role for the EU as distinguished from that of the individual member states. For example, the Commission represents the EU in the so-called G-24 (group of countries) as the coordinator of assistance from the West (including the United States) to the countries of the region, and relations with Central and Eastern Europe are largely carried out under the framework of a series of agreements negotiated with the EU.

In many respects, the EC's response to the Gulf War exposed the weakness of its system of political cooperation and accordingly was the subject of much criticism or at least hand-wringing. That was somewhat unfair in that the weakness was largely the result of the absence of an EC security role, which until the Maastricht Treaty clearly did not fall within the competence of the EC. In fact, the EC took several steps, with little delay, at the outbreak of the war in August 1990: it imposed an embargo on oil imports from Iraq and Kuwait, and it suspended military cooperation with Iraq and its eligibility for tariff reductions under the Generalized System of Preferences (GSP). Throughout the war it supported the series of UN resolutions establishing the basis for combined economic and military action against Iraq. The EC's inability to play any military role, however, did provoke serious consideration of an eventual EC security policy, which subsequently was reflected in the Maastricht Treaty.

The failure of the EU, as well as of the Western world as a whole, to prevent the outbreak, escalation, and ferocity of the civil war in ex-Yugoslavia is, of course, one of the great tragedies of the second half of the twentieth century.[13] Historians and politicians will undoubtedly argue for many years over whether the fighting could have been prevented or at least stopped and, if so, how. Even had the EU been able to carry out a "real" foreign policy in that area, it is by no means certain that the situation would have been appreciably different.

Two somewhat conflicting conclusions can be drawn from the EU's experience with the civil war insofar as EU political cooperation is concerned. On the one hand, the EU's role as a political participant was clearly enhanced, even if in small, incremental steps. The EU developed common policies, the Council Presidency and troika undertook peace missions and delivered statements on behalf of the EU, the EU sent observers to monitor so-called cease fires, and perhaps most important, the EU took the lead at the outset in seeking a negotiated settlement to the war. Later it was entrusted with the administration of the divided city of Mostar. All those steps have contributed to increasing the EU's "political identity"; although the concept is vague, the development is significant.

On the other hand, the conflict showed, in stark terms, the very real limits to political cooperation. The diversity of views among the member states hampered the development of rational and consistent policies: Germany's insistence on recognition of Croatia despite strong opposition by most other member states is believed by many to have been an important contributor to the war, Greek sensitivities with regard to Macedonia forced the EU to forgo recognition, and the day after the European Council in Lisbon agreed to a closer coordination of member state policies French President François Mitterrand left for an unannounced "peace and solidarity" visit to Sarajevo. Finally, through a combination of developments, the EU's negotiators became increasingly marginalized, first to the United Nations and then to a five-country "contact group" and by mid–1995, to the United States. The contact group included three EU member states—France, Germany, and the United Kingdom—along with Russia and the United States. Although these three countries nominally represented the EU in the contact group, their participation was largely independent of the views of the other member states. In any event, the negotiation of the Bosnian peace agreement in late 1995 was orchestrated and dominated by the United States with the other members of the contact group relegated to minor supporting roles.

Last, mention should be made of the EU's role in the Middle East peace process. Although several member states have traditionally carried out an active foreign policy in the area, they were not significantly involved in peace efforts through the 1980s. However, in 1991, the United States agreed to give the EC a seat at the peace conference, which began the process that subsequently led to the creation of a Palestinian state. It did so in response to the general shift in the European attitude to a less pro-Arab attitude and, more important, to the potential economic contribution of the EC (or at least some of member states) to an eventual settlement.

In sum, during the pre-Maastricht era, the EC significantly expanded its activities in the field of political cooperation, although its influence on developments outside its borders remained modest at best.

Since the entry into force of the Maastricht Treaty, the EU has agreed on a number of common positions and joint actions. In October 1993, i.e., just before entry into force of the treaty, the European Council called for joint actions to be taken in a number of areas, with others subsequently added. By early 1995, the list of joint actions agreed upon by the Council covered humanitarian aid in Bosnia and Herzegovina and EU adminis-tration of Mostar; support for the democratic transition in South Africa (monitoring the elections and organizing an assistance program); conven-ing of a Conference for a Pact on Stability in Europe (a French initiative seeking to establish mechanisms to resolve minority and border disputes among the nations of Central Europe); engagement in the Middle East peace process (including providing regional economic assistance); moni-toring of the Russian parliamentary elections; preparations for renegotia-tion of the Nuclear Non-Proliferation Treaty; and control of exports of "dual-use" goods (i.e., products with both civilian and military uses).

Although those actions were limited in scope and none required a major policy change or initiative by member states, the fact that the member states agreed on such joint actions represented an important step toward political integration. It is also significant that on no occasion has the Council agreed on the subject of a joint action and then failed to reach a decision on its content.

Similarly modest in scope and noncontroversial, most common posi-tions agreed on through early 1995 pertained to the reduction of economic and financial relations or trade sanctions. The first category contained two common positions relating to Haiti, one to the Serbian-held portion of Bosnia-Herzegovina, and one to Libya; the second contained common positions relating to Sudan (imposition of arms embargo) and the former Yugoslavia (lifting of trade restrictions). Apart from another common position relating to the satisfaction of claims in ex-Yugoslavia, there have been three common positions setting objectives and priorities.

The first such common position, concerning Rwanda, occasioned a heated jurisdictional battle between the Council and the Commission, with the Commission asserting that the common position pertained to economic issues, for which it has the exclusive right of initiative (not exercised in this case), while the Council countered that it was acting within its prerogatives because the common position did not go beyond setting a general policy. Subsequently, similar common positions were agreed for Burundi and Ukraine (though under a somewhat different formula that avoided re-igniting the jurisdictional dispute). The dispute between the Council and the Commission, which may recur with future common positions and will probably not be settled before the Intergovernmental Conference's review of the Maastricht Treaty, reflected the two institutions' efforts to maximize (or maintain) their competence in new areas of activity in the context of the treaty's ambiguity, which does not define the procedures for determining common positions as it does for joint actions.

Finally, though least important, have been CFSP declarations on a lengthy list of foreign policy issues, primarily reactions (such as to "congratulate," or to "deplore") to specific events in other countries. The significance of the declarations is limited, despite their large number—fifteen during the last months of 1993 (following entry into force of the Maastricht Treaty), 110 in 1994, and thirty-two in the first three months of 1995—although some countries, especially aid recipients, do take note. In addition, the EU makes a number of confidential démarches, usually by the troika.

Security Policy

The member states took their first tentative security policy steps in the Single European Act. The logic of moving in that direction was clear enough: security policy is a component, not always easily separable, of foreign policy. Thus, as the member states proceeded to intensify their political cooperation, the argument for including some form of security dimension became increasingly compelling. However, determining the appropriate dimension was no simple matter because European security was the subject of other, long-standing institutional arrangements in which the EC member states participated to differing degrees.

Since 1949, the North Atlantic Treaty Organization (NATO), an alliance in which the United States plays the predominant role, has been the security guardian of Western Europe. At the time of the Single European Act, NATO's membership included all member states of the EC, with the exception of Ireland. However, two major European members (France and Spain) did not participate in NATO's integrated military structure. The other organization was the Western European Union (WEU), created in the late 1940s to promote intra-European cooperation. However, it became irrelevant soon thereafter because of the establishment of NATO and the EC. WEU members by the late 1980s included nine EC members

(all except Denmark, Greece, and Ireland). With these overlapping organizations and, more important, with responsibility for security firmly
anchored in NATO, it was understandable that the EC would tread tenta-
tively into the security area.

Thus the provisions regarding security policy that were included in the
foreign policy section of the Single European Act were hardly far-reaching. Nor were they particularly clear. The key paragraph encouraged
"closer cooperation on questions of European security" (significant for
inclusion of "security," hitherto unacceptable to some member states) and
asserted that the member states were "ready to coordinate their positions
on the political and economic aspects of security."[14] This meant that
member states could undertake common activities relating to all aspects
of their external relations except for defense. The paragraph continued
with an opaque reference to maintaining "the technological and industrial
conditions necessary for ... security," designed to provide a political justification for cooperation among member states on industrial projects in the
defense sector and to permit the development of a common procurement
policy. Finally, the paragraph declared that none of its provisions would
impede closer cooperation under the aegis of NATO or the WEU.

By the time the intergovernmental conference was convened to negotiate what ultimately became the Maastricht Treaty, the European security
scene had changed dramatically with the collapse of the Soviet empire.
Thus, consideration of whether and how to strengthen the EC's involvement in security policy took place as the countries of the West began to
face the question of adapting their Cold War policies and institutions to
the post–Cold War era. The issue of future EU security policy was necessarily intertwined with the need for evolution in European security
arrangements.

In essence, the two issues were how far should the EU proceed with
an identifiable EU policy, and how would that policy and any supporting
institutions be linked to the existing structure, i.e., NATO. The main protagonists on the one side were the Netherlands and the United Kingdom,
which were anxious to maintain the primacy of the United States in the
defense of Europe and which were fearful of any diminution of NATO's
role; and on the other side France and to a lesser extent Germany, which
were eager to begin to develop a security policy and the beginnings of a
defense force with a genuine European identity.

The outcome of the negotiations "tilted more toward the Europeanists
than the Atlanticists,"[15] largely the result of the shift in the US position
from unease, if not hostility, to acceptance of the concept of a European
security identity. The treaty upgraded the largely moribund WEU into
what was intended to be an operational arm of the EU, serving as a link
between the EU and NATO. At the same time, it was explicitly stated that

the new arrangements would not diminish NATO's role, but rather would enhance the EU's contribution to European security by integrating the WEU more closely into the EU framework. Indeed, the treaty referred to the WEU as "an integral part of the development of the Union," and it specified that the EU's security policy would be compatible with that established under NATO.[16] The latter was a major condition of US support, as a senior US official subsequently expressed: "[A] stronger European pillar of the [security] alliance can be an important contribution to European stability and transatlantic burden-sharing, provided it does not dilute NATO."[17]

The imbalance between EU and WEU memberships was lessened when Greece became a WEU member in 1992. Denmark and Ireland became observers, permitting them closer access to deliberations, while reflecting Danish concern over undercutting NATO and Irish neutrality. To enhance coordination between the EU and the WEU, it was also decided to establish a WEU Permanent Council, and the WEU Secretariat was moved from London to Brussels.

The Maastricht Treaty also increased the potential for the development of an EU security identity, both by determining that CFSP encompasses "all areas of foreign and security policy" and by broadening the definition of security to include not only economic and political aspects, covered in the Single European Act, but also military aspects. Security now specifically includes "the eventual framing of a common defence policy, which might in time lead to a common defense."[18]

Since entry into force of the Maastricht Treaty, the WEU's membership has grown not only in number as noted above but also in complexity. It now consists of ten EU members (Belgium, France, Germany, Greece, Italy, Luxembourg, the Netherlands, Portugal, Spain, and the United Kingdom), five observers (the other five EU member states, i.e., Austria, Denmark, Finland, Ireland, and Sweden), associate members (the other NATO members, i.e., Iceland, Norway, and Turkey), and associate partners (six Central European countries plus the three Baltic states).

The role of the WEU and its relationship to NATO has evolved slowly. While in theory the WEU will enhance the Atlantic alliance by working out, with NATO, "separable but not separate" defense capabilities,[19] it is not clear how, or indeed whether, that will happen. The main focus of discussion in this area has been the development of combined joint task forces, agreed upon at the NATO summit in 1994. Although not fully refined, the concept is that units from various countries, possibly including non-NATO members, will be formed for specific actions outside the NATO area that do not involve the United States.

In fact, the WEU has played a role, albeit minor, in a number of operations. The first instance predated the upgrading of its status in the Maastricht Treaty—minesweepers of WEU member states were sent under a WEU banner to the Persian Gulf in 1988, and the same procedure was repeated with warships during the Gulf War in 1990. Subsequently, the WEU contributed to the effort to resolve the civil war in ex-Yugoslavia by participating in the Adriatic naval blockade of Serbia, by applying the blockade on the Danube, and by providing the police force for the EU administration of Mostar. The latter operation is the only instance in which the WEU has been used in a joint action under CFSP, and this is presumably why the Commission concluded that the "connection [between the EU and the WEU] has been used rarely and with limited success."[20]

A more visible manifestation of efforts to develop an EU security policy has been the Franco-German initiative to establish a so-called Euro-corps. A unit consisting of French and German troops was established in 1992, with Belgian, Luxembourg, and Spanish troops added subsequently. However, indicative of the difficulty of achieving European integration was the Belgian insistence that the unit's languages be not only French and German but also Dutch so that the Flemish contingent could understand; Spanish was later included. Furthermore, it is unclear what role this unit will play and where it will fit into the existing European security structure. Apart from Euro-corps, a decision was taken by the WEU foreign ministers in 1995 to create two joint military forces, a land-based Euroforce and a naval unit called Eurmarforce, in which France, Italy, Portugal, and Spain will participate. However, a more striking, though purely symbolic, example of incipient security cooperation was the inclusion of German troops in the 1994 National Day parade in Paris—an event unimaginable in earlier years.

While these various forces exist in the abstract or at best in preliminary form, a tangible expression of security cooperation among EU member states was the formation of an Anglo-French rapid reaction force in 1995 to support political and military objectives of the two countries in Bosnia. However, this action was taken totally outside the EU and the WEU context. The two militarily strongest member states simply decided bilaterally to take joint action.

Third Pillar

The pace of action under the third pillar—justice and internal affairs—has been slow. This is not surprising for a new area of responsibility for the EU, at least in a formal sense, and one dealing with sensitive issues on an inter-governmental basis (where decisions must be taken by unanimity). The two main areas of activity have been the establishment of a European Monitoring Center for Drugs and Drug Addiction (in Lisbon) and

Europol (in The Hague). The European Monitoring Center, which entered into operation in the mid-1990s, is charged with coordinating the collection and distribution of information and developing uniform methodology for maintaining statistics on drug addiction.

The establishment of Europol was proposed, in response to rising crossborder criminal activity, as an intelligence service to collect and analyze information. At least some envisage that it will develop into an EU version of the US Federal Bureau of Investigation. Although a precursor organization has operated since 1993 (with a limited area of responsibility), agreement on the convention establishing Europol has been delayed for some years by controversy over two issues: the disposition of personal data (i.e., how to balance the civil rights of individuals against the needs of police organizations); and accountability (i.e., how much autonomy should it be given and what institution(s) should oversee its operations—specifically, what role if any should the European Court of Justice play). The latter issue has proven particularly contentious and remains unresolved. Although the member states signed the Europol convention in July 1995, ratification will necessarily have to await resolution of this issue. Irrespective of when Europol is officially launched, working out problems of communications and harmonizing its procedures will take time.

In addition to the establishment of these two organizations, third pillar activities have included the adoption of resolutions, recommendations, statements, and conclusions on issues ranging from the interception of telecommunications and responsibility of organizers of sporting events to common forms and procedures and the financing of terrorism. Furthermore, work is under way on a number of conventions covering subjects such as crossing external frontiers and extradition. In addition, agreement was reached in 1995 on a simplified procedure for voluntary extradition—the first convention to be concluded under the third pillar—followed by agreement on a customs information-sharing convention concerning the use of information technology for customs purposes.

Decision Making

The process of European political integration in the sense of limiting member states' sovereign powers began with the Treaty of Rome.[21] This reduction of member states' prerogatives took two forms: the treaty assigned the Commission certain executive powers; and it provided that decisions in some areas would be taken by the Council with less than unanimity beginning in 1966. Although it can be argued that the Commission's general responsibility for supervising and implementing Council decisions involves a pooling of member state powers rather than a diminution, it is undeniable that its power, exercised independently of the Council as in competition policy, or as delegated by the Council as in the Common Agricultural Policy (CAP), impinges on the normal prerogatives of national governments.

The provision in the Treaty of Rome for some decisions to be taken on a basis other than unanimous approval by the member states similarly represented a degree of political integration. Its inclusion indicated the negotiators' recognition that the Community could not function effectively if each member state could exercise a veto over every piece of legislation. Accordingly, the treaty provided for the introduction of voting by a "qualified majority" on a number of issues by 1966, the end of the transition period for the customs union. Votes were distributed among the member states roughly on the basis of population (but with over representation by the smaller countries), and more than two-thirds of the votes were necessary for approval. However, despite the treaty provisions, qualified majority voting was not put into operation because of French intransigence and because individual member states continued to exercise a de facto veto when they considered "very important interests" to be at stake (the so-called Luxembourg compromise).

The member states' failure to surrender exclusive use of unanimous voting was one of the motivating forces behind the Single European Act; it was self-evident that a program to remove the barriers to free movement in the EC had no chance of success under the prevailing voting arrangements. Thus, a great achievement of the Single European Act was the acceptance of new procedures providing for qualified majority voting on an extensive list of specified categories, essentially those falling under the rubric of single market harmonization measures. Under the voting system, the four largest member states (France, Germany, Italy, and the United Kingdom) were allocated ten votes each and Spain eight, while the smaller countries had five or three, with a minimal two votes for Luxembourg. A blocking minority consisted of at least three large states, or two large states and one small one, or five small states. Exempted from this procedure (i.e., requiring unanimity) were issues such as taxation, social legislation, and some forms of environmental legislation.

An important component of the decision-making changes in the Single European Act was the increased role given to the European Parliament, another manifestation of the transfer of power from the member states to EC institutions. Prior to the Single European Act, the Parliament's functions were largely consultative, with the notable exception of the Community's budget, which could not be adopted without its approval (incidentally, the Parliament has control over expenditure but no influence over revenue). The Council voting changes described above were part of the "cooperation procedure" under which legislative proposals subject to a qualified majority vote require two readings by the Parliament. The Parliament can approve amendments, which must then be considered by the Commission and the Council and, under certain circumstances, can be rejected by the Council only unanimously.

Although the Maastricht Treaty left unchanged the ratio of member state votes needed to block a qualified majority (see Chapter 7), it extended the range of issues subject to qualified majority voting and significantly expanded the powers of the Parliament by introducing a "codecision procedure." On a broad range of issues—including the single market, research and development policy, and a portion of the environmental agenda—the Parliament can force a negotiation on the contents of proposed legislation with the Council (analogous to the conference committee procedure in the US Congress), and if that fails to produce an agreement, it can force withdrawal of the proposal. During the short life of this procedure, the Parliament has not hesitated to use these new powers.[22]

In addition to further diminishing the member states' ability, acting through the Council, to determine legislation, the Maastricht Treaty gave the Parliament two further powers over the Commission: it was required to give its opinion on the nomination of the president of the Commission (named by the European Council) and to approve the collective Commission (whose members are appointed by the member states). When the first post–Maastricht Commission was named in late 1994, the Parliament made the most of its new powers by subjecting the nominated Commission president, Jacques Santer, to sharp questioning and by adopting a favorable opinion by a narrow margin; by insisting that each nominated commissioner appear before the appropriate committee of Parliament for a hearing (rather than appearing together, reflecting the collegial nature of the institution), where each was also sharply questioned; by issuing a report, sometimes criticized, on each nominee; and by then seeking the withdrawal of four nominees and some reallocation of the commissioners' portfolios as the price for approval. Although the Parliament ultimately was satisfied with only a minor change in the portfolios— whereupon it approved the Commission by an overwhelming margin—it aggressively exercised its powers at the expense of the member states that had nominated the commissioners and of the Commission.

Notes

1. Lily Gardner Feldman, "The EC in the International Arena: A New Activism?" in U.S. Congress, House Committee on Foreign Affairs, *Europe and the United States: Competition and Cooperation in the 1990s* (Washington: Government Printing Office, June 1992), p. 143.

2. Single European Act, Article 30(1).

3. Ibid., Article 30(2).

4. Maastricht Treaty, Article B.

5. Feldman, "The EC in the International Arena," p. 144.

6. Maastricht Treaty, Article J.1.

7. Ibid., Article J.2.

8. Ibid., Article J.1(3).

9. Ibid., Article J.3.

10. Ibid.,Title V, Articles J.7, 8, and 9.

11. Feldman, "The EC in the International Arena," p. 146.

12. Michael Calingaert, "The European Community's Emerging Political Dimension," *SAIS Review,* Winter-Spring 1992, pp. 69–83.

13. For an account of the earlier stages of EU policy in ex-Yugoslavia, see David Buchan, *Europe: The Strange Superpower* (Aldershot [U.K.]: Dartmouth, 1993), Chapter 6.

14. Single European Act, Article 30(6).

15. Desmond Dinan, *Ever Closer Union? An Introduction to the European Community* (Boulder: Lynne Rienner Publishers, 1994), p. 472.

16. Maastricht Treaty, Article J.4(2) and J.4(4), respectively.

17. Richard Holbrooke, "America, a European Power," *Foreign Affairs*, March/April 1995, p. 47.

18. Maastricht Treaty, Article J.4(1).

19. WEU Kirchberg Declaration, May 9, 1994.

20. European Commission, "Report on the Operation of the Treaty on European Union," SEC(95) 731, May 10, 1995, p. 69.

21. Technically, such integration began with the EC's precursor organization, the European Coal and Steel Community, established by the Treaty of Paris in 1951.

22. In July 1994, the Parliament rejected a Council text that would have guaranteed open access to telephone networks. It did so as a matter of principle—the Council had not accepted its amendments. The following March it went further, rejecting the text that its own negotiators had worked out with the Council in the conciliation committee on the legal protection of biotechnology inventions, thereby terminating legislative active on the proposal.

PART TWO

Facing the Future

5

Prospects: Internal Conflicts

The foregoing chapters have described recent developments regarding economic and political integration in the European Union, presenting a status report of the situation prevailing as the EU moves toward the end of the twentieth century. An obvious question is to what extent integration has taken place. The answer necessarily depends on the scale of measurement. "Progress" in integration can be measured by a variety of standards, such as theoretical or historical models, objectives, or aspirations. Perhaps most meaningful is to compare the present state of integration with the situation that obtained at a point in the past. Although undue precision should be avoided, an appropriate general benchmark is 1985, which marked the negotiation that led to the Single European Act and the launch of the EC 1992 program.[1]

A substantial degree of integration has clearly taken place in the EU. This is decidedly the case with respect to economic integration, the result not only of the corpus of single market legislation, but also of the reaction of economic operators to the incentives and opportunities offered by the legislative changes as well as by other developments affecting the market. This is an ongoing, self-perpetuating process, or as one observer put it, "the incremental logic of the integration process itself."[2] Although the situation as regards political integration is more ambiguous, considerably more foreign and security policy coordination exists than did previously, and member states have yielded significant decision-making powers to the EU institutions, first in the Single European Act and then in the Maastricht Treaty.

Nonetheless, it is equally clear that the momentum in favor of continuing the process of integration—strong in the case of economic integration, less so in the case of political integration—which was so evident up to the signing of the Maastricht Treaty in 1991, had abated by the mid–1990s. The oft-cited "Euro-phoria" was shattered on June 2, 1992, when the Danes narrowly voted in a referendum to reject the treaty.[3] Although some national referenda had been held in the past, the citizens of the European Community (or, more accurately, throughout the member states) were given the first opportunity on a pan-European basis, either through a national referendum or at least a national debate, to express their views on European integration. The issue on the table, of course, was the Maastricht Treaty, but the debate over its ratification ranged well beyond the treaty provisions to more fundamental questions concerning the EC.

The debate unleashed a multitude of forces that challenged the pre–1992 consensus. Public support for the EC and its institutions had clearly waned. The French voted only narrowly in favor of ratification (though in a referendum that largely became a vote of confidence in President François Mitterrand), and public opinion polls indicated that the Germans might not have approved the treaty if a referendum had been held. The focal point of the upsurge in discontent was "Brussels," usually equated with the European Commission, although the respective roles of the different EC institutions were seldom distinguished. The criticism was directed at what people viewed as overregulation and intrusion, the perceived danger that national cultures and traditions would be submerged in the Union, and the opaqueness of the decision-making process. In sum, the debate reflected a growing concern on the part of ordinary citizens that they were uninformed and uninvolved in a system of governing that directly affected their lives.

The Danish voters' rejection of the Maastricht Treaty had a salutory effect in that it revealed a significant disconnect between the EC's political leadership that had negotiated and approved the treaty (the Danish Parliament had voted by a three-to-one margin for approval) and a citizenry that revealed itself in large measure skeptical about European integration.

Thus, "Euro-phoria" has been replaced by "Euro-pause," as the EU seeks to catch its breath, react to a vastly different set of circumstances, and ponder its next steps. It began this phase with a new institutional cast: a new Commission, headed for the first time in ten years by someone other than Jacques Delors, the first one filling a five-year term and requiring approval by the European Parliament; a newly elected (June 1994) Parliament, with less than half its members having sat in the previous Parliament, and its powers in EU decision making enhanced by the Maastricht Treaty; and an enlarged EU, with increased membership for the first time since 1986.

However, the EU, and its citizens, will have little time to adjust to the vast internal and external changes of recent years and to ponder their implications before being called on to decide what direction they would like the EU to take. In the second half of the 1990s, they will be called on to take a number of basic decisions that will determine the future path of European integration. As indicated in the Introduction, the decisions relate to three central issues:

- the launch of economic and monetary union (EMU), foreordained in the Maastricht Treaty, which will bring about a far higher degree of integration but at the same time create a major distinction between participating and nonparticipating member states;
- the inevitable enlargement, to the east, of the EU, which will even further increase the differences and disparities in conditions and perceptions among the member states; and
- changes in the EU's decision-making and institutional structures, generated by a variety of internal pressures and made necessary by the impending enlargement.

Although decisions relating to the first two issues follow their own path and timetable, the focal point for deliberations on the future of European integration will be the Intergovernmental Conference (IGC) that begins in 1996.

Mandated by the Maastricht Treaty "to examine those provisions of th[e] Treaty for which revision is provided" (see Chapter 7),[4] the IGC will not limit its review of possible treaty changes to those specific provisions but, rather, will include essentially all aspects of the structure and operation of the EU. For that reason, decisions taken at the IGC will directly affect the conditions under which EMU and enlargement take place. And they will significantly determine the shape of the Union as it enters the twenty-first century.

In assessing the prospects for integration in the coming years, account must first be taken of the contrasts and conflicts inherent in the EU. To a certain extent, these have always been present. However, their resolution, or at least management, was easier in an EC of six or even twelve member states than in an EU of fifteen and potentially many more. Thus, these contrasts and conflicts present a greater challenge to continued movement toward integration.

Determination of Goals and Objectives

The overriding challenge facing the member states is to achieve, or move toward, a consensus on the type of Union its citizens consider desirable. The option of a single federal state—some form of a "United States of Europe"— can be defined with reasonable clarity. However, it is a politically unrealistic goal. The likelihood of sufficient support being generated to reach it in the coming years, if not decades, is minimal. Elimination of that option leaves an almost infinite choice of alternatives not only on the continuum from a loosening of the bonds of integration thus far achieved through maintenance of the status quo to further integration. And because few models can be easily characterized, the selection process is rendered all the more difficult.

Three basic questions must be answered, implicitly if not explicitly, by the people of Europe.

1. What is the basic purpose of the Union, i.e., what is it meant to accomplish?
2. How much national sovereignty should be ceded to collective decision making and the EU institutions, i.e., to what extent should supranationality replace an inter-governmental system deriving its legitimacy through national electorates?
3. What degree of diversity of interests and national objectives is compatible with EU membership and to what extent should the EU be willing to depart from the EC's original concept of universal application of the corpus of programs and legislation in adapting to that diversity?

Until the controversy broke out over ratification of the Maastricht Treaty, these issues were not in the forefront of public debate, if they were debated at all. However, even had there been ample discussion, controversy would undoubtedly have reigned, as it now does, over the desired form of the EU. This would have occurred not only because of the fundamental nature of the required decisions but also because the development of the EU is necessarily an evolutionary process. Under conditions of minimum change in the external environment and maximum well-being, it takes time to develop a consensus on a new set of institutions and methods of governing among nation states with a long history of separate existence—and the decade from 1985 to 1995 can hardly be characterized as one of "minimum change and maximum well-being." Furthermore, it is impossible to forecast at what point the body politic will conclude that the process is "completed," to the extent that such is ever the case. The historical experience of the United States in that regard indicates, albeit under quite different circumstances, that the development of a union takes many decades—in the US case from the late eighteenth century to the early twentieth.

However, public attention has been increasingly drawn to the issue of the future direction of the EU, first with the controversy over ratification of the Maastricht Treaty and then with the approach of the IGC. In essence, the debate has revolved around two issues: the powers of the EU institutions (vis-à-vis those of the member states and relative to each other); and the replacement of "uniformity" with "differentiation." Within the range of important questions encompassed by the first issue, the key subject for resolution is what changes, if any, should be made in the balance between the EU's intergovernmental and supranational elements. Although rhetoric and posturing by the member states will play an important role during the run-up to the IGC, some generalizations can be made. The two clearest, and most extreme, positions are those of Germany and the United Kingdom: Germany seeks to expand the powers of the EU institutions, particularly those of the Parliament, while the United Kingdom, at least under the Conservative government, wants to preserve, if not increase, the preponderantly inter-governmental nature of the EU.

Regarding the second, EC's underlying assumption was that all member states would take similar decisions and implement them at the same time; in other words, that the EC represented "single-speed Europe." In fact, however, the EC became a "multi-speed Europe" by granting some member states a longer transition period for implementing certain legislation, a practice that became widespread with the entry of less advanced member states.

Under the Maastricht Treaty a new principle was established: all policy actions and treaty provisions do not necessarily apply to all member states. The clearest manifestation of this principle was the British opt-out of the EU's social protocol (see Chapter 4). Even if, as appears likely, the British Labour Party comes to power and carries out its commitment to "opt in" to the social protocol, the precedent has been established for "Europe a la carte," i.e., an EU in which member states can select the programs in which they wish to participate. The other manifestation of the principle is contained in the provisions for EMU, which set conditions for participation that cannot possibly be met by all member states—establishing the principle of "two-speed" or "multispeed" Europe—and gave the option to Denmark and the United Kingdom of not participating in the final stage of EMU if their governments or electorates so decide.[5]

The introduction of differentiation represents the EU's acceptance of the inevitable consequences of an expanding membership. It is by definition more difficult to reach a consensus and arrive at decisions among fifteen member states than among six, even with the introduction of qualified majority voting. Furthermore, the differences among the member states in economic situation and political interests and orientations are such that the EU risks facing a basic choice between taking minimalist decisions on the basis of the lowest common denominator and permitting like-minded member states to undertake activities that will not involve all member states.

This issue was directly posed in a discussion paper issued by the German government's parliamentary group, the CDU/CSU, in September 1994, which attracted widespread interest in the EU and in a sense became the focal point of debate on the IGC.[6] Although this so-called Lamers or Schaeuble report made five "dependent and reinforcing" proposals, public attention focused on its strong support for strengthening the EU's "hard core," thereby proposing differentiation—although open to all member states that were able and willing to participate—as a key feature of the future EU.[7] This will indeed be an important element in the debate leading to the IGC, where efforts to reach a consensus among the member states will culminate (see Chapter 7).

Diversity of Culture and Language

As the membership of the EC and EU has expanded, the differences among the member states in culture, customs, historical tradition, and language have become more accentuated. In a narrow sense, the president of the European Parliament is accurate when he asserts that "Warsaw and Prague, Budapest and Bratislava, Sofia and Bucharest are just as European as Madrid or London, Berlin or Helsinki, Rome or Copenhagen."[8] A similar statement could be made about Aberdeen and Athens or Goteborg and Granada. However, more relevant is the degree to which people in these different cities feel a kinship with one another or that "Europe" binds them together sufficiently to make them want, or at least agree, to work jointly in an EU context. National rivalries, misperceptions, and misunderstandings—and prejudices—inevitably exist. Although these differences are likely to diminish as the peoples of Europe increasingly interact, the range of diversity inevitably grows with the geographical extension of the EU.

Language is an important divisive factor (there are now eleven official languages for fifteen member states) even if people from different countries communicate in one or another common language. Although the point should not be exaggerated, the necessity of communicating in a language other than one's own native tongue is an impediment to developing mutual understanding and confidence. To this must be added the inefficiencies—unavoidable politically—that arise from the equal official status given to the eleven EU languages.

Diversity is obviously not a bar to European integration. However, it limits, in a political and practical sense, the extent to which integration will take place. In addition, growing public concern in certain member states—triggered by the campaign of opponents in Denmark to ratification of the Maastricht Treaty—that recent and prospective developments in the EU threaten the maintenance of distinctive national cultures adds weight to the forces opposing further integration.

Small Versus Large Member States

Tensions will inevitably continue between the interests of the small member states and the large ones. The former want to maintain what they consider to be adequate influence over decision making. In other words, they want to limit the large member states' ability to determine EU actions and policies over their objections. Although this concern was probably more pronounced during the early days of the EC, when the small countries feared that the large member states would establish a sort of "directory," it has remained close to the surface. This was evidenced when France and Germany in effect determined between themselves in 1994 that Belgian Prime Minister Jean-Luc Dehaene would succeed Jacques Delors as president of the Commission, a form of decision making that clearly annoyed the small member states, but which became moot when the United Kingdom vetoed the nomination.[9] Conversely, the large member states want to limit what they deem to be the dispropor- tionate (as measured by population and economic strength) blocking power of the small members, a situation likely to be exacerbated when further enlargement takes place. This conflict is manifested in each of the three main EU institutions.

The small member states regard the Commission as a defender of their interests because its perspective embraces the Union as a whole and thus it tends to oppose policies that would favor large member states at their expense. In the words of Belgian Foreign Minister Eric Derycke, "the Commission is the main ally of the small powers."[10] For that reason they generally defend the Commission against attacks on its prerogatives and actions, just as the large member states are among the most prominent critics of the Commission (although Denmark and Germany are notable exceptions, respectively, to these two generalizations).

In the Council, the small member states obviously benefit from voting by unanimity because any one of them can block action, which they occa- sionally do, e.g., Greece held up the customs union with Turkey for several years, and Portugal blocked agreement on the Uruguay Round until its concerns over the consequences for its textile industry had been satisfied. However, qualified majority voting, which has increasingly become the norm, has diminished these countries' ability to determine the outcome of Council action. In the fifteen-member EU, a measure can be blocked by three large countries (or two large and three small ones), whereas, it takes six small countries to block a measure.

Although the United Kingdom obtained minimal support from the other member states in its effort during the negotiations on the 1995 enlargement to keep the blocking minority unchanged (i.e., not to raise it in proportion to the increase in membership), the large member states could seek a change in the qualified majority formula at the IGC. On a scale from least to most likely, this effort could take the form of changing the number of votes assigned to each member state, of changing the percentage of votes required to block an action, or of adopting a two-tiered system, under which a blocking minority will require not only a minimum number of votes but also a minimum percentage of the EU's population (see Chapter 7).

Finally, the small countries are overrepresented on a per capita basis in the European Parliament, an inevitable consequence of the vast differences in member state populations. Luxembourg has one member per 66,000 inhabitants, whereas in the five large EU countries one member represents over 600,000 people (and in the case of Germany, over 800,000).[11] With Parliament's membership of 626 (as of 1995) already straining, if not exceeding, the limits of logic and efficiency, any diminution of the disparities would necessarily involve some reduction in the number of seats provided for the small member states, an issue that will have to be resolved at the IGC (see Chapter 7).

Rich Versus Poor Member States

The gap between rich and poor in the EU is large, and it will widen when enlargement to the east takes place. In 1995, per capita gross domestic product (GDP), using 100 as the average of the fifteen member states, ranged from 168 in Luxembourg (followed by Germany, Denmark, Austria, France, Sweden, Belgium, and the Netherlands) to 46 in Greece and Portugal (joined by Ireland and Spain at the bottom of the list). This ratio of about one to four[12] makes for considerably different perspectives among member states as to what the aims and policies of the EU should be.

Not surprisingly, the poorer member states place high priority on direct financial benefits from EU membership. In this context, it is noteworthy that the proponents of approval of the Maastricht Treaty in the Irish referendum based their campaign almost solely on the very substantial inflow of funds and related benefits to Ireland resulting from membership in the EU.

Spain has taken the lead in promoting the interests of the four less developed countries (the other "cohesion states," as mentioned earlier, being Greece, Ireland, and Portugal). These interests are largely financial, i.e., maximizing the availability of funding under the various EU programs, notably the structural funds for regional development. Spain has not hesitated to use its leverage as a large member to ensure that the other member states do not lose sight of their obligations in this regard. These obligations contained in the Single European Act and Maastricht Treaty are to promote "economic and social cohesion" among the member states,[13] and, as stipulated in the political agreements reached among the member states, to sharply increase expenditures for the poorer countries as the price for supporting the launch of the EC 1992 program and for agreeing on the European Economic Area (EEA). However, a particular concern of the poorer member states is that the eventual accession of Central and Eastern European countries will result in a diminution of the resources that would otherwise have been available to them—a not improbable outcome (see the following section on "Northern Versus Southern Member States").

The other way in which the interests of these member states are pursued is by negotiating longer transition periods for implementing legislation. This is usually justified by the need to overcome a weakness in administrative structure and to cushion attendant costs.

On the other side of the ledger are the "paymasters" of the EU. The net contributors to the EU's budget are led by Germany, traditionally the principal benefactor. Historically, Germany has advocated, or at least accepted, a relatively liberal spending policy because of what it considered the political imperatives of confirming its "European credentials" and promoting the integration process. However, there are clear limits to such benevolence. Because it assumed the substantial financial burden of reconstruction of East Germany virtually single-handedly, in particular with the reintroduction of the "solidarity tax" in 1995, Germany has begun to scrutinize proposed EU expenditures more critically, and member states that have recently become net contributors to the EU budget have shown little enthusiasm for substantial increases in the EU's spending.

Although the main source of EU revenue is the value-added tax (VAT), a significant component is a levy intended to reflect each member state's ability to pay, based on its GDP. A major effort was made in 1992 to increase in 1997 the ceiling of the EC's budget from 1.2 percent of EC GDP to 1.37 percent. However, even that relatively modest proposal was rejected in favor of a smaller 1.27 percent increase which was not to be reached until 1999. Thus, the financial margins within which the EU operates will remain relatively restrictive for the foreseeable future.

Northern Versus Southern Member States

A final member state split is geographic, essentially a north-south divide, although the precision of its delineation should not be overstated.

To some extent this split mirrors that of rich (northern) versus poor (southern) countries. However, neither France nor Italy can be classified as poor, and in any event, France straddles the north-south divide, but fits predominantly in the southern category because of its location on the Mediterranean, much of its political and administrative philosophy, and its general *Weltanschauung*.

This geographic split is most relevant with respect to the EU's relationship with its neighboring countries. The northern members are particularly interested in promoting closer relations with—and eventual membership for—the countries of Central and Eastern Europe because of proximity and economic and cultural ties. Germany's position has been unambiguous: it has consistently pressed for the integration of the former Soviet satellites into the EU's ambit, leading eventually to EU membership. The Scandinavian member states have assumed the position of sponsors of the Baltic states.

On the other hand, the southern member states have shown considerably less enthusiasm—beyond the minimum required by "correct" behavior in European political terms—for such a policy for two reasons. First, they have fewer economic and political interests in those countries. Second (as mentioned earlier), to the extent the southern member states are synonymous with the poorer member states, they are concerned that concessions granted the Central and Eastern European countries and, eventually, accession will diminish the benefits they enjoy through membership. In particular they are concerned that the EU's regional development funds would be divided among a larger number of countries and that existing members' agricultural sectors would be threatened by the access granted to new members' agricultural production.

The counterpart of the southern member states' tepid attitude toward Central and Eastern Europe is their conviction that the EU has neglected its relationship with its Mediterranean neighbors. This view reflects the far closer ties these countries have historically maintained around the Mediterranean basin than with Central and Eastern Europe.

The EU's relationships with the two areas are quite different because it is closer culturally, ethnically, and historically to Central and Eastern Europe than to the Mediterranean countries and, in part for that reason, there is no question of eventual membership for the Mediterranean countries. EU policy in this area has largely centered around economic issues—determining the appropriate form and amount of assistance to be given to these countries as well as the conditions of access for their exports. However, the EU's policy has been increasingly affected by concerns about rising immigration from the North African countries—generated by the growing wealth gap (average incomes are roughly one-twelfth of the EU level)[14]— and the perceived threat from Islamic fundamentalism. As a result, the EU has sought to intensify its relations with the Mediterranean countries, both economically and politically.

Although the balance of attention and resources has clearly favored the EU's eastern neighbors since the end of the Cold War, the gap is likely to narrow because of the efforts of the southern member states to achieve greater "symmetry" between the EU's actions vis-à-vis its neighbors to the east and those to the south. The attitude of the northern member states is similar to that of the southern member states vis-a-vis Central and Eastern Europe, i.e., unenthusiastic recognition of the necessity to take some action. Thus, in 1994, the Commission proposed that a "new partnership" be built with the Mediterranean countries, including closer economic ties. The rationale, in the words of the responsible commissioner, was that "we must offer a political framework for anchoring the economies of these countries to the European Union."[15]

At its meeting in Essen at the end of 1994 the European Council pledged to maintain an appropriate balance in the geographical allocation of EU expenditure and commitments between Central and Eastern Europe and the Mediterranean. As it turned out, "appropriate balance" was somewhat less than parity: the Council divided the aid funds budgeted for the period 1995–99 on a 60–40 basis between Central and Eastern Europe and the Mediterranean region, respectively. The European Council also called for early conclusion of association agreements with Israel, Morocco, and Tunisia (that was accomplished by the end of 1995).

Following up on that, the Spanish Presidency organized a conference of foreign ministers of the EU member states and twelve Mediterranean countries in November 1995 to discuss the relationship and obtain agreement on economic and political guidelines for cooperation between the EU and the Mediterranean countries, including both additional resources and improved access by the Mediterranean countries to the EU market. The Spanish strategy called for creation of an EU-Mediterranean association to establish a Mediterranean "peace and stability area," a new focus on economic and trade relations (with the long-term goal of forming a free trade area), and new aid instruments drawing on the EU's experience in Central and Eastern Europe.[16]

Spanish objectives were largely achieved. The conference produced a declaration of principles focusing on three areas of cooperation: a political partnership, an economic and financial partnership with the goal of achieving a free trade area by 2010, and a partnership for social and humanitarian cooperation. Accompanying the declaration was a five-year aid package of ECU 4.7 billion ($5.9 billion). Although it will be a long time before any of these generalities are transformed into reality, the conference was a significant event. It initiated and institutionalized a process under which the EU, the northern as well as the southern component, gives comprehensive, high-level attention to its relationship with the Mediterranean countries.

While the EU's new focus on the Mediterranean will probably contribute to mitigating northern-southern antagonisms, time will tell to what extent the EU in fact maintains an economic and political balance between the interests of its northern and southern member states. However, irrespective of the outcome, some friction between the two groups is likely to remain.

The north-south distinction is also relevant in a more general, though less easily definable, sense. The northern member states tend to espouse more liberal economic policies—less regulation of the domestic economy, a greater role for the private sector, and freer trade—than those of the south. In addition, the administrative structures of the south are generally less efficient and developed than in the north. These differences are often reflected in debates over policies and in the degree and quality of implementation of legislation.

Member State "Unilateralism"

Throughout the forty-odd years of existence of the EC and the EU, occasions have arisen when a member state—for reasons relating to its history or self-defined cultural, economic, and political interests—considers that it must pursue a policy or undertake an action that violates EU policy or legislation, disrupts EU operations, or otherwise goes beyond the bounds of what is implicitly recognized as acceptable behavior. The most notable example in earlier years was France's "empty seat" at the Council table,[17] which led to the so-called Luxembourg Compromise that effectively prevented important decisions being taken by less than unanimity from the mid–1960s to the mid–1980s.

More recent instances relate largely to foreign policy coordination—or lack thereof. Perhaps the most serious consequences resulted from Germany's unilateral decision to recognize the independence of Croatia in early 1992, even though recognition was opposed by the other member states and Croatia did not meet the EU's criteria for recognition.[18] However, when the member states were presented with a choice between maintaining EU solidarity (i.e., joining Germany in granting recognition) and avoiding exacerbation of the incendiary situation in Yugoslavia, they opted for the former. Subsequently, Greece violated EU trade policy by instituting an embargo on trade with the Former Yugoslav Republic of Macedonia because of fears that the latter's self-proclaimed independence implied territorial claims on the Macedonian region of Greece. This was clearly a case where the Greek government determined that national interests took precedence over compliance with its obligations as an EU member. In addition, actions have been taken in the economic area that violated EU legislation, for example the French ban on waste imports from Germany and the German ban on imports of British beef (because of concerns over mad cow disease).

However, there is a more ambiguous issue of how long and in what manner a member state should fight to protect its interests. The United Kingdom was widely criticized by the other member states for Prime Minister Margaret Thatcher's tone and tactics in fighting to revise the calculation of its contribution to the EU's budget in the 1980s. On a number of occasions, a member state has either undertaken action that the other members states were forced to accept or has unilaterally blocked actions, e.g., the French threat not to ratify the Uruguay Round and the British veto of the nomination of Dehaene as Commission president.

A further refinement—and in many respects the most threatening form—of unilateralism is holding a measure hostage to settlement of another, unrelated issue. For example, in 1994, Italy blocked approval of the 1992 budget reform until the Council agreed to decrease the fine levied on it for exceeding the EU's milk quota, and Spain blocked completion of the ratification process for the accession of the EU's new members until it had received satisfactory access to North Sea fishing zones.

Although these actions can be justified by member states as protecting their legitimate national interests—and only some, not all, constituted a violation of EU treaty or legislative obligations—they impaired the effectiveness of the operation of the EU. The EU's decision-making system offers wide opportunities for member states to make aggressive use of their voting leverage, and thus it is not surprising that these opportunities are used on occasion. What remains to be seen is the extent to which such tactics will be used in the future and how disruptive they are of the EU's operations.

Conclusion

As indicated at the outset, none of these many areas of conflicting interests is new; all have been present since the inception of the EC. The key—and at this time, unanswerable—question is whether the conflicts will intensify as the EU seeks to resolve the critical issues facing it.

Notes

1. Negotiations for the Single European Act took place in 1985, it was ratified in 1986, and it came into effect in 1987.

2. Peter Ludlow, "Beyond Maastricht: Recasting the European Political and Economic System," Centre for European Policy Studies, Working Document No. 79, Brussels, July 1993, p. 12.

3. The vote was 50.7 percent in favor and 49.3 percent opposed, with less than 30,000 voters determining the outcome.

4. Maastricht Treaty, Final Provisions, Article N.2.

5. Although those exemptions form part of the Maastricht Treaty, the requirement that the Bundestag confirm conformity with the convergence criteria as a precondition for German participation is a national, not an EU issue, because it is not contained in the treaty but rather results from the German Constitutional Court's interpretation of the German constitution.

6. "Reflections on European Policy," CDU/CSU Group, September 1, 1994.

7. The other proposals were the further development of EU institutions, raising the quality of Franco-German relations, improving the capacity for effective action in foreign and security policy, and expanding the EU toward the East.

8. Klaus Haensch, as quoted in "EU/East Europe: Pre-Accession Strategy Gets into Gear," *European Report*, No. 2013, April 8, 1995, p. V/6.

9. Despite their displeasure over the principle, the small member states were not prepared to contest the nomination, which, in fact, they welcomed.

10. Speech given by Eric Derycke, at "L'Elargissement de l'Union Européenne: Enjeux et Implications Politico-Institutionelles," Brussels, Foundation Paul-Henri Spaak, October 13, 1995.

11. These numbers were calculated by the Institute of European Studies, Free University of Brussels, December 10, 1994.

12. European Commission, *Eurostat news release*, No. 60/94, December 13, 1994.

13. Title V of the Treaty of Rome as amended by the Single European Act, which was strengthened by Title XIV of the Maastrict Treaty.

14. "To South, EU Has Its Work Cut Out," *International Herald Tribune*, July 17, 1995.

15. Ibid.

16. "Priorities for the Spanish Presidency of the Council of the European Union," July 12, 1995, Spanish government document reproduced in *European Report*, supplement to No. 2058, July 15, 1995.

17. France boycotted Council sessions to prevent qualified majority voting. See Desmond Dinan, *Ever Closer Union? An Introduction to the European Community* (Boulder: Lynne Rienner Publishers, 1994), p. 58.

18. Ibid. p. 486.

6

Prospects: Determining Factors

The previous chapter described a number of conflicts among competing interests in the European Union—both of a general nature in the debate over goals and objectives and arising from disparities of size, wealth, and location among the member states—that could impede efforts to further the process of integration. However, a number of factors cut across member state borders that will play a more significant role in determining the course of European integration. These factors are assessed in this chapter.

Perception of External Political Threat

In many respects, the European Community thrived, or at least grew, on the existence of a threat. The first threat, which provided the basic motivating force for embarking on the process of European integration, was fear of yet another Franco-German (or other intra-European) war. This was obviously not an immediate threat, but rather a recurrent pattern of European history that the architects of postwar Europe wanted to end. That clearly was the rationale for the establishment of the European Coal and Steel Community in 1951 and one of several for the creation of the EC in 1957.

While that threat receded sharply in the early postwar years and had effectively disappeared by the early days of the EC, it was replaced by the threat of Soviet aggression. It is, of course, not possible to measure the degree to which the existence on the EC's eastern borders of a hostile, and at times threatening, Soviet empire provided an impetus to European integration. However, its existence undoubtedly played a part in the creation and further development of Western European integration, quite apart from the direct security response made through the creation of the North Atlantic Treaty Organization (NATO) in 1949.

With the collapse of the Soviet empire and the consequent disappearance of the Cold War threat, one external pressure for integration was removed. Could another one arise in its place? Although none is evident at present on the political side, potential replacements—unlikely though they be—should not be dismissed out of hand. In any event, the key factor is whether there is a perception of a threat, irrespective of its likelihood.

One potential threat is a resurgent and belligerent Russia, developing out of the debilitated and fragmented remains of the Soviet system. More likely reflecting the weakness than strength of post-Communist Russia, that threat could take the form of extreme nationalism arising from frustration over the internal problems—exemplified by the radical politician Vladimir Zhirinovsky, with backing, if not leadership, from the Russian military—and destabilize the political and possibly the military situation in Central Europe.

Another potential threat is Islamic fundamentalism. The most immediate manifestation of this threat, geographically and culturally, is the fundamentalists' fight against the military regime in Algeria. To some extent, that fight has already spilled over into France, with its large North African population, in terms of political and physical conflict among the participants and exodus (or attempted exodus) of people fleeing Algeria. In more general terms, the threat, in the eyes of many Europeans, is the disruptive effect that the spread of Islamic fundamentalism to the EU could have in the political, cultural, and religious fields.[1]

Neither of these potential threats is of the same magnitude as a Franco-German war or Soviet belligerency. Nor is the level of people's concerns as great. In addition, there is no clear link between these threats and the "protection" that would be offered by further progress toward integration, except in the very general sense of promoting common approaches to the problems created by the threats.

Economic Threat

The more immediate threat to the EU is economic: competition from other parts of the world. This is not a new threat. In fact, the fear of increasingly intense competition, especially from Asia, and its counterpart—declining European competitiveness—provided a major impetus to the single market program. Not only has that fear not abated, it has intensified, largely because of the increased globalization of the world economy (see Chapter 1). As a result, there has been a growing public awareness in the EU of the seriousness of this threat and an increasing acceptance of the view that a European response is necessary.

Concerns over Europe's competitive position have engendered a wide-ranging discussion on the appropriateness and costs of government's role in the economy. That discussion has revolved around subjects such as the social welfare system, government ownership of and assistance to industry, and government regulation. And it has highlighted the conflict between (a) the universally accepted responsibility of government to provide an extensive underpinning of social services to its citizens (a system whose origin dates back to nineteenth century continental Europe, but in its present form is a post–World War II compact between government and the electorate); and (b) the economic costs of this system to governments and business, which has diminished the competitiveness of European firms.

Although these many, interrelated issues fall clearly within the competence of the individual member states, they became increasingly the subject of consideration at EU level in the early 1990s, mainly at the initiative of the European Commission. Anxious to make a contribution toward resolving the most serious economic problem facing the EU, unemployment, and eager to burnish its image after the barrage of criticism directed at it during the debate over ratification of the Maastricht Treaty, the Commission published a white paper in 1993, at the request of the European Council, on "Growth, competitiveness, employment."[2] The white paper identified the EU's economic problems—declining growth potential, secular rise in unemployment, worsening competitive position—and offered recommendations in the form of guidelines for member state policies and actions to improve competitiveness and what it termed the "employment environment."

The white paper also indicated areas where EU policies could contribute to promoting growth, employment, and competitiveness. One of these is bringing to fruition the single market. Two others, to which the white paper attached particular importance, were laying the foundations for the information society (see Chapter 3) and developing major European infrastructure networks, as called for in the Maastricht Treaty.[3] In fact, the white paper referred to these trans-European networks (TENs) in energy, telecommunications, and transportation as "fundamental to the competitiveness of European businesses."[4] Needless to say, the TEN program has important implications for economic integration as well as for promoting growth and competitiveness. Expert groups have developed a number of TEN proposals, notably in the transportation field, where fourteen priority projects were approved by the European Council in December 1994. However, by their very nature, these projects are extremely expensive—about ECU 90 billion ($113 billion)—and doubts exist that the necessary funding will become available, particularly from EU sources (the Economic and Financial Affairs Council, i.e., the economic and finance ministers of the member states, proposed that the EU contribution be limited to 10 percent). In addition, ten priority energy projects were selected, costing about ECU 4 billion ($5 billion). Work on the trans-European telecommunications network is less advanced.

Concern over the economic threat posed to European business from other parts of the world will remain a constant in the foreseeable future. Accordingly, the issue of European competitiveness will continue to receive high attention in the EU. In all probability, policies and actions at the EU level will reflect the general shift in attitude toward strengthening market forces rather than government support. One indication of that philosophy was the Commission's industrial policy statement, adopted by the Council in 1994, that tied industrial policy directly to competitiveness and moved away from a sectoral and protectionist approach to an emphasis on opening markets, effective use of research and development, and competition policy.[5] Another indicator was the establishment of a Competitiveness Advisory Group in early 1995, consisting of thirteen leading industrialists, trade unionists, academics, and retired political leaders, and chaired by Carlo Ciampi, former governor of the Bank of Italy and Italian prime minister. The group was charged with drafting an independent report on the current state of competitiveness before each semiannual European Council meeting.[6]

There is, of course, no way of knowing how long and how deeply such attitudes and policies relating to competitiveness will be held. However, as long as they are, they will constitute a force for further economic integration as a means of enhancing Europe's ability to face outside competition.

Economic Situation

A more immediate, and more direct, determinant of future developments in Europe will be the economic situation—in particular, the speed and strength of the recovery. The greatest opposition to integration has come during periods of economic stress; conversely, the periods of greatest movement toward integration have coincided with a favorable economic situation. Thus, for example, the faster-than-scheduled removal of internal customs duties took place during a period of high economic growth; the oil shock-induced downturn of the 1970s and early 1980s was characterized by integration gridlock; and the single market euphoria burst forth during the economic prosperity of the late 1980s.

That period of prosperity was followed in the early 1990s (see Chapter 1) by a severe and lengthy recession with the attendant problem of sustained high levels of unemployment. However, by 1994, the European economy had turned the corner. The recovery first took place in the United Kingdom (which had been among the earliest to fall into recession) and then moved to the Continent, where Germany, after negative

growth in 1993, registered 2.5 percent growth in 1994 with annual incre-
ments of 0.5 percent expected in the succeeding two years. For the EU,
after three years with growth in the range of −0.5 to +1.5 percent, gross
domestic product (GDP) grew 2.7 percent in 1994, and growth was forecast to remain in the 2.5–3.0 percent range through 1997.[7] This favorable
economic climate will increase receptivity to integration.

However, the economic picture is clouded by the gloomy unemployment situation. As mentioned in Chapter 1, the consensus among econo-
mists is that despite expected economic growth in the next few years,
there is little likelihood that unemployment will decrease significantly or,
conversely, that there will be a significant increase in employment before
1997. The Commission forecasts that unemployment will remain over 10
percent through 1996. The persistence of high unemployment can be
expected to exercise a negative influence over integration efforts, as
people are more likely to view integration as exacerbating the unemployment problem rather than mitigating it.[8] As one French official com-
mented privately, "People ask whether 'Europe' is the cause of
unemployment or at least why it does not help."

Political Leadership

How will the present and prospective political leadership within the
EU affect the integration process? To what extent will it seek and obtain
popular support for further integration?

At the beginning of 1993, the notional inauguration of the single
market, the prospects were far from bright. The preceding decade had
seen remarkably little change in government and leadership in most
member states: Christian Democrat-dominated coalitions in Belgium and
the Netherlands headed by Wilfried Martens and Ruud Lubbers, respectively, conservative coalitions in Denmark under Poul Schluter (until
1992), Socialist governments in France dominated by François Mitterrand, the Christian Democrat-led coalition under Helmut Kohl in Germany, rotation of power among a narrow stratum of party chieftains in
Italy, a Socialist government under Felipe Gonzalez in Spain, and a Conservative government in the United Kingdom dominated until 1991 by
Margaret Thatcher.

Although this leadership represented continuity and experience, it
was also increasingly discredited by the national electorates. In fact, by
1993, as one observer described it, there was a "growing disenchantment
in almost every European country with the established political class."[9]
This resulted from two interrelated factors. One was political weariness;
people were losing their enthusiasm for and confidence in leaders who
had remained on the scene too long. The other was the economic crisis, in

particular the perceived inability of the leaders to solve or at least miti-
gate the problems the crisis was causing.

By the mid–1990s, some change had taken place. The most radical
upheaval occurred in Italy, where the entire post–World War II leadership
was effectively swept from office in March 1994 in the wake of corruption
scandals; however, it was not replaced with a stable alternative. In France,
the Socialists lost control of the National Assembly, and thus the government, while Mitterrand remained as a semi-lame duck president until the
spring of 1995, when the center parties completed their sweep of the
Socialists from power with the election of Jacques Chirac. The Dutch coalition was voted out of office in 1994, ending the long tenure of Prime
Minister Lubbers, and it was replaced by a Socialist-led coalition.

Others remained in power, though often in a weaker position. In Germany, Kohl was returned to office yet again in October 1994, though with
a sharply reduced majority for his coalition, while in Spain, the Gonzalez
government was re-elected by a narrow margin in 1993, with its hold on
power increasingly tenuous. In the United Kingdom, the slim majority of
John Major's government limited its room for maneuver, and its defeat at
the hands of Labour in the next general election (which must be held not
later than the spring of 1997) is likely.

To what extent have these changes of government, and prospective
further changes, affected the outlook for integration in the EU? On balance, the changes are unlikely to influence significantly the movement, or
lack thereof, toward integration. A Social Democratic victory in Germany
in 1998 or a Conservative victory in Spain earlier will not fundamentally
change those countries' attitudes and policies vis-à-vis the EU because of
the existing cross-party consensus. In any event, it is not evident that such
victories would bring with them more vigorous leadership.

On the other hand, the expected Labour victory in the next British
election will alter the British position on European integration. Labour
leader Tony Blair has adopted a more pro-EU stance than the present government,[10] and the party program calls for greater use of qualified majority voting and co-decision on economic issues. One policy change will
definitely be made: the Labour Party will carry out its commitment for
the United Kingdom to opt-in to the social protocol. The question is how
much farther it will move toward "Euro-friendliness."

A Labour government will have to take into account the widespread
wariness, if not hostility, toward the EU within the United Kingdom, an
attitude the Conservatives will undoubtedly play to in the electoral campaign. In addition, it will have to contend with a vociferously anti-EU
popular press and a vocal anti-EU minority within the party, similar to
that of the Conservatives though probably more manageable, particularly
if Labour wins with a comfortable majority. Thus, one can expect a shift,

but not a sea change in British policy. As an aspiring Labour politician told a private gathering a few years ago, "Labour loves the EU far more in opposition than it will in government." In any event, its prospective prime minister has vowed to stand up firmly for British interests and not relinquish the right of veto in crucial areas such as border controls, taxation, security, and treaty amendment.

Whatever leadership is exercised in the EU, it will take place in the context of rising anti-EU views. To some extent, this reflects opposition to existing regimes—for example, as was mentioned earlier, the anti-Maastricht vote in France was in part an anti-Mitterrand vote. However, it also reflects the growing strength of critical, if not hostile, views on the EU, as became manifestly apparent during the debate over ratification of the Maastricht Treaty. Anti-EU views are also reflected in the secular decline in public support for the Union, as registered in the periodic public opinion surveys carried out by the Commission. These show, for example, a substantial drop in the percentage of Europeans who consider that EU membership has been a "good thing" and that the respondent's country has benefited during the first half of the 1990s.[11] In some countries—for example, the Benelux countries, Germany, Ireland, and Italy—support remains high. However, in others, notably France and the United Kingdom, an important anti-Europe element exists. Although the French right has always contained its share of Euro-skeptics, the latter's views have increasingly been felt in the French conservative governing coalition. In the United Kingdom, a small but determined group of anti-EU members of the prime minister's party has severely limited the government's freedom of maneuver on European policy.

On balance, there are no indications that fresh political blood is waiting in the wings to infuse Europe with new enthusiasm. Such enthusiasm cannot be expected in four of the five major EU member states, whether because of conviction (the United Kingdom), political weakness (Spain), focus on domestic issues (Italy), or changing popular mood (France). The major exception is Germany, where Chancellor Kohl has consistently pressed for greater economic and political integration in the EU. As he represents the strongest country in the EU and one with a political consensus on European policy (at least on a philosophical level), his views will carry considerable weight in the councils of the EU.

Transparency and Participation

The Maastricht ratification debate revealed a strong sense among the European people that they have little input or influence over decisions affecting their daily lives. Furthermore, they feel that they have insufficient knowledge of the actions being taken by the EC institutions and that these actions are not subject to sufficient controls. Thus, the degree of future public acceptance and support for integration will depend in part on the extent to which Europeans consider that the Union's institutions are operating transparently, are democratically accountable, and reflect their interests—in other words, that the EC's citizens are participating in the Union's decision making.

Although some of this perception is unfocused, being directed at a far-away "Brussels" allegedly making rules without reference to the wishes of the people, the two principal targets are the Commission and the Council. The Commission is an obvious target because it is a bureaucracy, hence unelected and relatively independent in its operations, with substantial powers that it has not hesitated to use. The Commission's institutional bias is to seek EU solutions to problems—which implies expanding the scope of its activities and those of the EU—and that does not always meet favor with the EU's citizens. In addition, much of the Commission's activities are conducted outside public scrutiny, particularly its key function of developing legislative proposals.

A further source of criticism of the Commission is fraud in the expenditure of EU funds, largely agricultural support and structural assistance. The scale of fraud is substantial; according to one estimate, fraud and other financial irregularities drain between 2 and 10 percent of total EU spending.[12] Although the Commission has combatted fraud through the years, its efforts do not appear to have been particularly successful, and in any event, these attempts have not attracted the public's attention. However, the Commission entering office in 1995 has adopted a high public profile. It has increased its focus on fraud by giving a commissioner specific responsibility for fighting fraud, by publicizing the increase in fraud detection, and by instituting a fraud telephone hot-line, a special database, and a program to improve the training of officials. In addition, the Commission responded positively when the annual report of the EU Court of Auditors was issued in November 1995. Shedding much of its previous defensiveness, it provided detailed responses and promised firmer action against fraud and irregularity (though noting that member states, where 80 percent of EU moneys are spent, bear a share of the responsibility). The Commission's activism in this area should contribute over time to improving its image with EU citizens.

Although Brussels is usually equated with the Commission, in fact the objects of criticism are frequently the results of actions taken by the Council, i.e., the member states taking collective decisions. The oft-quoted phrase of British Foreign Secretary Douglas Hurd complaining about "Brussels" inserting itself into every "nook and cranny" of daily life referred largely to Council decisions, although the phrase was not generally understood in those terms. The activities of the Council are far from transparent. Its consideration of legislative proposals, from the working groups of experts from the national capitals to the permamment representatives in Brussels and then the ministers of the member states, takes place exclusively in private, although information on the deliberations is usually obtainable on an informal basis by interested parties. Nonetheless, the privacy of the Council sessions has one distinct advantage: it greatly facilitates decision making in that member state representatives can make compromises and cut deals far more easily *in camera* than they could in public.

Public concerns about transparency and accountability did not begin with Maastricht. They have been a recurrent theme in recent years, particularly as the single market program has expanded the scope of EU rule making. One reflection was the discussion, and subsequent adoption in the treaty, of the principle of subsidiarity, under which actions in areas where there is not exclusive EU competence are to be taken at the EU level only if the objectives cannot be "sufficiently achieved" by the member states (see Chapter 7).[13] While subsidiarity will not in itself affect transparency and accountability in the EU, it is expected to reduce the level of EU regulation, and that would diminish the criticisms of Brussels. Another reflection is the campaign to rectify what many perceive to be a "democratic deficit," for which the main solution is seen to be an increase in the powers of the Parliament (see Chapter 7).

Recognizing the importance of transparency of the decision-making process, including for public confidence, the Maastricht negotiating conference, in one of the thirty-three declarations appended to the treaty, recommended that the Commission submit a report to the Council no later than 1993 "on measures designed to improve public access to the information available to the [EU] institutions."[14] The theme of openness was also stressed in the report of a high-level group headed by a highly respected former commissioner, Peter Sutherland, in October 1992, which asserted that "[t]he need is for a more effective and clearly expressed dialogue between Community institutions and European citizens and business."[15]

Subsequent to the Maastricht Treaty and the Sutherland report, the Commission issued a number of communications describing its actions to increase openness. In late 1992, it announced a series of improvements in its procedures that were designed to increase public awareness of the transparency of its activities. These included broadening the consultation process, increasing the amount of information released to the public, codifying legislation, and announcing new initiatives well in advance. The Commission also set out a policy governing its relations with special interest groups. Two years later, it set up a Users' Advisory Council to obtain feedback on its efforts to achieve greater transparency, and it organized "Internal Market Weeks" in every member state, at which Commission officials explained policies and invited comments and questions. These various steps move in the direction of greater openness and should contribute to diminishing the public's concern about transparency and, perhaps to a lesser extent, accountability. Nonetheless, such efforts, even if highly successful, can change attitudes only gradually, and thus will affect public perceptions only over the long term.

Meanwhile, there has been little change in the modus operandi of the Council. The member states have been split over the desirability of opening at least part of their meetings to the public (the discussion but not the voting). However, the preponderant view has been negative, and the results unimpressive. Although the Council's rules of procedure were changed in December 1993 to provide for public sessions (decisions to do so are taken by unanimity on a case-by-case basis) and to require a public session on the Council Presidency's program each semester, the number of such Council meetings represent a minuscule percentage of the total, and most have covered the introduction of work programs. In fact, more public meetings (twelve) were held in 1993, especially during the Danish Presidency (before the change in the rules) than in the following year (only five in 1994).[16] The first public session of the General Affairs Council featured a televised round of opening statements, which proved to be a public relations disaster—a series of brief, stale speeches aimed at an audience outside the Council. Although the accession of Finland and Sweden will add to the pressures for transparency, the Council's basic procedures are unlikely to change unless decisions to do so are taken at the Intergovernmental Conference (IGC).

Future of the Franco-German Alliance

A central feature of the EU's development has been the leadership provided by France and Germany, working closely together. The 1957 Treaty of Rome establishing the EC was largely based on a Franco-German understanding, and in the years following, particularly since the mid–1970s, under Presidents Valéry Giscard d'Estaing and Mitterrand and Chancellors Helmut Schmidt and Kohl, the two member states have taken the lead in setting the agenda and taking the decisions in the EC and the EU. No major decisions have been taken, nor could they have been, without the consent of France and Germany.

To some extent, this situation reflected the close personal relations between the incumbent French President and German Chancellor, until recently Mitterrand and Kohl, whose bond was their respective experiences in World War II.[17] More important was recognition that the two countries shared the same objectives and strongly believed that working together served their mutual interest. However, in the words of one German observer, it has been "a marriage of convenience, not love." The relationship has encountered difficult moments that exposed its fragility, yet the continuation of the Franco-German partnership was never threatened because both governments gave the highest priority to maintaining the alliance.

With Mitterrand's departure from the scene in 1995 and the dramatic changes that have taken place in Europe, it is relevant to consider the future of that relationship. The replacement of Mitterrand by Chirac introduces an element of uncertainty in that (a) his views on Europe are less clear—and in any event, less passionately pro-European—than those of his predecessor, and (b) he does not have the same personal relationship with Kohl, at least at the outset of his presidency. The strength and effectiveness of the relationship will be tested by two significant developments.

First, prior to German unification, the fiction of equality between France and Germany was maintained; now Germany is clearly the predominant member of the partnership. Although on the surface no change may become apparent, France may find it more difficult to influence Germany, and Germany, in turn, may be more reluctant to defer to France as a "coequal." Second, there is a divergence between French and German objectives on the future of Europe. France seeks to promote its interests through the EU; therefore, it supports integration and is eager to proceed with economic and monetary union (EMU). However, it wants weak EU institutions so that it can wield power and influence through the intergovernmental process.[18] On the other hand, Germany firmly supports further integration, in particular an expansion of the Parliament's powers (seen as the quid pro quo for EMU), but also a strengthening of the Common Foreign and Security Policy (CFSP) and the third pillar through the use of qualified majority voting; it also supports enlargement of the EU to the east. This divergence will undoubtedly strain, and possibly weaken, the Franco-German relationship.

Alliance-building among member states is a continuing process, and with the increase in EU membership and expansion of qualified majority voting there is greater scope for shifting alliances. In the run-up to the IGC, the United Kingdom has sought to persuade France that its objectives, especially that of preserving the EU's intergovernmental nature, are closer to those of the United Kingdom than Germany. Although it cannot realistically hope to replace the Franco-German partnership with an Anglo-French one, a careful campaign could achieve some success, particularly if the negative bias of British policy were abandoned.[19] Nevertheless, it is difficult to imagine that either France or Germany will permit their relationship to unravel in the coming years. France recognizes that it cannot achieve its objectives in Europe without German support, and Germany wants to be firmly tied into the EU without being cast as the "leader" or dominant decision maker in the EU. That, at least, is the present situation.[20] What remains to be seen is whether changing circumstances and perceptions will result over time in greater German assertiveness in the determination of EU policies.

Membership

Decisions on the accession of new members—the number, their identity and the timing of their entry—will directly affect the member states' ability and willingness to proceed further toward economic and political integration of the Union.

A major change in the composition of the EU took place on January 1, 1995, with the accession of Austria, Finland, and Sweden, three highly developed market economy, democratic countries (see Chapter 1). Although the accession negotiations (including those over the European Economic Area, EEA) were lengthy and at times contentious, the level of development and the economic and political systems in the new members were very similar to those of the more advanced EU countries. Thus, their entry into the Union required relatively little adjustment on either side. The one issue that had set them apart, their historical policy of neutrality, became largely irrelevant with the ending of the Cold War, and all three accepted the required undertakings of the CFSP as part of membership.[21]

Now, however, the new Union of fifteen member states finds itself facing applications, or at least clearly expressed desires for membership, from a numerous countries. The eastern boundary of the EU, already reaching Russia in the north (Finland and Sweden), could shift from that of the ex-Iron Curtain to the border of ex-Soviet Union, if not farther. Thus, the prospect is that in the next decade or two, the European Union will more or less coincide with the geographic expanse of Europe.

The applicants or potential applicants fall into a number of categories. First in line are the pending applications of Cyprus, Malta, and Turkey. Cyprus and Malta applied to join in 1990. However, until recently both applications were largely ignored, not only because of the member states' involvement with more pressing issues (negotiating new relationships with the countries of the European Free Trade Association (EFTA) and Central and Eastern Europe and the Maastricht negotiations), but also because there was no compelling economic or political reason (and little cultural affinity) in EU eyes for accession by these countries. Cypriot accession remained out of the question with the island divided and a bone of contention between Greece and Turkey, and Malta could not hope to emulate the Luxembourg example as a micro-state member because it was neither centrally located, economically linked, nor culturally related to the mainstream of the EU.

Nonetheless, the EU recently turned its attention to these two applications. Cyprus's application became unblocked in early 1995 as part of a deal whereby Greece lifted its veto over conclusion of a customs union between the EU and Turkey (see below) in return for a commitment that accession negotiations for Cyprus would begin six months after conclusion of the IGC. Once that decision had been taken, there was no rationale for treating Malta differently. Accordingly, the Commission committed itself to concurrent accession negotiations with Malta. In any event, it would have been difficult to justify entering into accession negotiations with countries of Central Europe (see below) without addressing longer-standing applications, and the "sponsors" of Cyprus and Malta (Greece and Italy, respectively) might well have used their veto to prevent the eastern applicants from "cutting into line."

The case of Turkey is sui generis. Its 1964 association agreement was considered, as was that of Greece two years earlier, to be a first step toward eventual membership. However, it soon became clear that there was little support among the member states for Turkish accession. Their concerns ranged from its size (it would have the largest population of any member state), to religion (Muslim), economic level (its per capita GDP is half that of the poorest EU member state) and human rights (its treatment of the Kurdish minority). Irrespective of these considerations, it is difficult to imagine circumstances under which Greece would lift its veto of Turkey's entry; hence, the issue is moot for the indefinite future. Thus, rather than acting on Turkey's 1987 application for admission, the EC and then the EU have sought an alternative structure for its relationship with Turkey. In 1995 Greece lifted its long-standing veto of the EU–Turkey customs union and the European Parliament gave its grudging assent (despite concern over Turkey's human rights record), thus enabling it to enter into effect in 1996.

The only Western European countries not presently desiring membership in the EU are Iceland, Liechtenstein, Norway, and Switzerland. Although the Norwegian government successfully negotiated accession, the electorate rejected membership in a referendum in 1994. This decision reflected the majority's belief that EU membership threatened Norwegian control over its oil and gas resources and its generous welfare system while offering few tangible benefits—Norway already benefited from a free trade agreement with the EU and enjoyed a strong economy based on its energy resources. Iceland, as a small, distant country, with a single-commodity economy (fish, the subject of hotly contested catch regulations in the EU), would not fit easily into an integrated Union. In any event, it will not pursue membership now that Norway's electorate has rejected that option, an issue that will not be reopened in the foreseeable future.

On the other hand, the conflict continues in Switzerland between the economic logic of joining the EU and the political reality of deep conservatism and suspicion of the majority of the electorate. Although the formal Swiss application for membership remains on the table, the voters' rejection of the EEA in December 1992 pushes the date for any application far into the future.

Now that the EU's relationships with the present and future EFTA countries have been settled, the immediate issue is Central Europe—what countries among the former Soviet satellites should become members, when, and under what conditions. The post-Communist governments of these countries have given the highest priority to obtaining the EU's commitment to membership, an objective they consider not only desirable but also essential for their transformation from Communist satellites to Western democracies. In addition to the moral argument that these countries should not be punished for the historical tragedy of having been subjugated by the Soviets but rather "welcomed back" by the West, the governments assert that in the absence of such a commitment their electorates will not support the painful changes that are a necessary ingredient of the construction of democratic countries with market-driven economies.

The ex-Soviet satellites consist of two distinguishable groups. The so-called Visegrad countries, named after the Hungarian city in which they met in 1990 and agreed to undertake a common approach to the West, are the most advanced economically and politically. These include the Czech Republic, Hungary, Poland, and the Slovak Republic; although the latter is somewhat less advanced economically and politically, it has participated in the group from the outset as part of what was then Czechoslovakia, and there is no disposition to demote it from the first tier Central European states. The second group of ex-Soviet satellites comprises Bulgaria and Romania, whose level of economic and political development trails substantially behind that of the Visegrad countries, and Albania, which is in a uniquely backward class of its own.

As of the mid-1990s, the only viable candidates for EU membership are the members of the Visegrad group. Bulgaria and Romania, to say nothing of Albania, will not be seriously considered for at least another decade. The EU has moved cautiously on the issue of membership for the Visegrad four, seeking the progressive expansion and deepening of the economic and political relationships. Thus, it has undertaken a substantial economic assistance program to the Central European countries under PHARE (so-called because of the original, but discarded, name of

Poland and Hungary Assistance to the Restructuring of the Economy), with an annual budget that grew from ECU 500 million ($625 million) in 1990 to over ECU 1 billion ($1.3 billion) in 1992 and 1993 (which has declined somewhat since then), and it assumed the coordinating role for assistance being provided by the Western donor nations. Parallel to that effort, the EU entered into a series of bilateral agreements providing for progressively closer economic and political relations, culminating in "Europe Agreements" that provide both enhanced trade benefits and closer political ties.

However, the trade dimension has proven contentious. Although the EU recognized the important contribution that expanded exports from Central Europe would make to the development of these countries, the areas of their greatest export potential—agriculture, steel, and textiles—are characterized by overcapacity in the EU, and thus strong political opposition developed within member states to granting trade concessions. This caused considerable embarrassment to the EU, particularly as it enjoyed a sharply increasing trade surplus with the area. Nonetheless, under strong pressure from the Commission, the European Council agreed to a relatively liberal import regime in June 1993, which was expanded into a free trade area with the Visegrad four plus Bulgaria and Romania in 1995. The arrangement is unbalanced in that import restrictions will be lifted more slowly in the Central European countries. Agriculture is excluded from the free trade area, and EU restrictions on steel and textile imports will be removed in 1997.

The political argument for enlargement is strong and obvious. There is no a priori bar to membership. Once the decision was taken in 1981 to admit Greece on political grounds (i.e., the perceived need to nurture democracy following the overthrow of the "colonels regime"), the EU in effect lost its ability to deny admission to an applicant country (or, more precisely, individual member states lost their ability to block admission) when a political rationale existed and other basic conditions (including, of course, geography) were met. Furthermore, it is clearly in the interest of the EU member states to promote the stability and economic well-being of their neighbors to the east, and achievement of those goals would be facilitated by membership in the EU.

On the other hand, the economic implications of enlargement are serious and negative. Per capita GDP in these countries is considerably lower than in the rest of the EU. In 1993, compared to an EU average of ECU 16,000 ($20,000), that of the Visegrad four plus the richer Slovenia was only ECU 2,300 ($2,900).[22] In addition, these countries need to put in place a Western legal and economic framework and adopt legislation mirroring that of the EU. Despite substantial progress, it is doubtful that the Visegrad countries could withstand the competition of the single market without a long transition and significant exceptions. Most important, if no changes were made in the EU's agricultural and structural adjustment programs, the Visegrad countries would be major beneficiaries, adding a massive burden to the EU's budget. Estimates of the cost, which must be viewed with caution, vary considerably, running as high as ECU 64 billion ($80 billion) annually, a sum roughly equal to the entire annual budget of the EU.[23]

Despite these obstacles, the European Council, at its meeting in Copenhagen in June 1993, formally invited the countries of Central Europe to join the Union as soon as they have met the required economic and political conditions. Although formally that declaration did not break new ground, it was an important signal to the aspiring members. The member states also set out the following criteria for membership: appropriate and compatible political systems based on democracy and respect for human rights; a functioning market economy capable of competing in the EU; and acceptance of the body of EU law and regulations (the *acquis communautaire*) and the political objectives of the EU.

Thus, the question is no longer whether Central European countries will join the EU, but rather when. Germany has been the most active promoter of the EU's forging ever closer links with Central and Eastern Europe, leading to membership by these countries, and thus it will have the greatest voice in determining the answers to that question. For a combination of historical, economic, and political reasons, Germany has stressed its need to be bound on the east, as well as the west, by the EU. Its foreign minister made that clear, describing as "a primary goal of the German Presidency [July–December 1994] ... we see ourselves as [these countries'] primary advocate in their request for integration in Europe,"[24] and Chancellor Kohl has made that a constant theme in his public statements. However, the political impetus and rationale have to fit within the bounds of economic feasibility, and it will take time to work out the modalities. Thus, by 1995, the encouraging messages from within the EU, including those from Chancellor Kohl, had become more tempered, urging upon the Central European applicant countries patience and "realism."

The process leading to accession is under way. The heads of government of the six Central European countries that are parties to Europe Agreements (the Visegrad four plus Bulgaria and Romania) were invited to attend part of the December 1994 European Council meeting, which also endorsed a strategy (a sort of "road map") for preparing these countries for accession. The EU foreign ministers met with their six Central European counterparts at that session as the first of regular semiannual meetings, and periodic meetings of other counterpart ministers began in the first half of 1995. In a follow-up to the strategy document, the Commission published a white paper in May 1995, identifying legislation that is essential for the functioning of the EU internal market, suggesting the sequence in which applicant countries should bring their national legislation into conformity, and describing the administrative structures that will be necessary to make the legislation effective.[25] While the white paper is clearly identified as a guide and not part of the accession negotiations, applicant countries will obviously need to make sufficient progress along the lines it indicates before accession negotiations can begin. These negotiations will not start until the conclusion of the IGC, which convenes in 1996 and meets for an indeterminate period, certainly until 1997.

Accession agreements with these countries will undoubtedly include a long transition period and significant derogations from the *acquis communautaire*. In particular, the realities of the economic costs and the political unwillingness of present beneficiaries of existing programs to reduce their share significantly mean that new entrants will have to resign themselves to less favorable benefits from the EU's agricultural and structural adjustment policies—a sort of second-class membership—than is enjoyed by the present membership. They are in a weak bargaining position—eager to join but possessing little leverage.

The EU will conduct the negotiations with individual applicants, not with the Visegrad four as a bloc. The most likely "first wave" will consist of the Czech Republic, Hungary, and Poland; Slovakia's ability to meet the economic and political tests of membership remains less certain. Despite the inevitability of enlargement to the east, it is unrealistic to contemplate accession before the turn of the century, and a number of statements to that effect have been made by European leaders. These have elicited a sharp reaction from the Visegrad countries; Czech Prime Minister Vaclav Klaus reacted with typical vigor, "[that] is much too late, unacceptably too late."[26] Nonetheless, when it occurs, enlargement will probably be premature economically but concordant with political necessity.

Two other groups of Central and Eastern European countries are also potential EU members: parts of ex-Yugoslavia and the Baltics. While the fighting has raged in what used to be Yugoslavia, Slovenia, the first state in the former republic to declare its independence, has succeeded in distancing itself from the conflict, largely because of the small percentage of non-Slovenes within its borders. It has also benefited from its economic links with its neighbors, Austria and Italy. Thus, once negotiations on a Europe Agreement (initiated in mid–1995) are concluded, Slovenia will become eligible for membership. It will probably be included in the first wave of new members, provided it can reach a settlement with Italy on the latter's claims for compensation for property lost in the area that was within pre–World War II Italy and is now part of Slovenia.[27]

Depending on the durability of peace in the area, membership for Croatia in the coming years is also possible. However, prospects are dim for membership by other parts of ex-Yugoslavia.

The case of the three Baltic republics represents an exception to the notional geographic limits of the EU. Whereas it is generally accepted that a line must be drawn between "Europe" and "Asia" along the border of ex-Soviet Union (despite Russian claims to being a European nation), the status of Estonia, Latvia, and Lithuania is special: their incorporation into the Soviet Union dates only from 1939, and it was not recognized by most Western countries. Culturally and historically, these countries are readily distinguishable from the other components of the former Soviet Union. Not only does that enhance their claim for EU membership (all submitted applications in 1995), but the three Scandinavian neighbors that are now EU members can be expected to press for their admission to the Union. Although their request will have to be considered in light of their economic circumstances (i.e., they are considerably less developed that the more advanced Central European countries)[28] and of the generic problem of the conditions under which the EU should accept membership by small states, it is likely that Estonia, Latvia, and Lithuania will eventually join the EU. Conclusion of Europe Agreements in 1995 gave them formal status equivalent to that of the six Central European countries; thus, they now participate on an equal footing in all relations between the EU and the potential applicants to the East.

The prospective enlargement of the EU has very direct, significant implications for the future of the Union. It will increase its size and diversity, thus forcing important decisions to be taken regarding the EU's institutions and policies.

These differences—in economic activity, structure, political interests, culture, and traditions—will have to be reconciled, or at least dealt with, within the EU. As a result, the EU will find it more difficult to arrive at decisions: it will face the choice between further reducing the ability of one or a small number of member states to block decisions—in other words, further restricting the extent of voting by unanimity and reducing the blocking minority—or weakening the integration process and giving member states greater latitude to determine the extent of their participation in EU programs and activities. In addition, size, structure, and modus operandi of the EU institutions will have to be reviewed, notably the size and composition of the Commission, but also the size of Parliament and the rotation of the Council Presidency. Finally, the budgetary implications of enlargement will force a review of spending programs, both the structural programs and particularly the Common Agricultural Policy. These issues are addressed in the next chapter.

Notes

1. One example that is interpreted by some as "disruptive," and that certainly has engendered controversy, is the insistence of some Muslim girls on wearing head scarves in French schools.

2. European Commission, "Growth, competitiveness, employment: The challenges and ways forward into the 21st century," White Paper, *Bulletin of the European Communities*, Supplement 6/93, Office for Official Publications of the European Communities, Luxembourg, 1993.

3. Treaty of Rome as amended by Maastricht Treaty, Article 129b, c, and d.

4. European Commission, "Growth, Competitiveness and Employment—Note for the Council of Ministers (Economy/Finance) on the economic elements of the White Paper," Brussels, November 18, 1993, p. 11.

5. European Commission, "An industrial competitiveness policy for the European Union," *Bulletin of the European Union*, Supplement 3/94, Office for Official Publications of the European Communities, Luxembourg, 1994.

6. In its first report, presented to the June 1995 European Council in Cannes, the Competitiveness Advisory Group called for far-reaching action, including faster liberalization and deregulation, early implementation of economic and monetary union (EMU), removal of obstacles to the trans-European networks, and an overhaul of education and training. It remains to be seen how much influence the group will have.

7. European Commission press release, "Economic Forecast for 1995 and 1996," IP/95/491, May 17, 1995, and Communication from Commissioner de Silguy to the European Commission, "The Outlook for the Community Economy 1995–97: Autumn 1995 Economic Forecasts," November 22, 1995.

8. Indicative of this view was the Commission's minimalist proposal in 1995 for liberalization of postal services, which took into account strong member state concerns about the negative implications for employment in a sector with over 1.8 million employees.

9. Peter Ludlow, "Beyond Maastricht: Recasting the European Political and Economic System," Centre for European Policy Studies, Working Document No. 79, Brussels, July 1993, p. 20.

10. As Blair told the Royal Institute of International Affairs, "opinion polls probably would push us towards a sceptic approach," but that would be "folly," as quoted in "Monsieur Oui," The Economist, April 8, 1995.

11. European Commission, *Eurobarometer*, No. 41, July 1994, pp. vi and 8. After a secular climb during the 1980s, peaking at 72 percent in 1991, those considering membership a "good thing" dropped to 54 percent in 1994. Similarly, support for "benefits" from membership peaked in the late 1980s at 59 percent before falling to 47 percent in 1994.

12. "Hot on the trail of the EU fraudsters," *Financial Times*, April 3, 1995.

13. Treaty of Rome as amended by Maastricht Treaty, Article 3b.

14. Maastricht Treaty, declaration 17 on the Right of Access to Information.

15. "The Internal Market after 1992: Meeting the Challenge," Report to the Commission by the High Level Group on the Operation of the Internal Market, October 1992.

16. See Annex III of *Report of the Council on the Functioning of the Treaty on European Union*, No. 5082/95.

17. According to a frequent participant at Franco-German summits, Kohl and Mitterrand invariably harkened back to World War II in their references to the basis of the bilateral alliance.

18. In the words of a French Commission official, "France wants decisions taken by phone calls between France and Germany."

19. As Ian Davidson wrote in "Weak kind of wooing," *Financial Times*, January 18, 1995, "British negativism on Europe has lost its capacity to impress or deter ..."

20. Post-unification Germany has thus far downplayed its predominance in the EU, e.g., it did not seek to upset the parity among the major member states in the staffing of the Commission, and the increase in German representation in the Parliament was carried out in a low-key manner.

21. Austria, Finland, and Sweden also brought a strong welfare state tradition and a long history of government involvement in the economy, both present throughout much of Europe but more pronounced in these three countries. However, the welfare state and corporatist traditions are under economic and political pressure in most European countries, Sweden being a prime example.

22. According to "EU/East Europe: Commission Unveils Study on Agricultural Prospects," *European Report*, No. 2061, July 26, 1995, p. V/10, Central European country averages were as follows: Hungary ECU 3,150 ($3,950), Czech Republic ECU 2,600 ($3,250), Poland ECU 1,900 ($2,400), and Slovakia ECU 1,650 ($2,050).

23. Richard E. Baldwin, *Towards an Integrated Europe* (London: Centre for Economic Policy Research, 1994), p. xvii. Although the Commission has made no official estimates, its Regional Policy Directorate General has informally calculated ECU 38 billion ($48 billion) as the cost of extending current EU policies to ten potential member countries in Central and Eastern Europe (the Visegrad four, the three Baltic republics, Bulgaria, Romania, and Slovenia). Even that figure reportedly includes only a part of the benefits provided under the Common Agriculture Policy. See "The EU goes cold on enlargement," *The Economist*, October 28, 1995, p. 37.

24. "CEEC the focus of upcoming German Presidency," *European Report*, No. 1958, June 15, 1994, p. I/5.

25. European Commission, "Preparation of the Associated Countries of Central and Eastern Europe for Integration into the Internal Market of the Union," COM(95) 163, May 3, 1995.

26. William Drosdiak, "Former Communist States Feel Stranded by EU Club," *International Herald Tribune*, April 18, 1994.

27. With per capita GDP of $5,800, Slovenia is the richest of the Central European countries, *Central European Economic Review* map of Central and Eastern Europe, 1993.

28. According to "EU/East Europe," p. V/10, per capita GDP in the Baltic republics is about one-third that of the Visegrad four plus Slovenia, which, in turn is about 15 percent of the EU average.

7

Prospects for Integration

The fundamental questions facing the European Union as it moves toward the twenty-first century concern the future of European integration. Will the EU opt for maintenance of the status quo, leaving the present level of integration more or less unchanged? Will it reverse the process of integration by repealing some of the measures that have been taken? Or will it move the process forward, tightening the bonds among the member states?

There is a body of opinion in the EU that believes it essential to move forward to avoid moving backward. This "bicycle theory" holds that unless further integration takes place, the forces of retrogression will succeed in shifting the balance in favor of the opposite direction—"disintegration." Standing still, it is asserted, is not a viable option.

The likelihood that the EU will start to dismantle the integration thus far achieved is remote. The supporters of this theory overestimate the intensity of the pressures for rolling back the tide of integration, whether among member state governments or organized groups among the population, and the ability of these forces to do so given the momentum of integration.

The real battle will pit the proponents of status quo against those of forward movement. It is a battle that will involve a multitude of participants—national governments, political groups, sectors of business and society, and other interest groups. It will take place, as described earlier, in the context of a growing disparity of interests among member states and the virtual certainty of a significant expansion of membership in the near future. And it will be fought on many fronts—across the range of economic, political, and institutional issues.

Thus, any forecast of future developments must necessarily be based on a review of the various components of integration in the EU. Although that review logically begins with the single market program, in many respects the key issue is economic and monetary union (EMU)—the symbolic cornerstone of economic integration, as yet incomplete, and the structure that will codify the division of the EU into two categories of members. Apart from EMU, the major focal point for determining the future of integration will be the Intergovernmental Conference (IGC), where the gamut of institutional issues will be considered.

The "Four Freedoms" of the Single Market Program

In two respects integration is proceeding under the momentum developed by the single market program. First, as described earlier, most of the legislation takes effect in the member states at a date later than that of its adoption, sometimes with further delays for certain member states, particularly the less developed ones; thus, additional integration will take place in stages. Second, the European Commission and the European Court of Justice, despite their relatively limited resources and slow procedures, respectively, over time can be expected to bring about greater adherence to the legislation that has been adopted.

A potential countertrend relates to the Maastricht Treaty's introduction of the principle of "subsidiarity." Formalizing a doctrine that had already gained a certain degree of acceptance in practice, the treaty provides that in areas where it does not have exclusive competence, the EU shall take action only when the objectives "cannot be sufficiently achieved" at member state level and when the "scale or effects" of the proposed action can be better achieved by the EU.[1] This principle was given further prominence by the reference to "respect for the principle of subsidiarity" among the treaty's objectives.[2]

As a result of the introduction of this principle, the European Council called on the Commission at its Edinburgh summit in December 1992 to review existing EU legislation and make proposals for annulling or amending those parts that did not conform to the requirements of subsidiarity. The Commission then drew up a work program to put subsidiarity into effect. In its first annual report on the application of the principle of subsidiarity, the Commission described (a) its new procedures for reviewing the conformity of proposed legislation to subsidiarity, which resulted in fewer initiatives and greater use of alternative approaches; (b) its withdrawal or revision of a number of proposals in the legislative process; and (c) its program for modifying some existing legislation.[3] However, these alternatives affect only a small percentage of EU legislation, and the measures in question do not fall particularly under the category of hard-core integration issues (e.g., withdrawal of the proposed harmonization of the conditions of animals in zoos).

In any event, the Commission's focus is prospective rather than retrospective. The significance of subsidiarity lies in its effect on future legislation because the Commission is now required to demonstrate that all legislative proposals conform to that principle. That will undoubtedly force the Commission to exercise some restraint as regards the nature and scope of proposed new legislation. However, irrespective of the introduction of subsidiarity, the volume of legislative proposals has declined substantially since 1990 because the bulk of single market measures had been introduced by then. Thus, the Commission's 1996 work program contained only 19 legislative proposals, less than one-third the number in 1990.

Subsidiarity responds to a genuine need to limit the scope of legislation harmonizing member state laws and regulations that is required to ensure free movement in the EU. Examples of proposed and approved legislation that do not meet that requirement are legion.[4] However, the potential conflict between subsidiarity and free movement must be recognized—if subsidiarity is taken too far, it will threaten the EU's ability to maintain common policies. Hence, there will necessarily be controversies over whether proposed legislation meets the test of subsidiarity, with one side claiming that a harmonization proposal is not necessary and the other accusing the opponents of seeking to thwart legitimate efforts to eliminate barriers to the single market or otherwise to take action at the EU level. The European Parliament will be a vigilant defender of EU legislation. In any case, a member state's interpretation of subsidiarity will likely vary at least as much according to its interest in a particular issue as its philosophy of regulation.[5] The net result of the introduction of subsidiarity will be to codify the already existing predisposition to lighten the regulatory framework of the single market.

A further force for lightening the regulatory framework is the European business community. In a variety of forums, the private sector has pressed for the simplification or abolition of regulations: the Anglo-German Deregulation Group established by Chancellor Helmut Kohl and Prime Minister John Major issued a scathing report in 1995, charging that "over-regulation is stifling growth, reducing competitiveness and costing Europe jobs" and offering a twelve-point action program; the Molitor Group established by the Commission to look at the effect of EU legislation on employment and competition;[6] and a similar group set up in UNICE (the union of national employers' and industry confederations) in conjunction with the small and medium-sized business unit of the Commission to study the impact of legislation on competitiveness called for urgent action to improve the quality of regulations and reduce their number.[7]

Turning, then, to the prospects for the single market program, regarding both the unfinished legislative agenda and the situation in the marketplace, and using the categorization of measures contained in the 1985 single market white paper:

Physical Barriers

- *Control of goods.* This is essentially completed.
- *Control of plants and animals.* The progressive harmonization of plant and animal health controls is likely to continue without major impediments.
- *Control of people.* Controls over movement across the borders between countries participating in the Schengen Agreement will gradually disappear. However, other countries will find it difficult for geographical and policy reasons to join this arrangement. Similarly, the Commission's effort to legislate the extension of Schengen, by proposing a set of directives in 1995 that would abolish internal border controls and provide non-EU citizens the right to travel freely from one member state to another, will be blocked by strenuous British opposition, backed by the rule of unanimity in this area. Furthermore, concerns over the ability of Schengen, and non-Schengen, countries to police their borders against illegal entry from third countries will remain, and progress in establishing common visa and asylum policies, a necessary adjunct for the free movement of people, will be slow.

Technical Barriers

- *Harmonization of standards.* EU legislation has established procedures and provided the impetus for the development of European standards. With fifteen to twenty manufacturing categories or sectors covered (or in the process of becoming covered) by "new approach" directives (see Chapter 2), national standards for an important segment of manufactured products will be harmonized, and subject—at least in theory and, to an increasing extent, in practice—to mutual recognition among the member states. The pace of development of European standards and the nature of these standards (particularly whether they represent global standards or are restrictively written) will depend in part on the relative strength of two sets of business interests: that recognizing the advantages to be gained from the internationalization of standards, and that seeking to use standards as a form of protection from competitors. The presumption is that the first group will remain dominant. Work on standards-writing is proceeding, albeit slowly relative to the demand, and the preponderance of standards are being drafted through a reasonably open process that takes account of global interests.

- *Harmonization of testing and certification of standards.* Progress is likely to be relatively slow in the development of mutual recognition of products, based on decisions that they meet the relevant standard, through national testing and certification procedures for two reasons: genuine concern about the quality and reliability of testing carried out by bodies and authorities in certain member states with less experience and expertise in such activities; and professional concern that mutual recognition will result in a reduction of the workload (and thus employment) of the body in question. Progress in testing and certification will require the development of accreditation programs for testing, inspection, and certification at the EU level. Bodies have been established in specific sectors (e.g., certification and laboratories) to ensure mutual recognition based on technical competence, and the Commission is encouraging the European Organization for Testing and Certification and other relevant bodies to ensure the technical competence of certification accreditation bodies and harmonize the technical procedures they use. The success of these efforts will require that governments devolve responsibility for testing requirements to these bodies.
- *Approximation of laws in specific industrial sectors.* The single market legislation contained a rather heavy component of sector-specific legislation—e.g., chemical products, food, and pharmaceuticals— that is, overall, on the way to implementation. However, a number of contentious issues in the food sector will be difficult to resolve.
- *Public procurement.* The stakes in the EU's vast public procurement market are enormous, both for suppliers who benefit from the previously existing closed system and the potential beneficiaries of the opening up envisaged in the EU legislation. The strength of the vested interests in the old regime and the inherent difficulty of administering and enforcing the EU legislation will slow the process of liberalization of public procurement in the EU. In addition, conflicts will arise in which important political interests and sensitivities are at stake, rendering more difficult the task of ensuring a fair process and effective enforcement. Nonetheless, a steady, if gradual, shift from protection to transparency and fairness is likely to take place.
- *Free movement for labor and the professions.* Movement of working people within the EU is limited by tradition, culture, and language, and often by economic constraints such as availability and cost of housing. Thus, under the best of circumstances one should not expect mobility of the EU populations on anything approaching the US scale. In any event, a major obstacle to the movement of people to another member state for work is the absence of EU-wide

pension schemes. Normally, it is impossible for an individual to carry a pension from one member state to another; thus, moving often results in a significant reduction in retirement benefits. Since most pension systems are government-funded and government budgets will remain a national government prerogative, any progress toward alleviating this constraint will be slow.

- *Financial services.* Despite differing national government approaches to regulation in the financial services sector, the scope for crossborder activities is vast under the single market legislation. However, it will take place more quickly at the corporate level than under conditions where the private individual comes into contact with the nonnational company, e.g., retail banking or the sale of personal insurance policies, because individuals generally feel more comfortable dealing with home country businesses on personal financial matters. Nonetheless, over time these markets will become far less compartmentalized on a national basis as companies, both buyers and sellers of services, look for economic advantages. On the other hand, the liberalization of securities trading is likely to take longer.

- *Transportation.* Liberalization of air transportation is clearly under way, and competitive pressures, combined with enforcement by the Commission and the European Court of Justice, will continue to move the process forward. However, progress will be limited by member states' continued subsidization of their national carriers, to the extent that will be permitted, and it is likely the Commission will achieve only modest success in limiting such actions. The phasing out of the quota system for road transportation will progressively lower costs and increase this sector's competitiveness. While there has been talk of loosening the national monopolies over the rail transportation sector, that is unlikely in the foreseeable future. Similarly, although the Commission has shown interest in developing coordinated policies for the transportation sector as a whole rather than considering each mode of transportation independently, such thinking is unlikely to produce tangible results for many years.[8]

- *New technologies and services.* Although it is difficult to generalize about the range of subjects covered under this category, the Commission will continue to give prominence to efforts to develop the information society in the EU, essentially by seeking to facilitate the ability of market forces to develop and utilize new equipment and services. One issue will remain high-profile and contentious: the harmonization of rules on audiovisual broadcasting, in particular the limits on non-EU programs, which combines cultural and political with economic considerations (see Chapter 8).

- *Capital liberalization.* All restrictions have been removed, and it is most unlikely that any member state will reimpose controls on the movement of capital, short of a massive currency crisis exceeding those of 1992 and 1993.
- *Company law and taxation.* Progress is likely to remain slow, primarily because of the strenuous opposition of the business community to the inclusion of provisions on worker participation in decision making in much of the pending legislation. These proposed provisions go farther than the works council directive (the latter relates to information rather than decision making), and agreement on that directive was reached only after a decade-plus of debate and with British abstention from the voting (because it was taken under the social protocol). Thus, the variation in member state company laws and regulations is likely to remain significant. Similarly, there is little prospect for an alignment or approximation of the different systems and rates of taxes, especially regarding direct taxation, to which corporations are subject. In any event, pressure from the private sector for harmonization is mitigated as companies have of necessity learned to operate within the context of multiple jurisdictions—many consider that their ability to function under the existing structure gives them a competitive advantage—and to a certain extent they prefer stability to change.
- *Intellectual property.* Now that the EU has adopted most of the basic legislation necessary for harmonizing intellectual property rights, attention will shift to action at member state level, particularly in those countries, essentially the southern members, lacking a strong tradition of protecting such rights. Spain, for example, not only blocked action on trademark regulation for several years over the site of the EU trademark office, but it opposed most of the legislation relating to industrial property (patents and trademarks) on the grounds that, in its view, the EU does not have the necessary competence. However, the issue was taken to the European Court of Justice, which ruled in 1995 that the EU had competence to adopt measures harmonizing member state laws or to create EU titles of industrial property. Spain has accepted that ruling. Nonetheless, there will probably be some foot-dragging at member state level, countered, however, by the efforts of the EU's private sector that stands to gain significantly from the EU legislation.

Fiscal Barriers

- *Excise tax.* There is little reason to expect any change in the loosely-harmonized EU excise tax system that has been established. There is neither strong pressure nor rationale for altering the system, nor is there a plausible alternative.

- *Value-added tax (VAT)*. The key issue is whether the member states will reach agreement on a "definitive" VAT system. Although the Commission is making a determined effort to bring forward a proposal that stands a reasonable chance of obtaining member state agreement, its effort is not likely to succeed. The main stumbling block is concern in at least some member states that they will not be adequately protected by the establishment of a clearing system against the loss of tax receipts that would otherwise accrue to them under the existing "origin-based" VAT system. It is not clear how effectively such a system would work and what would be the administrative and financial implications. In the last analysis, the question is whether the member states will be prepared to agree to such a system. That is a virtual impossibility, because unanimity is required and the majority favor continuation of the "destination-based" VAT system rather than adoption of an origin-based one.

Follow-up on the Single Market Program

As described in Chapter 3, the single market program is far more than a set of EU legislative enactments. EU legislation constitutes merely the first step in the process of economic integration, and it is a step that has been largely completed. Although some legislation remains pending, relatively few new legislative proposals are envisaged. Rather, the Commission plans increasingly to place the emphasis on deregulation and toleration of diversity. As one Commission official put it, "Harmonization is a dying industry."

The extent to which the single market ultimately becomes a reality will depend in large measure on the response of the member states—in the way they apply EU legislation and in the degree of confidence and cooperation developed in working with other member states—and that of individuals and organizations inside the EU. It is to these that the Commission has directed its attention. Following extensive consultations, it drafted a "strategic program," published in December 1993, in which it set forth what it considered the main priorities of the EU in completing, managing and further developing the single market—constituting, in the words of the same Commission official, "a road map" for future action. In it the Commission points out that "the establishment of a genuine single market ... is a continual process of ensuring that [the] common legal framework is applied, widely understood, enforced and, where necessary, developed in a coherent way to meet new needs."[9]

The first priority is to ensure that member states adequately transpose EU legislation because "an essential condition for the internal market to function well concerns the quality of implementation of internal market measures."[10] It is reasonable to assume that the member states will take the necessary legal and administrative steps for transposition, albeit with some delays.

Less certain is the assiduousness with which they will carry out the letter and spirit of the single market legislation. In part this will reflect member states' perceived need to protect what are deemed (at least polit-ically) to be important national interests; such instances have occurred in the past, and they will undoubtedly recur. To what extent will the other member states accede to these actions, how forcefully will the Commis-sion react, will the courts be used prevent such actions, and if so, will judicial mandates prove to be effective? These questions cannot be answered categorically. The responses to member state actions will depend on the circumstances, including the identity of the member state (realistically, a large member state is more likely to have its way than a small one) and the intensity of its action. However, momentum of the integration and enforcement process is likely over time to lead to a dimi-nution in the ability of a member state to depart from the legislative intention.

A related problem is the lack of uniformity in the sanctions imposed by member states for noncompliance with EU legislation. The French Presidency (from January to June 1995) urged that action be taken to remedy this situation, for example by including in each regulation and directive a section on penalties. Accordingly, the Council adopted a reso-lution calling for transparency in the national systems of penalties as the basis for achieving balance among member state sanctions. Member states agreed to advise the Commission of any national provisions for penalties for infringement of single market legislation, and the Commis-sion was instructed to make legislative proposals should problems arise. All that, of course, is far from a harmonization of member state sanctions.

The other aspect of member state noncompliance with single market legislation is the lack of confidence in the administrative capabilities of some member states. Although to some extent this attitude serves as an excuse for failure to carry out EU legislation for other reasons (e.g., mutual recognition of other members' technical standards implies a reduction in the number of standards officials in the member states), it does reflect genuine differences among the member states in the level of administrative competence and reliability of enforcement.

To a considerable extent, this is a north-south, rich-poor split. The ease with which illegal immigrants can enter the EU varies widely; customs controls are less rigorous in certain countries than in others; standards testing is far less sophisticated in the industrially less advanced member states. The Commission is seeking to narrow these gaps—and to foster cooperation among regulatory authorities—by promoting exchanges of officials and organizing meetings and conferences;[11] developing communications and data exchange networks among member state administrations; and issuing interpretative guidelines to EU legislation. Such actions will undoubtedly contribute to raising administrative standards and increasing uniformity among authorities in the member states. However, under the best of circumstances this will be a long-term process, and thus the disparities in competence and level of enforcement will continue to constitute a significant barrier to genuine integration.

Needless to say, the determinants of the future course of economic integration do not lie solely in the hands of the member states. As indicated earlier in Chapter 3, Commission enforcement, competition policy, and the European Court of Justice rulings will all continue to play important roles, and they will undoubtedly continue, on balance, to enhance the integration process. At the same time, it should be recognized that political realities—i.e., the political strength of member state interests, particularly in the present anti-"Brussels" climate—will limit the scope for pro-integration solutions.

The Commission can be expected to enforce the Maastricht Treaty and EU legislation with rigor and dedication, yet with more care than in the past to guard against accusations of overstepping its prerogatives. By limiting private sector restrictive activities and member state subsidies, competition policy will remain an essential tool for removing intra-EU barriers, thereby contributing significantly to the achievement of the single market objectives. Nonetheless, particularly in the state aid area, the Commission will have to take member state interests into account, as was evident in its relatively permissive 1994 decisions regarding bailouts of national airlines. It is more difficult to generalize about the European Court because of the opaque nature of its deliberations. However, the Court will continue to play an important role as a contributor to removing internal EU barriers, although probably in line with its recent tendency (see Chapter 3) to narrow the scope of its decisions.

Economic and Monetary Union

Progress, or lack thereof, toward establishing EMU will be a key indicator, both substantively and symbolically, of the EU's ability and willingness to move the process of integration forward. As described in Chapter 3, the blows dealt by the money markets to the exchange rate mechanism (ERM) in 1992 and 1993 were overcome, and by late 1994/early 1995, the

EU was addressing the prospects for introduction of EMU as agreed upon in the Maastricht Treaty. Before that can happen, however, several issues of an economic and political nature have to be decided.

The first relates to the convergence criteria. Although the criteria regarding inflation, interest rates, and exchange rate fluctuation do not present significant problems for most member states,[12] the criteria regarding budgetary deficits and government debt constitute serious obstacles for many countries.

In fact, as was discussed in Chapter 3, by the end of 1993, only Luxembourg had met all the criteria; it was joined only by Germany in 1994. According to calculations by the German Finance Ministry in early 1995 (which did not include the exchange rate criterion), four countries met none of the criteria—Greece, Italy, Portugal, and Spain[13]—and the European Monetary Institute's first annual report (1995) lists Germany, Ireland, and Luxembourg as the only countries meeting the budgetary deficit criterion. Among the other member states, only two member states' budgetary deficits fell in the 3–5 percent range in 1994; those of the remaining seven member states all exceeded 5 percent.

At the other end of the scale, the debt-to-gross domestic product (GDP) ratios of Belgium, Greece and Italy all exceeded 120 percent (double the permissible level), and as national governments and their electorates are increasingly aware, the political and social costs of the tight fiscal policies required to reduce the deficits and debts are very high.[14] Thus, governments will find it difficult, even if they are willing, to carry out and maintain deflationary programs over an extended period of time.

Which countries, then, will meet the convergence criteria and thus be eligible to participate in EMU? It is taken for granted that EMU cannot be established without France and Germany and that Austria and the Benelux countries, as economic satellites of the Franco-German axis, will join at the same time (see below). However, although Austria, France, and the Netherlands are within striking distance of the convergence criteria, Belgium is not, and that creates a serious dilemma. On the one hand, the linkages among the economies of the Benelux countries, Belgium's longstanding monetary union with Luxembourg, and the tight bond between the Belgian franc and the deutsche mark—to say nothing of the symbolism of Brussels as the "capital of Europe"—make it difficult to envisage Belgium's not being among the founder members of EMU. On the other hand, it is inconceivable that Belgium will be able to meet the debt criterion before well into the next century. The unspoken, but pervasive, assumption is that a way will be found to enable Belgium to join EMU, while keeping out other countries not meeting the criteria, but it is by no means certain that that circle can be squared. [15]

There is no realistic possibility for the members of the EU's southern tier to participate in EMU from its inception. This is a particularly serious issue for Italy and Spain. Although they recognize that they do not meet the convergence criteria, they are disturbed by the prospect of remaining outside EMU. The problem for them is partly psychological: for Italy as one of the founding member states of the European Community and a member of the Group of 7 (G–7) countries, and Spain as one of the EU's five large member states, aspiring to be among the EU's leaders. Both will find it embarrassing, if not demeaning, to be labeled with what will be seen as second-rank status. For that reason they may look for ways of delaying EMU—not an impossible task in view of their blocking minority in the Council, which will have to identify the member states that meet the criteria. They could, for example, block Belgian participation in EMU or link the establishment of EMU to other, unresolved issues.

However, their main tactic will be to seek interpretations of the criteria that would qualify them for participation, in particular that they are moving in the direction of meeting the criteria, e.g., Italy is running a surplus on its budget net of interest payments. An alternative tactic, less likely of success, is to request what one Italian official called a "political evaluation of the situation," i.e., seek to convince the other member states that political considerations for participation override a country's failure to meet the criteria.

Such efforts are not without justification because the Maastricht Treaty provides for flexibility in determining whether the criteria regarding the budgetary deficit and public debt have been met. The debt criterion can be met if the debt ratio "is sufficiently diminishing and approaching the reference value at a satisfactory pace," while the deficit criterion can be met if the deficit ratio "has declined substantially and continuously and reached a level that comes close to the reference value."[16]

Thus, when the Commission drew up its first report in 1994 on member states not meeting the convergence criteria, it did not include Ireland despite a debt-to-GDP ratio of about 90 percent because it judged Ireland's performance of lowering that ratio by almost 25 percentage points over the previous seven years (a remarkable feat, taken at considerable cost to Ireland's economic growth) and its low budgetary deficit as indicating sound fiscal policies.[17] Interestingly, other than a sharp protest from Germany, which feared this was an initial effort by the Commission to weaken the convergence criteria,[18] no other objections were registered by the member states, and the Economic and Financial Affairs Council sent recommendations on policies affecting debt and deficit to all member states except Ireland and Luxembourg.

Since the 1992–93 currency crises, the public debate over EMU has been carried on more in political than in economic terms. EMU has been used as a sort of litmus test of the pro-European credentials of the country, group, or person involved; the arguments in favor of accelerating, or at least maintaining, the timetable have to a considerable extent been political. On the other hand, many of those who will be directly affected by EMU, particularly central bankers, have voiced concern that the political forces are not taking sufficient account of economic factors. As one expressed it, "political aspirations may get the better of economic realities ... [T]his would bring progress in the EU to a halt."[19] These factors include the importance of strict adherence to the convergence criteria, the difficulty of many member states in meeting those criteria, and the mechanical and technical problems involved in introducing a single currency.

Little public attention has been paid until recently to the massive complexity, time, and cost involved in converting national currencies into a single currency. Although a decision was taken in 1995 to call the single currency the Euro, highly political decisions will have to be taken concerning its design, particularly whose picture(s) appears on it and whether it includes identification of an individual member state. Printing and coining a completely new system for several highly developed market economies take years, not months, and the withdrawal from circulation of national currencies and their replacement with the EU currency is enormously time-consuming. Furthermore, every account in the world denominated in one of the previously existing national currencies will have to be recalculated, as will automatic teller machines and computers. Every financial instrument in those currencies will have to be redenominated and an "amalgamated" interest rate fixed. In sum, the political decision to proceed with EMU will require a process of conversion seldom, if ever, encountered in the world's financial system.

As recognition of the nature and extent of these problems has grown, so has debate over how quickly the single currency can and should be introduced after the decision has been reached to enter the third and final stage of EMU (i.e., establishment of the European Central Bank and the "irrevocable" fixing of exchange rates of the participating countries). The two main questions are how long "irrevocably fixed" exchange rates can be defended against an attack by market forces (days, months, years?), and how long the many-faceted physical conversion to a single currency will take. The answer to the first question is "not long" if the market chooses to test the exchange rate grid and to the second "a long time." Thus, a diligent effort will be required to satisfy the resultant conflicting requirements.

Although some argued for a "big bang" approach, i.e., implementation of the single currency and the concomitant adjustments within a very short period, a consensus emerged during 1995 on a phased approach.

This was reflected in a green paper issued by the Commission on introduction of the single currency in May 1995, which identified problems, offered a scenario, and proposed a communications strategy to gain public support.[20] The scenario was largely mirrored in a separate report of the European Monetary Institute several months later, and it was in turn approved by the Economic and Financial Affairs Council (finance ministers of the member states) and, finally, by the European Council by the end of the year. The European Council decision established the following three-phase schedule:

A. *In early 1998.* Identification of the participants and the establishment of the European Central Bank.

B. *At the beginning of 1999.* The official launch of the third stage of EMU, consisting of irrevocable fixing of exchange rate parities, establishment of the Euro as a currency, and introduction of single monetary policy for the participating countries. The progressive changeover to the single currency will begin—public debt must be issued in Euro, and private operators may use the Euro (the intention being that over the succeeding three years the use of the Euro will achieve a "critical mass").

C. *During the first half of 2002.* Introduction of new notes and coins, the withdrawal of national currencies, and the complete changeover by public and private operators to the single currency.

In any event, before the third stage has been reached, the IGC will be convened in 1996, and EMU will undoubtedly be a subject for review. Specifically, issues for discussion will be whether to change (i.e., weaken) the convergence criteria, whether to change (i.e., extend) the timetable for arriving at EMU, and whether to alter any other fundamental components of EMU. In arriving at decisions on these issues, the position of Germany, as the undisputed leader of the EU's currency bloc,[21] will be a critical, if not the determining, factor. It is most unlikely that any change will be made to the basic provisions for EMU, since the rationale—to enable the free movement of goods, services and capital to take place, thereby reducing costs and providing economic benefits throughout the EU—remains valid, and, more generally, the member states will be reluctant to reopen the package that was laboriously negotiated at Maastricht.

As regards the convergence criteria, although with the benefit of hindsight one could question the appropriateness of some of the criteria negotiated in the Maastricht Treaty (in particular, the public debt-to-GDP ratio), it would be politically impossible to contemplate adjustments. An effort might be made to introduce a criterion regarding unemployment as a way of offsetting the deflationary (i.e., anti-employment) effect of the measures needed to meet the existing criteria.[22] However, apart from the fact that selecting an appropriate criterion would be difficult (including selecting one that would not conflict with the existing criteria), such a step would represent a fundamental change that would be unacceptable, particularly to Germany. The latter will, in fact, block any proposals for change. Not only has the German government made a commitment to that effect to the Bundesbank, but the German Constitutional Court has ruled, in connection with a legal challenge to German ratification of the Maastricht Treaty, that the Bundestag will have to determine that the intended participants in EMU have met the criteria. This will enable Germany to prevent any reinterpretation of the Maastricht Treaty criteria. The Bundestag's vote will constitute a political, though not legal, commitment by the government when it votes on EMU membership in the Council.

The key questions, then, are whether EMU will come into operation and, if so, when and with what member states participating. The answer to the first question is affirmative if France and Germany agree; without the participation by both countries, EMU is not politically sustainable, and probably not economically either. Both countries remain firmly in favor of EMU. The strongest pressure comes from France, which sees EMU as a means of anchoring Germany to the EU and gaining a measure of influence over European monetary policy that is now virtually monopolized by Germany. However, French participation will require the pursuit of economic and financial policies that are compatible with those of Germany. In particular, France will have to exercise tight fiscal restraint to reduce its budgetary deficit (amounting to about 5 percent of GDP in 1995). However, doing so entails a high political cost—witness the strikes that brought the French economy to a standstill in late 1995—and that brings into question France's ability to meet the convergence criteria in time.

On the other hand, Germany will need to be convinced that the convergence criteria have in fact been met and satisfied that EMU has been accompanied by significant steps toward political union. The latter concept, though not clearly defined but undoubtedly encompassing an increase in the powers of the European Parliament, runs counter to French objectives, and thus it will constitute a point of friction. Nonetheless, EMU clearly meets the overall economic and political objectives of the two countries.

This does not mean, however, that the path to EMU is clear. Many uncertainties remain. EMU will not take place under the optional alternative provided in the treaty, i.e., as the result of a vote before 1997 with a majority of member states (eight) meeting the criteria. Not only is it excluded that a sufficient number of member states will meet the criteria, but there will not have been time to have resolved the many attendant technical problems, and the EU will not be politically prepared to take this momentous step so quickly. The European Council tacitly, though not explicitly, accepted that inevitability at its June 1995 meeting in Cannes.

On the other hand, the situation will be different in 1999, when the treaty provides that EMU will come into being with whichever member states meet the criteria. It is generally assumed that the founder members will be a nucleus of five member states (Austria, France, Germany, Luxembourg, and the Netherlands), presumably Belgium (see above), and possibly Finland, Sweden, and Ireland (the latter's close links with the British economy may preclude participation without the United Kingdom). However, it is by no means certain that all these countries will meet the criteria as of the beginning of 1998, particularly if economic conditions worsen in the interim. On the other hand, both Denmark and the United Kingdom are expected to meet the criteria, but because of their opt-outs of EMU (see Chapter 3) Denmark's participation is highly unlikely and that of the United Kingdom uncertain at best.

Furthermore, foreign exchange markets remain subject to shocks, and the political debate over EMU has intensified. Both were clearly evident in the fall of 1995 in reactions to (a) remarks by the German finance minister that Italy would not qualify for participation in EMU in 1999 and that Belgium had little chance of meeting the criteria by then, to which he added doubts about France and the Netherlands; and (b) German proposals to impose new and more stringent conditions on member states that join the EMU. These German actions reflected concern over the strength of opposition to EMU in Germany. Although a strong political consensus favors EMU (government and the opposition Socialists), doubts persist among the German public,[23] which has always worried that EMU would limit Germany's ability to maintain its rigorous anti-inflationary policy.

Unease over EMU exists in varying degrees in the member states for a number of reasons:

- (most countries except Germany) the budgetary stringency required to meet convergence criteria conflicts with many (particularly short-term) political and social objectives;
- (weak currency countries) inability to meet the criteria will give a country a second-class status in the EU;
- (particularly Germany) because exchange rates will no longer provide an adjustment mechanism for economic differences among member states, EMU participants in economic difficulties may require budgetary transfers or adopt inflationary fiscal policies;
- (strong currency countries) nonparticipating member states will enjoy a competitive advantage (perceived to have been the case with Italy since it left the ERM) through the absence of fiscal discipline and the ability to depreciate their currency.

Nonetheless, the provisions of the Maastricht Treaty, the momentum developed since then, and the continued firm commitment given by the European Council dictate that EMU will take place. However, it is distinctly possible that its introduction will be delayed. Although that would require amendment of the Maastricht Treaty, a step that would not be lightly or easily taken, political and economic reality could force such an action.

Social Agenda

The questions facing the EU are whether to complete the "unfinished business" of the 1989 social agenda, whether to proceed beyond that, and, if so, in what directions. Consideration of these questions will take place on three levels: on a philosophical or theoretical level, i.e., in the context of what is judged to be the appropriate role of the state and the "contract" between the citizen and the state; on a political level, i.e., in the context of what is the perceived requirement to offset the economic benefits given the economic operators through economic integration and how much political pressure is there for such measures; and on an economic level, i.e., in the context of the debate over how best to attack the problems of competitiveness and unemployment in Europe.

As regards the philosophical basis for social legislation, with the exception of the United Kingdom (at least under a Conservative government), it is generally accepted that EU-wide standards should be set in protecting what may loosely be called "basic rights" of workers (the definition of which is, of course, open to interpretation). However, the degree of political support for social legislation is difficult to gauge because it undoubtedly includes a certain element of rhetoric. While one observer's view that "[a]lthough the rhetoric might suggest otherwise, virtually nobody is in favor of a genuine social dimension of EC–1992 regulation"[24] is an overstatement, it accurately reflects the existence of some ambiguity of views. For example, there is some concern in less developed member states that they will lose a competitive advantage by maintaining a lower level of protection for their workers.

However, concerns have focused more generally on the costs of social legislation as they affect efforts to revive European economies and reduce unemployment. As described in Chapter 6, it is increasingly recognized in the EU that the inflexibility of labor conditions and the cost of labor (including nonwage costs) are among the factors responsible for the low growth of employment in Europe, particularly compared to that in the United States.[25] However, this recognition is balanced by the strong, long-standing consensus in Europe in favor of government protection of workers and working conditions. That explains the political groping for a middle path between what is widely viewed as an "inhumane" system of minimal safeguards in the United States and an excessively generous safety net that is increasingly unsustainable in the EU.

One of the many examples of concerns over finding the right mean between flexibility and worker protection is contained in the Commission's progress report on the white paper on growth, competitiveness, and employment, which urges that labor market efficiency should not include a "dilution" of the European model of social protection but "through the adaptation, rationalization, and simplification of regulations … a better balance [be established] between social protection, competitiveness and employment creation."[26] A similar thought was expressed by the in-coming Commission president, Jacques Santer, in his first address to the European Parliament: "[r]eforms are … necessary to reconcile a high level of social protection with economic reality."[27]

The prospects, then, are for social issues to remain firmly on the EU's agenda, although proposals for action will now be considered in their relationship to competitiveness. The passage of social legislation will be facilitated by the provisions of the protocol on social policy attached to the Maastricht Treaty—the extension of qualified majority voting and the British opt-out. If Labour wins the next British general election, it will carry out its commitment to "opt in" to the social legislation. Nonetheless, Britain's position on social issues will probably remain more reserved than that of most, if not all, continental member states. On balance, however, relatively little social legislation is likely to emerge in the near future. The consensus view in the Commission and member states is that further EU legislation will not provide many answers to employment and social problems and that the EU can play a more useful role by offering guidance and suggestions for actions, which can best be carried out by the member states.

Other Issues

The main "nonsingle market" issues will, of course, remain on the EU's integration agenda in the coming years: telecommunications, energy, and environment.

The revolution in information technology and the attendant focus on the shape and requirements of the information society point to a reduction in barriers both within and between EU member states, i.e., a combination of liberalization and integration, centered in the telecommunications field. Thus, despite the reluctance of some governments and national monopolies to move quickly in that direction—reflecting a combination of concern that services will not be adequately provided and reluctance to face competition—the trend in the EU is toward increasing deregulation under the combined pressures of Commission action and the imperatives of the marketplace.

Although the monopolies and other barriers to the purchase and operation of equipment and services will likely be eliminated over time, the critical question is whether that process will take place extensively enough and at a sufficiently fast pace to avoid damaging the competitive position of firms operating in the EU. Specifically: will voice telephony be deregulated throughout the EU before the presently established January 1, 1998, date; will full competition be granted among infrastructures; and will access be guaranteed to end-users? Based on past performance, progress in the EU is likely be mixed, and in any case to lag behind that of the United States.

Progress in integration of the EU's energy market in all probability will remain slow. Like agriculture, energy is a basic resource, but with national security implications. For that reason governments are loathe to loosen control, and there is little public pressure for deregulation. Despite the economic logic for the reduction or removal of barriers to the transmission and distribution of energy supplies, it is unlikely that sufficient political strength will be generated, either within the business community or among the public at large, to bring about a significant change in the existing pattern of national government controls. If the IGC adds a specific mandate on energy to the treaty, it will most likely be limited to a general statement of policy rather than involve new EU competences or activities.

Environmental issues, on the other hand, will no doubt continue to hold a prominent place on the political agenda throughout the EU. Pressures will remain strong to seek EU-wide solutions to environmental problems; indeed, they will be increased by the entry of Austria and the Scandinavian countries (whose environmental standards are higher than the EU average). The European Parliament will also play an important role because it contains a high proportion of "pro-environment" members, who dominate the strong and aggressive Environment Committee and are more than willing to use the maximum leverage on the Commission and the Council to promote environmental goals. At the same time, the basic conflict between the harmonization of environmental protection in the EU and the ability of member states to impose higher levels of protection (see Chapter 3) will continue; it is inconceivable that the latter option would be revoked. Thus, the EU can be expected to remain actively involved in the environment field, to some extent with new legislation, but also in ensuring effective implementation of existing legislation and in introducing different actions that do not entail legislation. Nonetheless, considerable differences among the measures adopted by member states will remain.

Foreign Policy

The prospects for the development of the foreign policy component of the Common Foreign and Security Policy (CFSP) are modest. Foreign policy cooperation among the member states started from a low base, with only a modest degree of cooperation, and the ambitions of the participants are restrained.

The starting point of any assessment must be recognition that the process of a convergence of member state foreign policies has been under way for a number of years through increasingly intensive consultation—in many cases on a daily basis—among the foreign ministries of the member states and the heavy foreign relations component of the deliberations of the General Affairs Council. The results, although difficult to measure, are significant and cumulative, and the consultative mechanism in all probability will contribute to an increasing coordination of foreign policies within the EU.

As described in Chapter 4, the EU has assumed a foreign policy role—as distinct from the policies and actions of its member states—in a number of areas. A modest continuation of that trend is likely, particularly in circumstances where there is a consensus on the nature of the policies and actions and where it is recognized that acting collectively will increase their effectiveness.[28]

EU foreign policy cooperation has largely taken place because the EU could exercise an economic interest and leverage. In most cases, this involved economic assistance. That was an essential element in the development of the new relationships with the countries of Central and Eastern Europe; it was deemed crucial to the effort to assist in the transformation of South Africa into a multiracial state; and it provided a rationale that had not existed previously (aid to the new Palestine state) for EU participation in the Middle East peace process.

However, the focus—for an assessment of progress and a forecast of the future—is necessarily on ex-Yugoslavia, where the EU's experience has shown the potential for and the limitations of EU foreign policy cooperation. Although the demonstration effect of joint action would have been more persuasive if the policies in ex-Yugoslavia had resulted in an end to the fighting, it should be clear that individual action by member states would only have exacerbated the situation. Nonetheless, it should be recognized that the EU's peace plan has formed the basis for negotiations with and among the warring factions and that the EU has undertaken a substantial humanitarian assistance program in ex-Yugoslavia.

The issues for the future relate to substance and structure. It is difficult to envisage a lessening of activity in foreign policy cooperation, if only because so little progress has been made. However, the EU will move slowly, at best, into the formal adoption of common policies. The procedures established in the Maastricht Treaty permit collective policy to take place only where a strong degree of consensus has been achieved.

The critical determining factor is that few member states, and particularly not the major players of France, Germany, and the United Kingdom, will agree in the foreseeable future to place themselves in a position where they are either forced to take an action of which they disapprove or prevented from taking an action because they have been outvoted in the EU. The member states will want to maintain their ability to carry out an independent foreign policy when they deem it to be in their national interest, and that is in fact what has happened in, for example German recognition of Croatia, French peace initiatives before the Gulf War, and unauthorized contacts by Greece during its Council Presidency with Serbian President Milosevic. In addition, inevitably there will be areas where a member state will have a recognizably special interest—e.g., France in Algeria and Greece in the Former Yugoslav Republic of Macedonia—that the other member states will, for the most part, let them pursue independently.

As regards the structure of foreign policy cooperation, it is most likely that the principle of intergovernment decision making will, for the reasons described above, not be breached. Nonetheless, other options are under discussion. The most far-reaching is the German proposal for the introduction of qualified majority voting in the CFSP. Others include various formulations under which a sufficiently large majority of member states could act together or, alternatively, a small minority could abstain from a particular policy (as Ireland and Italy did in connection with the embargo of Argentina during the Falklands War in the early 1980s).

The more likely outcome will be a general trend in the direction of coordinating the policies of the member states, but little progress on the development of what could be termed an EU foreign policy. Rhetoric aside, the desire of member states to move ahead in foreign policy cooperation is limited; however, any move in the opposite direction would be viewed as damaging to the Union.

Security Policy

The development of a common security policy in the EU, while a logical adjunct to the development of a common foreign policy, is necessarily intertwined with the broader, and unresolved, issue of how to organize European collective security in the post-Cold War era. In the first instance, it involves determining the most appropriate roles for the United States and the countries of Western Europe and their interrelationship. However, beyond that, it involves dealing with the desire of the ex-

Soviet satellite countries of Central Europe to join the Western European security system, the concerns of Russia that it will face a military alliance consisting of all European countries on its western border, and the possible need to involve former members of the Soviet Union (particularly the Baltic countries, a sensitive issue for Russia, and Ukraine) in European security arrangements.

Under these circumstances, the obvious questions are what an EU security policy should consist of and how that policy and attendant organizational framework should relate to the central locus of European security (the North Atlantic Treaty Organization NATO), and to the EU. The focal point of the EU's security policy, as provided in the Maastricht Treaty, is the Western European Union (WEU). However, the elevation of what had been a moribund and obscure organization to visibility and prominence also raised questions about what role it could realistically be expected to play.

The WEU is groping toward that role and a relationship with the EU and NATO. Its focus has been establishing its identity through the combined joint task forces and new military groups (see Chapter 4), and undertaking specific tasks—the main one thus far being the administration of Mostar. However, it will undoubtedly take a number of years before a clear consensus emerges on where to place the WEU in the European security framework. The overlapping membership among the three institutions—EU, NATO, and WEU—creates some problems, and various suggestions have been made that all members of the EU be required to join the WEU or that all members of the WEU join NATO. In addition, the difference in the defense commitments of NATO and the WEU must be taken into account; the WEU commitment is stronger, but, of course, that of NATO is more credible. This difference is relevant for the potential new EU members in Central Europe, who also desire membership in the WEU, which would formally move the boundaries of European mutual defense to the east.

The WEU's activities thus far have been modest, and its relationship with NATO remains unclear. The outstanding question is what it can and should do that is distinct from NATO and that makes a useful contribution to enhancing the EU's security interests, while not duplicating the existing, well-developed integrated military structure of NATO. The various joint force initiatives represent the beginning of a potentially meaningful role for the WEU. However, as the Gulf War and subsequent events have shown, the EU's military capabilities are decidedly limited, and in the present environment of budgetary stringency and perceived higher domestic priorities, national defense expenditures will not increase substantially in the foreseeable future. Only two member states,

France and the United Kingdom, have significant military strength and the ability to use it outside its borders,[29] and European countries, individually and collectively outside the NATO structure, lack rapid deployment, communications, and, especially, lift (the ability to move large numbers of troops and equipment over long distances) and intelligence capacity.

Two further factors add to the uncertainty surrounding the future of a common security policy. One is the possible renegotiation of the treaty establishing the WEU (optional, but not compulsory, as of 1998). Renegotiation would offer an obvious opportunity to review the WEU's purpose and effectiveness in light of today's vastly different circumstances from those at its inception. The other is that the three new EU (and WEU) members bring with them traditions or policies—albeit different ones—of neutrality, which implies a lukewarm approach to the development of an EU common security policy.

Institutional Structure

The negotiations that led to the Maastricht Treaty left unresolved questions and controversy over many of the issues tackled under the heading of "political union," i.e., CFSP and the institutional structure and decision-making procedures of the EU. Accordingly, it was agreed to convene another Intergovernmental Conference in 1996 to reconsider these issues, taking into account the experience gained under the Maastricht Treaty provisions. In a formal sense, the IGC is being convened to examine those treaty provisions for which revision is provided, in accordance with the EU's objectives set out in the Common Provisions of the treaty.[30] The provisions subject to revisions include the scope of issues subject to the codecision procedure, CFSP, security policy and role of the WEU, institutional arrangements for the second and third pillars, competence in three areas (civil protection, energy, and tourism), and establishment of a hierarchy among the different categories of EU acts.[31] A number of other institutional issues have been added by the European Council and by agreement of the Commission, the Council and the Parliament.[32] In fact, however, all provisions of the Maastricht Treaty will be on the table.

The issues of institutional structure and decision-making will be central to the deliberations of the IGC for a number of reasons. First, the structure of the Union and the interrelationships among the EU institutions are clearly subject to modification. Unlike the situation in the United States where a consensus on these issues was reached almost a century ago (though after many decades of experience and debate), controversy continues over many basic elements of the EU's organization and decision-making structure, to say nothing of the constitutional form the Union should eventually take. Second, it is widely recognized that inefficiencies exist, particularly in the bewildering variety of voting procedures and legal bases for taking action under the treaty.[33] Third, the recent enlargement and the presumption of further accessions increase the urgency of adapting the institutions and decision-making procedures to the requirements of a Union of 15-plus members.

Finally, pressures are mounting to increase the democratic accountability of the EU institutions. The popular slogan is that the EU must eliminate the "democratic deficit" that is usually equated with the subordinate position of the Parliament—the only institution directly representing the citizens of the Union—to that of the Commission and the Council. In fact, however, the issue of the democratic deficit is far less clear-cut. On the one hand, member state governments represent the views of and are responsible to their citizens through the latter's election of national parliaments and, in some instances, governments. On the other hand, the "deficit" is also a function of the nontransparency of the Council's deliberations, the lack of effective independent oversight over the Commission's activities, and the weakness of the link between the Parliament and the public, including the indirect method of election of most members of the European Parliament,[34] the absence of a systematic consideration of views by interested parties on pending legislation, and voting decisions on the basis of private caucuses of political groups.

Unlike the process leading to negotiations for the Maastricht Treaty, considerable public attention has been focused on the IGC. Extensive debate and discussion has been held among the institutions of the EU, political groups, academic and research organizations, and the general public. In accordance with a decision taken by the European Council at Corfu in June 1994, the Commission, the Council and the Parliament have issued reports on the functioning of the Maastricht Treaty,[35] and a "Reflection Group" was established to examine and develop suggestions for treaty revision (but not to initiate the negotiations).

The group—consisting of one personal representative of each member state foreign minister, two members of the European Parliament, and one commissioner, and chaired by the Spanish State Secretary for European Affairs—conducted an intensive review of the issues and options and produced a report for the Madrid meeting of the European Council at the end of 1995. The report called for action in three areas—making Europe more relevant to its citizens, improving the efficiency of European institutions in the context of prospective enlargement, and increasing the EU's capacity to undertake common actions in foreign and security policy.

However, reflecting the diversity of government positions, unanimity was reached only on generalities. On specific proposals the group limited itself to citing the views of "many of us," "some of us," and "one of us" (the United Kingdom). The net result of the various reports and discussions should be greater clarity in exposing the issues and range of political possibilities, thereby, it is hoped, increasing the likelihood of producing well-considered and publicly acceptable treaty changes.

Five main institutional issues will be addressed at the IGC.

1. The composition of the Commission, i.e., the number of the commissioners and their distribution among the member states. At present the large member states have two commissioners and the small member states one; thus, in 1995 their number increased from seventeen to twenty. Although that number is universally recognized as excessive to the effective operation of the Commission, the political problem is agreeing on a method for decreasing the number. One option would be to limit the number of commissioners to one per member state. However, that would increase the existing imbalance of member state representation on a per capita basis (at present 400,000 Luxembourgers have one commissioner, while 80 million Germans have two), and therefore is politically unrealistic.

Although there are many variables at play, any solution would probably require the small member states to "share" a commissioner on a rotating basis (as is the case in the international financial institutions), presumably coupled with the large member states' reducing their number from two to one. One intriguing suggestion has been made by British Commissioner Sir Leon Brittan that there be "full ministers" and "junior ministers"; the large member states would always have a full minister, while the small member states would alternate between both categories.[36] In any event, organizational logic is unlikely to accord with political reality. The reluctance of member states, particularly the small ones, to accept a reduction in their representation on the Commission will make agreement on any major change difficult to achieve.

2. Voting in the Council. At issue will be the distribution of votes, voting formulas (qualified majority and other possible options), and the decision on which voting formula to use for the different issues. Although the weights given to the votes of the member states under qualified majority voting are the result of a political compromise among the member states, the large member states may well re-open the issue out of concern over the blocking power of the increased (and prospectively increasing) number of small member states. That issue is directly related to voting formulas. The determination of what constitutes a blocking minority in the Council will certainly be placed on the agenda, the United

142

Prospects for Integration

Kingdom having unexpectedly (and unwelcomely) pressed for lowering the threshold during the debate over accession of the former members of the European Free Trade Association (EFTA).

Nonetheless, variations, alternatives and possibly additional formulas will undoubtedly be considered at the IGC. One recurring idea is to institute a two-tier voting system, whereby not only a minimum number of votes is required for approval (as under the present qualified majority voting system) but also a minimum under a formula based on population (or, conversely, a ceiling is set on blocking legislation both in terms of member state votes and population). Finally, proposals will be made to expand the number of issues subject to qualified majority voting or a voting scheme other than unanimity. As in the case of amending the composition of the Commission, the conflict among member state interests will limit the extent to which such expansion will be agreed.

3. The role of other representative bodies. The Economic and Social Committee is essentially an anachronism. Established as an advisory committee representing the views of employers, labor, and other interests, its opinions are largely ignored, and its functions have been largely overtaken by the development of direct lobbying by interested groups and their representative organizations. However, inertia, an aversion to upsetting the vested interests of that organization, and concern that abolition of the committee would be perceived as a diminution of representative and participatory democracy should suffice to guarantee the committee its continued existence.

Although also limited to advisory functions, the EU's newest body, the Committee of the Regions, established by the Maastricht Treaty, is potentially a more influential institution because it reflects an important component of the governmental structure of several member states (Germany is the most prominent, but others include Belgium and Spain). For that reason, some of these countries will probably press for the committee to be given a role in the EU's decision-making procedures (e.g., in the adjudication of subsidiarity). However, there is little likelihood that the committee will move beyond its advisory role. Not only would that run counter to efforts to simplify decision making,[37] but the wide variation in role and structure of regions among the member states raises questions as to how effective and representative a Committee of the Regions with substantive powers can be.

The other set of institutions that needs to be taken into account is the national parliaments. Although not involved directly in EU decision making, these parliaments have at least the potential for scrutinizing proposed EU legislation and, more generally, affecting policy through whatever control they exercise over their national governments. There are considerable differences in the extent to which national parliaments involve themselves in EU affairs. However, on the whole, their interest and influence in this area is increasing, the greatest control over government policy being that exercised by the Danish parliament.

Despite public assertions to the contrary,[38] it is inevitable that a certain degree of suspicion and jealousy of prerogatives exists between the national parliaments and the European Parliament. Some informal and formal exchanges (the latter are joint meetings called "assises") have taken place, and the Maastricht Treaty "encourages greater involvement of national parliaments in the activities of the European Union" through an increased exchange of information, intensification of contacts, and meetings "as necessary" of assises.[39] It is unlikely that this "encouragement" will result in significant substantive interchange between the European Parliament and the national parliaments. Although some suggestions have been made for inserting national parliaments formally into the EU decision-making process,[40] there is neither strong support nor a convincing rationale for adding to the already cumbersome decision-making process.[41]

4. The relative powers of the three nonjudicial institutions, an issue that is to a considerable extent subsumed in the foregoing issues. On a day-in, day-out basis the Commission, the Council and the Parliament interact with each other and seek to maintain, if not increase, their power and influence. This struggle will be transferred to the more formal setting of the IGC.

From the inception of the EC, the Council has had the last word in legislation, although its power was diminished by introduction in the Maastricht Treaty of the codecision procedure. While subject to some criticism for its lack of transparency (see Chapter 6), the Council is in the strongest position of the three institutions because the preponderant view among the member states is opposition to further significant erosions of the intergovernmental character of the EU. Thus, it is difficult to envisage circumstances under which the member states will agree at the IGC to any meaningful diminution of the Council's position as the "supreme organ" of the EU.

On the other hand, the Commission will enter the IGC in a relatively weak position as a result of the criticism, whether valid or not, it has faced for allegedly overstepping its powers and its lack of accountability. On balance, the Commission lost power in the Maastricht Treaty, primarily at the expense of the Parliament. However, it did gain a formal role in CFSP, the third pillar, and economic surveillance mechanism of EMU, and the extension of qualified majority voting increases the chances for its proposed legislation to be adopted. It will enjoy the support, in general, of the small member states, which look upon it as a defender of their interests against the large countries (see Chapter 4). However, realistically, the Commission's optimum position will be maintenance of the status quo, in particular its exclusive prerogative of legislative initiative.[42]

To a large extent, consideration of the respective roles of the institutions will focus on the Parliament, thus presenting the IGC with a dilemma. On the one hand, the IGC will find it difficult to reject the Parliament's argument that as the only directly elected representative body of the EU it should have increased powers—for example, extending the codecision procedure (possibility of Council-Parliament negotiations over text and rejection by Parliament) to all issues now subject to the cooperation procedure (two readings with possible amendments by the Parliament). However, on the other hand, if such powers are ceded to the Parliament, the degree of control exercised by the member states will be diminished correspondingly, and that runs counter to the now-dominant view that national prerogatives need to be protected against "encroachments" by the Union. Furthermore, institutionally and as a result of the proclivities of its members, the Parliament typically favors actions to increase EU powers; and that runs counter to the prevailing view among the member states.

However, one important ally of the Parliament is Germany, which has consistently urged that the Parliament be given a greater role in the decision-making structure. Germany has sought to make satisfaction on this issue a pre-condition for entry into force of EMU, which is France's primary goal. Although theoretically Germany cannot impose conditions beyond those contained in the Maastricht Treaty on EMU, in fact its efforts on behalf of the Parliament will probably result in the latter's achieving some success—presumably more than would otherwise have been expected.

5. The final issue is whether to change the institutional and decision-making structure of CFSP and the third pillar and, if so, in what way. The first question is whether to maintain the separate pillars as established in the Maastricht Treaty or to bring all three pillars under a single legal and institutional structure, as had been discussed during the negotiations. The latter is only a remote possibility because a single structure would weaken the intergovernmental basis of the second and third pillar, which is not in accord with the present political climate. That consideration will override concerns that the intergovernmental basis makes it difficult to take action under the third pillar, an area where considerable public support exists for EU solutions to important problems.

Two questions will be addressed: (a) decision making, in particular the possibility of moving away from the principle of unanimity; and (b) possible expansion of the role of the Commission and the Parliament. Although there may be some movement in these directions, fundamental changes are unlikely.

Conclusions

The EU finds itself in the mid–1990s at a turning point, facing a range of issues on which critical decisions will have to be taken. However, there is no clear deadline for such decisions. Maintenance of the status quo is an option for a limited time, and, indeed, it seems the course the EU is most likely to adopt as it approaches the twenty-first century. The range of conflicting interests and objectives among the member states, combined with the majority view that the essentially intergovernmental nature of the EU must be maintained, argues for a minimalist approach. Thus, the IGC will likely result in modest change. As one observer expressed it, "the scope for unbridgeable differences, ambiguous compromises and uninspiring language will be even larger than at Maastricht."[43]

However, decisions will eventually be forced upon the EU—notably the establishment of EMU and accession by countries of Central Europe—and they will produce substantial changes. Gone will be the pretence of a homogeneous Union in which all member states, over time, follow the same policies and participate in the same programs. The conflict between finding the lowest common denominator among an increasingly diverse membership and maintaining and promoting integration will necessarily result in a differentiated Union. An inner core of countries able and willing to continue the integration process will emerge—in the first instance as the participants in EMU. In a sense, then, the EU will revert to its origins, conceptually and geographically. However, differentiation will extend beyond EMU. A somewhat different constellation is likely to proceed in the areas of foreign policy and security. The same is already apparent with third pillar issues.

The result, then, will be a rather messy organizational structure, but one that corresponds more directly to the ability and willingness of individual member states to participate in particular activities. In sum, the European Union of the twenty-first century will be distinctly different from the EU as it is known today.

Notes

1. Treaty of Rome as amended by Maastricht Treaty, Article 3b.
2. Maastricht Treaty, Article B.
3. European Commission, "Report to the European Council on the Application of the Subsidiarity Principle 1994," COM(94) 533, November 21, 1994.
4. Among the more intriguing are proposals for harmonizing regulations regarding firefighter's uniforms and (mentioned above) the conditions of animals in zoos, enthusiastically approved by the European Parliament's Environment Committee but subsequently withdrawn by the Commission.

5. For example, the United Kingdom, which is strongly prosubsidiarity, pressed for EU legislation to establish rules regarding the transportation of live animals, not because differences in rules among member states affected the free movement of goods but rather because it (or at least a vociferous part of its population) believed that the conditions under which animals were transported in many member states were inhumane.

6. In its "Report of the Group of Independent Experts on Legislative and Administrative Simplification," COM(95) 288, June 21, 1995, the Group proposed a comprehensive action program, based on its study of four sectors: machine standards, food hygiene, the environment, and social legislation.

7. "Releasing Europe's Potential Through Targeted Regulatory Reform," *The UNICE Regulatory Report 1995*, Union of Industrial and Employers' Confederations of Europe, Brussels, 1995. This report is based on a survey of more than 2,500 companies in twenty European countries.

8. In 1995, the Commission proposed the deregulation of rail transportation, exposing international passenger and all freight services to competition by 1998. However, that is only the beginning of what will at best be a lengthy, controversial process.

9. European Commission, "'Making the Most of the Internal Market': Strategic Programme," COM(93) 632, December 22, 1993, p. 1.

10. Pierre Buigues and John Sheehy, "The Internal Market Programme—The Impact on European Integration," European Commission, Document II/133/95, p. 11.

11. A five-year exchange program of officials concerned with implementation of single market legislation, the Karolus program, was initiated in 1993, with the objective of arriving at a more uniform interpretation and application of EU legislation.

12. Because the formal bands of the exchange rate mechanism (ERM) have been widened to 15 percent, virtually all member states will presumably meet the normal currency fluctuation criterion by remaining within that range for two years, although there is some debate over whether the original 2.25 percent band should be used.

13. "London and Bonn still sceptical about 1997 deadline," *European Report*, No. 2018, February 22, 1995, pp. II/5–7.

14. It has been estimated that Belgium would have to run a 6 percent budgetary surplus (net of interest), i.e., nearly double the existing level, for fifteen years before it could achieve a 60 percent debt ratio. "EMU strain begins to show," *Financial Times*, January 17, 1995.

15. Belgium's argument, in essence, is that the market has shown the Belgian franc to be a stable currency for many years—it has moved in virtual lockstep with the deutsche mark. Its interest rate has been among the lowest in Europe, and it has consistently run a current account surplus. Thus, it asserts, reality dictates that Belgium should be among the founder members of economic and monetary union (EMU). Nonetheless, under the other reality—the convergence criteria—Belgium does not qualify.

16. Treaty of Rome as amended by Maastricht Treaty, Article 104c.

17. Belgian authorities have argued that recent and prospective reductions in Belgium's debt-to-GDP ratio likewise merit a determination that it has, or will, meet the debt criterion. However, the movement is quite recent and of small magnitude, and the ratio remains the highest of all the member states.

18. In the opinion of one German official, this effort represented a "premeditated softening-up for the reinterpretation of the criteria" on the part of the Commission.

19. The governor of the Bank of England, quoted in "UK warning about EMU," *European Report*, No. 1970, July 27, 1994, p. II/1.

20. European Commission, "Green Paper on the Practical Arrangements for the Introduction of the Single Currency," May 31, 1995.

21. Succinctly expressed by Reginald Dale in "Germany's Bludgeon Hits Both Ways," *International Herald Tribune*, September 30, 1995, "If Europe is to have a single currency it will be on German terms, or not at all."

22. A study commissioned by the European Parliament estimated that action by all member states to meet the convergence criteria could result in a loss of nearly 1.5 million jobs. Reported in "Maastricht 'may cost 1.5m jobs'," *Financial Times*, July 13, 1995.

23. A poll taken in the spring of 1995 showed that just over one-half of EU citizens favored the single currency, but that support in Germany (37 percent) was significantly lower. European Commission, *Europinion*, No. 5, July 1995.

24. Jacques Pelkmans, "The Significance of EC-1992," Centre for European Policy Studies, Working Document No. 82, Brussels, December 1993, p. 17.

25. However, it should be noted that this is not a universally accepted view. For example, the London-based Centre for Economic Policy Research concluded in *Unemployment: Choices for Europe*, issued in 1995, that the cost of labor regulation is not as high as it seems and that the European labor market is not as sclerotic as it is portrayed. See "Study supports labor regulations in Europe," *Financial Times*, April 5, 1995.

26. "Delors jobs plan wins backing," *Financial Times*, June 13, 1994.

27. Strasbourg, January 17, 1995.

28. This is a far more modest prediction than that of Adolph Spangenberg, who wrote in a letter to the *International Herald Tribune* on March 13, 1994, that "[i]n a few decades, French foreign policy will be about as important as the foreign policy of, say, Oregon today."

29. For example, Denmark's contribution of one ship to the Gulf War effort represented one-half of its navy, and according to a senior US military officer, the contribution of European countries was about 6 percent of the forces allied against Iraq.

30. Maastricht Treaty, Articles N.2 and A and B, respectively.

31. References in the text are as follows (all references are to the Maastricht Treaty, except for Article 189b(8), which is that treaty's amendment of the Treaty of Rome): codecision, Article 189b(8); CFSP, Article J.10; WEU, Article J.4(6); second and third pillars, Article B (by implication); three competences, Declaration 1 (referring to Article 3t); and hierarchy of acts, Declaration 16.

32. The European Council added the number of Commission members, the weighting of member state votes in the Council, and "appropriate institutional

arrangements" to ensure smooth operation of the EU after enlargement. The three institutions added budgetary procedures and executive powers to implement legislation adopted under the codecision procedure.

33. The four main voting procedures are assent, codecision, cooperation and consultation. Experts have identified 80 treaty articles providing the basis for legislative action.

34. The most common system among the member states is election in multiple constituencies on the basis of party lists; hence, a citizen cannot identify an individual member of the European Parliament as his or her representative.

35. European Commission, "Report on the Operation of the Treaty on European Union," SEC(95) 731, May 10, 1995; Council of Ministers, "Report of the Council of Ministers on the Functioning of the Treaty on European Union," Luxembourg, April 10, 1995; European Parliament, "Report on the functioning of the Treaty on European Union with a view to the 1995 Intergovernmental Conference —Implementation and development of the Union," A4–0102/95, May 4, 1995.

36. Leon Brittan, *Europe: The Europe We Need* (London: Hamish Hamilton, 1994), pp. 241–242.

37. An official of one of the other EU institutions referred to the committee as a prime example of "institutional excess."

38. One example of such an assertion was made by the President of the European Parliament, "I don't see [national parliaments] as rivals; I see them as partners," as quoted in "General of the Assembly," *Financial Times*, November 14, 1994.

39. Declarations 13 and 14.

40. One example is the proposal by Sir Leon Brittan that a Committee of Parliaments be established with specified rights and duties that influence the decision-making process. See Brittan, *The Europe We Need*, pp. 226–230.

41. In the words of one former official, "giving the national parliaments power would be a recipe for deadlock."

42. Although the Parliament has continuously sought to gain a share of the power of legislative initiative, its report on the Intergovernmental Conference (IGC) (see footnote 35 above) most surprisingly makes no mention of such a constitutional change. Rather, it recommends that the Commission maintain its right of initiative. In any event, proposals for reducing the exclusivity of the Commission's legislative initiative may come from certain member states.

43. Charles Grant, *Delors: Inside the House that Jacques Built* (London: Nicholas Brealey Publishing, 1994).

PART THREE

US Interests and Policies

8

Implications for US Economic Interests

It should be self-evident that the directions and manifestations of European integration will have a major effect across the range of economic interests of the United States. Because of the breadth and intensity of economic interaction between the United States and the European Union (see the "Introduction"), EU policies and actions will necessarily affect important US public and private sector interests.

Any assessment of the implications for the United States must start with the macroeconomic benefits. Although it is difficult, if not impossible, to measure with any precision the correlation between an increase in gross domestic product (GDP) and integration in its many possible forms, the general proposition is widely accepted that economic integration results in a higher level of growth than would otherwise have been the case. Just as the abolition of the internal tariffs between the six European Community founder members during the 1960s clearly contributed to the high level of economic growth during that period, the cumulative effects of the single market and related actions, which date from the late 1980s, are adding and will continue to add to the level of economic activity. Although integration adversely affects some economic operators, the net effect is clearly beneficial.

Thus, leaving aside whatever the implications of specific individual measures may be, the overall consequence of economic integration in the European Union has been enhanced advantages and opportunities for the US private sector arising from the reduction in barriers and, thereby, in costs of operation. These advantages and opportunities are available to US companies investing in the EU and to those exporting to it, although they are greater for firms in the former category simply by being inside rather than outside. However, these advantages and opportunities are available to all economic operators in the EU, irrespective of nationality or national origin. There is no statistical measurement to compare the extent to which US firms and others have benefited from the possibilities offered by the increasingly integrated EU, although undoubtedly some US companies have been major beneficiaries, particularly multinationals with skill and experience in operating across national borders.

A second general consideration is that the policies, regulations and general modus operandi of the EU are becoming more pervasive, not solely because of the geographic extension of the Union but because of the process of harmonization. Thus, for better or worse (from the US perspective), an "EU way" is being increasingly adopted throughout most of Western Europe, whether it is the system of agricultural subsidies under the Common Agricultural Policy (CAP), the procedures for obtaining authorization to market a pharmaceutical product, the standards applying to load-lifting machinery, or the establishment of works councils in the larger multinational enterprises. In other words, the EU market is becoming increasingly homogeneous in terms of the rules governing the activities of the private sector (as distinguished from what can be significant differences among the markets of the individual member states).

Naturally this offers both benefits and disadvantages. As a general proposition, the elimination of differences among member states lowers costs to the suppliers of goods and services, be they American or not. However, whether or not a benefit accrues will depend on the nature of the measures adopted in the EU and the way in which they are carried out. A pharmaceutical company, for example, gains from its ability to market a new product in the EU on the basis of a single application rather than separate applications in the 15 member states; on the other hand, the net result will be far worse if an unfavorable decision is taken on its application. The harmonization of controls of residues in animal products eliminates the necessity for exporters to meet multiple regulatory requirements; that is a benefit, but only as long as the resulting procedures do not conflict with those practiced in the United States. The EU's public procurement policy offers enormous possibilities for firms outside the member state in question to supply goods and services to government agencies; however, these possibilities can be nullified by action (or inaction) at member state and local level.

EC 1992 Revisited

Turning more specifically to the EC 1992 program and related economic integration measures, an assessment of their implications must start by recalling the fears that were raised in the United States when the legislative proposals began to emerge. To many observers, the EC single market risked becoming a protectionist, discriminatory regime in which a privileged position would be held by firms headquartered, or at least established, inside the Community. The phrase "Fortress Europe" was adopted to encapsule that fear, and before long it became an obligatory part of any discussion of the single market, even if only to assert that the EC would not develop into such a fortress.

The fortress was viewed more as a predisposition or policy objective than a specific set of potential measures. It was characterized by assertions by many within the Community that the purpose of the single market program was to provide benefits to Europeans, not to "outsiders" (however defined), who should not enjoy a "free ride" from the establishment of the single market. Nonetheless, a number of areas were identified where the danger existed that the EC could adopt Fortress Europe policies.[1]

In reappraising the situation in the mid-1990s it is clear that no Fortress Europe has been established; indeed, that phrase has to all intents and purposes disappeared from the lexicon of the US-EU dialogue. In fact, it was highly improbable from the outset that there would ever be such a phenomenon. Not only was it not a widely accepted, articulated objective in the EC, but economic and political realities limited the potential for such policies: the imperatives of the global economy, a preponderant view that the EC would derive more benefits from an "open" single market than a "closed" one, the espousal of generally liberal policies in several member states, and the constraints contained in the Treaty of Rome and the EC's international commitments.

However, beyond these generalities a balance sheet can be drawn of the areas where EU actions and policies, actual or potential, could impinge on US economic interests. The key issue is the manner in which internal market restrictions were eliminated and harmonization took place: was the effect market-opening, neutral, or market-restricting? Potential US concerns follow, in roughly ascending order of importance.

Restrictions at the External Border

With one exception, no significant US interests have been adversely affected by the EU's use of rules of origin, interpretation of antidumping rules, or import quotas. The latter had been a subject of concern among US automobile manufacturers because of the potential diversion into the US market of Japanese cars resulting from EU import restrictions imposed to replace some of the member states' import quotas. In fact, however, the EU-Japan agreement does not apply to Japanese-nameplate cars manufactured in North America, no such trade diversion has been discernible, and the interests of US companies manufacturing inside the EU have not been damaged by the EU's policies vis-à-vis Japanese imports (see the "Automobiles" discussion in the next section).

The case of one product where US interests have been adversely affected, bananas, is unusual in that it concerns US investment rather than trade, and the effects are indirect though substantial. In what was the last and most contentious replacement of import regimes in certain member states with a single, EU-wide system, preference was given to bananas produced in the African, Caribbean, and Pacific (ACP) states (ex-colonies of EU member states), thereby discriminating against the so-called dollar bananas from Central America, which had previously entered about half the member states without restriction.[2] US investments in Central and South American banana production have been adversely affected. After failing to get satisfaction through bilateral negotiations, the United States joined with several banana-producing countries in filing a complaint with the World Trade Organization (WTO) in late 1995.

National Treatment

A common concern at the outset of the EC 1992 program was that an effort would be made to dilute the national treatment provisions of Article 58 of the Treaty of Rome, under which all firms established in the EC, irrespective of the location of their headquarters or source of capital, are to receive treatment no less favorable than that accorded domestic ones. Despite the unambiguous language of the Treaty,[3] it was feared that distinctions would be introduced—either on the basis of national origin of firms or, in the case of non-EU firms, the nature and scope of activities carried out in the EU—in areas such as access to EU funding for research and development and public procurement bidding opportunities.

Thus far, however, national treatment has not been a significant issue. No effort has been undertaken to amend or redefine Article 58, nor have the EU or member states claimed a formal distinction between "EU" and "foreign" firms.[4] Nonetheless, the issue is not entirely dormant. US firms maintain that European governments, and more often competitors, occasionally assert that such a distinction does exist; however, that is difficult to document.

In addition, some recent legislation conflicts with Article 58. The 1994 hydrocarbons directive defines "non-EU firms" as those where effective control is exercised outside the EU, and the European Commission's draft directive on satellite networks and communications services provides that licenses can be denied to firms not 75 percent owned and effectively controlled by European nationals. To some extent, this erosion of Article 58 is the mirror image of developments in the United States, where a number of US laws were passed in the early 1990s imposing "conditional national treatment," i.e., permitting foreign-owned companies to participate in certain federal programs only if they meet specific conditions relating to their level of economic activity in the United States and reciprocal conditions in their home country. Thus, national treatment could become an issue on which a restriction imposed in the EU elicits an equivalent action by the United States or vice versa.

One issue of national treatment that affects US business and has been the subject of heated exchanges across the Atlantic merits mention: restrictions in the audiovisual sector. The issue is not new. Because television was being broadcast increasingly across national borders, support developed during the 1980s for a harmonization of regulations in the EC. The result, after considerable debate, was the 1989 broadcast directive, more popularly known as the television-without-frontiers directive. The provision relevant to the US film industry set a quota on the percentage of non-European programming on each broadcasting channel. Specifically, it provided that, "where practicable" (an important though ill-defined qualification, inserted to assuage British and German concerns and to provide a measure of flexibility in interpretation), a majority of programs other than news, sports, and game shows must be European. This meant that in the film sector (films, telefilms, and series), the share of US (and other non-EU) production would be limited to less than 50 percent of each channel's programming, although variety shows (invariably national) could be counted as part of the EU quota.

The issue is unique in that it relates not only to economic considerations but also to cultural policy. France, the driving force behind the directive and subsequent pressure for further restrictions, has alleged that Europe must protect itself against the "threat" of erosion of European cultures and languages at the expense of American culture—interpreted in a broad sense as ranging from McDonald's restaurants to lifestyles and forms of expression—which is spread by US films (although, it recognizes, by many other means as well). It is undeniable that many aspects of American culture have been progressively adopted in Europe since the end of World War II and that films have been an important vehicle for spreading that culture. And it is understandable that many Europeans are concerned over the resulting diminution of distinctive European cultures. That is a particularly sensitive issue for the French, whose language until recent decades was recognized as the world language, but has increasingly been replaced by English.

However, the issue has a clear economic dimension: the corollary of "cultural preservation" is trade restrictions on US films and protection for the European film-making industry. Indeed, the proponents of limiting the US film industry's access to the European market consider it essential that the European film industry be protected and otherwise helped to grow. That, of course, runs directly counter to the very substantial interests of the US film industry in Europe.[5]

Not surprisingly, the directive has been subject to interpretation by the member states, with varying definitions of "where practicable" and what constitutes a "European program." However, all member states have passed legislation along the lines of the broadcast directive, of which that of France is the most restrictive. Meanwhile, the situation regarding television broadcasting has changed substantially. Important technological changes have taken place with the development of satellite broadcast channels and pay-per-view television, and private television channels, virtually unknown in the EC in 1989 except in Italy, have proliferated. The latter's programs are heavily weighted to films and American serials, for which the demand cannot easily be met by European production, and in the case of European-produced serials, only at considerably higher cost.

The directive called for a review of the legislation after five years; thus, by the mid–1990s, the question of further legislative action had become a subject of debate. Predictably, France took the lead, calling in 1994 for more restrictions, such as tightening the quotas, narrowing the definitions, and establishing enforcement procedures. However, its efforts met considerable resistance among the member states. After much consultation and debate, the member states had moved by the end of 1995 toward a consensus on maintaining the existing quotas and the "where practicable" language. However, the views of the European Parliament had yet to be taken into account.

The United States made a major effort to bring the audiovisual sector within the ambit of the General Agreement on Trade in Services (GATS), which was negotiated as part of the Uruguay Round, a tactic that would have brought about a multilateral solution to a bilateral problem. However, the EU did not agree to its inclusion under the GATS, and thus that route will remain closed at least until the agreement is reviewed at the end of the decade.

Reciprocity Requirement

The main focus of the Fortress Europe debate was the clause in the proposed second banking directive that would have enabled subsidiaries of a non-EC bank to enjoy the benefits of EC-wide banking only if reciprocal treatment were accorded to EC banks in the country of the non-EC bank in question. Since banks were not permitted to establish branches across state lines in the United States, this provision could have barred US banks from establishing a single banking structure for the EU. After an acrimonious debate across the Atlantic (and despite a widespread— though erroneous—view in the EC that the United States had raised a "non-issue"), the reciprocity clause was modified to require simply that EC banks be accorded "national treatment reciprocity" (i.e., no less favorable treatment than that accorded firms in the home country of the non-EC bank) rather than "mirror-image reciprocity" (i.e., exactly the same treatment as provided for under EC legislation).

The latter is an eminently justifiable position—and, indeed, one that conforms to the 1976 National Treatment Instrument subscribed to by the members of the Organization for Economic Cooperation and Development (OECD), including the United States and the EU member states. National treatment reciprocity was subsequently required in other directives in the financial services field (insurance and investor services). However, mirror-image reciprocity was included in the 1994 directive on hydrocarbons. Although no US-owned firms were affected by these provisions in the initial years, the potential for exclusion from the EU market and the precedent established are unfortunate.

Regulations and Standards

In this critical area, US business was concerned that interested US firms would be effectively excluded from the EC standards-setting process and that the resulting standards would be designed to protect domestic industry and be at variance with internationally accepted standards. With a few exceptions, these fears have not been realized. On the whole, the system has not operated to the detriment of US private sector interests.

A key event was the agreement reached in 1989 between EC Commissioner Martin Bangemann and US Secretary of Commerce Robert Mosbacher, which marked the beginning of an on-going dialogue between EU and US officials on standards and testing issues and established a system under which the US private sector in effect became a party to the European standards-setting process. Specifically, the American National Standards Institute (ANSI), a federation that coordinates the development of American national standards, became the formal conduit for American views to the two European standards-setting organizations, CEN (the French acronym for the European Standards Committee) and CENELEC (the European Electrotechnical Standards Committee). ANSI receives all drafts produced in these organizations and provides the channel for the comments of US industry to the CEN/CENELEC process.

US concerns that Europe would not follow international standards have been largely assuaged by the smooth relationship between the two European organizations and their international counterparts, the International Standards Organization (ISO) and the International Electrotechnical Committee (IEC), respectively (ANSI is a member of ISO and the US national committee of IEC). According to ANSI, there is a great deal of positive interchange between CEN and ISO: about 40 percent of CEN standards are de facto ISO standards, a percentage that is growing; and in the case of CENELEC, any proposal for a new standard is automatically transferred to IEC, as a result of which 95 percent of standards become IEC standards.

For the most part, the US private sector interests (companies and their representative organizations) with sufficient desire and resources have been able to participate in or obtain adequate information about the European standards-setting process. However, firms exporting from the United States generally find that more difficult—because they must participate indirectly—than firms already established inside the EU, which in many respects are "insiders" to the process and therefore may on occasion prefer a market-closing standard to a market-opening one. Furthermore, some US sectors have basically opted out of the process in the belief that their efforts would be futile.[6]

In any event, the standards-setting field has not been problem-free. A serious problem arose in 1993 when the European Telecommunications Standards Institute (ETSI) proposed that a company would have to make any intellectual property contained in an approved standard available under patent licensing to any user of the standard. However, the issue pitted not Europe versus the United States, but rather European governments and technology users versus the US government and technology producers on both sides of the Atlantic, and it was satisfactorily resolved from the US perspective.

Testing and Certification

The beginnings of harmonization of the second stage of the standards process, i.e., testing that products meet the relevant standards and then certifying that such is the case, have not affected US companies differently from other operators in the European market. The critical issue, at least for US exporters, is whether a system can be devised that permits testing and certification of products destined for the EU market to take place in the United States, thus reducing the cost and risk. That issue is a key element of the ongoing dialogue between US and EU officials (see the section on "Implications for Government-to-Government Relations" below).

Public Procurement

The EU's legislation on public procurement contains significant opportunities and significant obstacles for the US private sector. As public procurement in the EU is opened up on a nondiscriminatory basis in accordance with the legislation, US firms will gain access to an enormous market. However, as described in Chapters 2 and 7, under the best of circumstances that will take place over time, and even then not without strenuous effort to counter entrenched interests.

On the other hand, the legislation governing public procurement in the utilities sectors (energy, telecommunications, transportation and water supply) contains discriminatory provisions—a 3 percent preference is given to EU firms (which includes the subsidiaries of US firms established in the EU), a bid with less than 50 percent EU content can be rejected, and in any case an equivalent bid with 50 percent EU content must be given preference. This clause was inserted to increase the EU's leverage in seeking to increase its access to the US public procurement market. Specifically, its purpose was to prevent the United States from gaining an advantage from the EU's market liberalization without having to "pay" something in return, i.e., improved access for EU firms in the United States, where many restrictions exist. The net result of the legislation in the key utilities area makes it more difficult for non-EU (including, of course, US) firms to compete in an expanding market. Because the issues are difficult to resolve (e.g., US access to the EU telecommunications market and removal of restrictions imposed at the subfederal level in the United States), the prospect is that public procurement will remain a contentious area between the United States and the EU.

The initial experience of US firms in this regard has been negative. The US government has complained publicly about the inability of US firms to break into the German market for power generation equipment since entry into force of the single market legislation, in particular General Electric's unsuccessful efforts, including its failure to obtain satisfaction in German review and appeals procedures.

Sectoral Examples

While the foregoing section has described the EU actions and policies that have affected US economic interests, it may be instructive to assess the implications from a different optic—by briefly describing the experiences of US businesses in certain illustrative sectors.

Automobiles

Beginning before World War II, the basic strategy of Ford and General Motors has been to establish a major presence in Europe in development, manufacturing, and distribution. They have succeeded in that and now account for about a quarter of the European market. As a result, they are accepted as European companies, engaged in sharp competition with the other large-volume European producers (Fiat, Peugeot, Renault, and Volkswagen). On the other hand, Chrysler has not been an important player in Europe in recent years. Its sales volume in Europe, based on exports from the United States (but expected to be augmented by the joint venture it entered into in the early 1990s in Austria), is vastly lower than that of its two US competitors.

The main issue to be addressed in the automotive sector under the EC 1992 program was the transformation of restrictions imposed on imports of Japanese automobiles by five member states (France, Italy, Portugal, Spain, and the United Kingdom) into an EU import regime. Following difficult negotiations, first within the EU and then between the EU and Japan, a memorandum of understanding was concluded in July 1991 between the European Commission and the Japanese Ministry of International Trade and Industry (MITI). Although the memorandum did not represent a formal agreement, the Japanese undertook to restrict their imports into the EU to an annually negotiated figure for the dual purpose of controlling the growth of Japanese penetration of the EU market and giving European manufacturers time to adapt to a declining market share.

The memorandum envisaged Japanese imports rising from about 12 percent of the market in 1990 to 16 percent by 1999, the date by which full liberalization was to be achieved. The negotiators forecast that the EU automobile market would grow from 12 million cars in 1990 to 15 million by the late 1990s, and they agreed that the Japanese could capture the bulk of the increase. In addition, although specific controls were not maintained on national markets, it was understood that the Japanese would see to it that undue disruption of the most highly protected markets (France and Italy) did not take place.[7]

Although the European manufacturers were relatively satisfied with the understanding (the two US companies more so than their European counterparts), a major difficulty was encountered early on, when the recession in Europe caused a decline in the size of the European market. The European manufacturers criticized the Commission for not sufficiently restricting Japanese imports under the new situation. However, the sharp increase in the yen's value rendered Japanese automobiles increasingly uncompetitive, and by the mid–1990s, the Japanese quota was no longer being fully utilized.

Once the EU's import regime for automobiles had been put in place, it was possible to conclude work on EU "type approval" for automobiles, i.e., a set of forty-three standards that all cars must meet to be marketed in the EU. Although agreement had been reached on most of the standards over a twenty-year period, some member states blocked approval of the remaining three (relatively minor) standards because they did not want Japanese automobiles to enjoy the benefits that would accrue from an EU-wide system. However, they ultimately lifted their objections so that the new system could come into effect in 1993.

Two other issues bear mention. Regulation of automotive emissions has remained high on the EU's environmental agenda. The Council has adopted a number of measures setting maximum emission levels, the most recent of which (1994) enters into effect in 1996. However, the process will continue: in response to strong pressures from the more environmentally conscious member states (supported by the European Parliament), the Commission has been instructed to draft proposals for further tightening of the permissible emission levels as of 2000.

The second issue is the system of exclusive dealerships for retailing automobiles in the EU that the manufacturers have been permitted to maintain under an exception granted in 1985 by the Commission's competition authorities. Although criticized by consumer groups for limiting competition among dealerships and contributing to the substantial price differences among EU markets,[8] it has been justified on the grounds of ensuring proper servicing while not detracting from interbrand competition. The exemption was renewed in 1995, albeit on terms less favorable to the manufacturers and for a shorter period than previously (seven years instead of ten).

Although the operations of the US companies are, of course, affected by the developments described above, there are no major areas in which the companies have been subjected to different or discriminatory treatment vis-à-vis the European manufacturers. In fact, the experience of US companies has been positive: the European operations of Ford and General Motors have on the whole been profitable, and Chrysler's exports, although starting from a very small base, have risen sharply.

Banking

The US banking industry has maintained a strong presence in the EU during the post–World War II period. The EC 1992 program offered it the potential benefits of a single market for banking (and financial services in general) on a scale considerably broader than that available in the United States. However, as indicated above, a serious concern was the proposed reciprocity legislation that brought into question the ability of US banks established in one member state to operate freely within the EU under the laws and regulatory control of the country of establishment. The prospect for discriminatory treatment was then removed by the change made in the final version of the directive that softened the requirements for reciprocity, thereby opening the EU's single banking market to US banks.

Nonetheless, US commercial banks (as distinguished from investment banks, not considered here) have not derived significant advantages from the creation of a single market for banking. On the one hand, the banking systems in the member states are quite different, and these market differences have limited the potential for economies of scale. On the other hand, the single market has increased competition in the banking sector, and, on the whole, European banks match their US counterparts in sophistication, range of services, and efficiency. In addition, European banks often have an advantage in terms of their knowledge of the market. In sum, there are few unique advantages US banks bring to the EU market. In addition, nationalized European banks generally have the additional advantage of being satisfied with lower profit levels.

At the same time, as business (and thus customer needs) has become increasingly international, it has become correspondingly important for US banks to develop a global presence or at least to be able to handle operations in any part of the world. US regional banks have experienced difficulty in generating profits from their European operations in the 1980s and 1990s, and thus their role has been limited. The large US banks have been more active, primarily catering to the needs of corporate business and devoting a significant part of their resources to developing niche markets. Their clients tend to be American rather than European, in most cases companies which are their customers in the United States. However, some observers maintain that their ability to service these customers in Europe has been reduced by the growing centralization of US company financial activities in the United States, the result of the information revolution.

US banks have made little effort to compete in retail banking, because retail consumers normally prefer to deal with nationally based institutions, and, in any event, it is very expensive to break into well-established retail markets. However, one notable exception is Citibank, which has developed a strong retail network in the EU as part of its effort to become a worldwide retail bank.

Insurance

EU legislation, adopted in the early 1990s, instituted a single market regime for insurance, under which a company established in one member state can operate in the other member states without the requirement of physical presence. The company's "home country" is responsible for financial oversight (primarily regarding the solvency and reserves of the company), while sales are regulated by the country in which they take place. This regime represents a radical departure from the previously existing situation that was primarily characterized by highly regulated and protected national markets and, in some instances, cross-subsidization of operations. Although the legislation was scheduled to come into effect in mid–1994, there have been delays in its implementation,[9] and not surprisingly some problems have arisen in terms of member state regulation.

A further step will be taken in 1998, when the insurance accounting directive enters into force. Its significance lies in the accounting system that companies will be required to use, which will result in far more transparency than in the past, forcing companies (especially German ones) to show their real value. Thus, the single market for insurance is becoming a reality, but gradually.

Nonetheless, competition has increased sharply in the commercial insurance sector, and prices have dropped accordingly. Consolidation among companies started in the early 1990s as companies in member states, looking to the advantages that would become available under the mutual recognition system, began to adopt pan-European strategies, including crossborder acquisitions. The resulting changes will affect financial markets—not simply the insurance market—in the EU because of the economic strength and range of activities of the insurance companies.

US companies—even those with preexisting operations in the several member states, some dating back many years—have not obtained significant benefits from the single market for insurance. In the nonlife sector the strength of US companies lies in new products. With their greater experience and greater willingness to innovate, US firms seek out unfilled needs in the market. However, it is nonetheless difficult for them to break into markets where universal banking exists (particularly Germany).

On the life insurance side, where liberalization has moved somewhat more slowly, US firms have been unable to make significant inroads into the EU market. That is partly a function of the intensified competition referred to above and the fact that, as with (and perhaps even more so than) retail banking, customers, who enter into what is essentially a lifetime relationship, generally feel more comfortable dealing with a "local" company. EU companies face the same problem, as well as that of needing to set up a distribution system in countries that do not have a strong independent intermediary sector (which includes most EU countries, with the exception of the Netherlands and the United Kingdom).

In any event, impediments remain to the development of life insurance in the EU—which, of course, affect all companies, not only American ones. These include the differences in tax treatment on pensions among member states, with the benefits normally being limited to policies taken out with local insurers;[10] government restrictions on the investments insurance companies can make; and the EU's inability (quite understandable in view of the enormous financial implications) to devise a system of portable pensions for EU citizens moving from one jurisdiction to another. The deficiencies in the latter respect include the lack of a transfer value (because most countries do not have funded schemes) and differences in vesting rights. The Commission intends to address this problem, but any solutions will take time.

Medical Devices

The US medical devices industry has developed an important market in the EU, where US firms account for 43 percent of total sales.[11] In part, this represents manufacturing by US firms in the EU, as US companies are increasingly moving their manufacturing operations to Europe. It also includes an important component of exports; more than 50 percent of which, according to the US Department of Commerce, is produced by small and medium-sized firms. The EU is the destination for 41 percent of US medical devices exports, and these, in turn, represent about two-thirds of the EU's import market.[12]

Unlike the situation in the United States where control is exercised by the Food and Drug Administration (FDA), medical devices were not subject to EU regulation (technical standards or requirements for placing a product on the market) prior to the EC 1992 program and only to little regulation by the member states. However, medical devices were targeted by the Commission as one area for regulation under the single market program. In developing the necessary directives—setting "essential requirements" under the "new approach" method of standards setting— the Commission consciously reached out to industry for its input, and the US industry involved itself in that effort. The result was a directive governing active implantable devices that came into effect in 1993; a more general medical devices directive that came into effect in 1995, though with a transition period until 1998, during which products could meet either EU or member state requirements; and an in vitro (outside the body) diagnostics directive scheduled for adoption in 1996 that will come into effect in the late 1990s. In proposing these directives the Commission sought to avoid overregulation, concentrating on safety and essentially leaving efficacy considerations to the market.

Interested US companies have participated in the technical work of developing the directives and subsequently the standards (in which CEN, CENELEC, and ISO are involved), both directly and through their relevant trade associations, and they have been largely satisfied with the results. US industry expects that significant benefits will accrue in the sector from the elimination of multiple regulatory schemes among the member states and from increased acceptance of standardized procedures and technologies.[13]

Nonetheless, some uncertainties remain. Testing and certification of products must be carried out by a "notified body" (one recognized by a member state authority). Thus far, these do not include US bodies because reciprocal arrangements have not been worked out for FDA recognition of European testing. Until that happens, US firms' decisions regarding the selection of the most appropriate European notified body will be critical to its success in the EU market.

In addition, the directives give considerable powers to "competent authorities" (usually national health authorities) in the member states, and it remains to be seen whether they will choose to exercise those powers to expand their regulatory activities. Nonetheless, despite the sharp increase in requirements for clinic testing, the regulatory environment in the EU is considerably less onerous than that in the United States, with the result that US companies have shifted much of their clinical testing from the United States to the EU.

Packaged Food

Legislating in the food sector is difficult because foods differ widely from country to country, account must be taken of questions of national pride and tradition, health and safety concerns must be satisfied, and a broad range of companies and economic interests is involved. The Commission's 1985 white paper setting out the EC 1992 program included a heavy legislative agenda in the food area. In accordance with the EU's objective of harmonizing member state regulations in areas such as product specification (in particular additives, coloring, and sweeteners) and labeling, much legislation was adopted, though not without controversy. These included directives on coloring, sweeteners, hygiene, processing, and miscellaneous additives. The focus was placed on horizontal legislation (i.e., generic legislation applying to all products) because it was deemed easier to adopt and more effective in achieving a single market for packaged food.

In earlier years, the thrust of the legislative effort had been to draft vertical product-specific legislation, primarily aimed at developing EC-wide definitions to replace the variety of national definitions. Products manufactured according to national requirements were subject to mutual recognition; however, in some instances, mutual recognition was overridden by considerations of health or environmental protection, which, in fact, were often merely an excuse for protecting domestic industry. However, the legislative battles over definitions were long, bitter, and divisive, reflecting differences in history and culture as well as protectionist pressures. As a result, only a handful of such directives was adopted (e.g., chocolate, coffee, and jam).

Although the relevance of these vertical directives has been diminished by adoption of horizontal legislation, efforts have recently been undertaken to update and simplify them and make them compatible with the horizontal approach—not always an easy task. To take one example, the debate over the definition of chocolate, contained in the 1973 directive defining 28 cocoa and chocolate products, pitted two groups of member states against each other: those in favor of permitting the use of vegetable fats (which give consistency to the texture) and those in favor of banning vegetable fats—hence requiring the use of cocoa butter (to protect the interests of the cocoa-producing countries in the developing world). If, as is likely, a compromise is eventually reached of maintaining the status quo (permission or ban, depending on national law), no harmonization will have taken place; rather, mutual recognition will remain the norm.

The net effect of the single market legislation affecting the packaged food sector has been a substantial lowering of national trade barriers, a development the industry considers very positive. Nonetheless, significant problems remain at member state level, most frequently in the areas of hygiene and labeling, particularly through insistence, by member state authorities or retailers, on compliance with national rules.

Some centralization of manufacturing and distribution has taken place in the packaged food sector in anticipation of the single market. However, although movement of national products across borders takes place, such activity is relatively limited. The European market remains largely fragmented: very little advertising is conducted on a pan-European basis, and many product formulations (e.g., coffee) continue to vary by region because tastes are basically local.

Although European firms predominate in this sector (especially British, French, German, and Swiss), the US presence is significant. The major US multinationals have established operations in Europe. Products manufactured in Europe account for the bulk of their European sales; US exports of packaged food are minimal. As is the case in most other sectors, US firms are not noticeably discriminated against or otherwise distinguishable from their European competitors. They share the latter's perspectives and concerns, and they participate in their representative organizations essentially on an equal footing.

Pharmaceuticals

The pharmaceutical sector is highly regulated in the EU not only because of government's role in protecting the health of its citizens but also because member state governments fund the major share of health care spending through their national social security programs. Regulation has been carried out by member states in three areas: marketing approval for new products; conditions of sale of products; and prices (by establishing maximum retail prices, patient reimbursement conditions, or a profit control system). However, beginning in 1965, the EU has developed a regulatory framework under which member state rules have been gradually harmonized. Thus, the single market program for pharmaceuticals represented the culmination, or at least acceleration, of an ongoing process.

The farthest-reaching action was taken on product approval. Building on a system of mutual recognition that achieved at best modest success, the EU adopted legislation in 1993 establishing a dual system of product approval that involved either mutual recognition or central approval. The two innovations were the establishment of a clear decision-making procedure so that, unlike under the previously existing system, the end result would be an agreed-upon EU decisions, and the establishment of a European Agency for the Evaluation of Medicinal Products (usually referred to as the European Medicines Agency) to oversee the regulatory process. As the legislation did not enter into effect until 1995, it is premature to pass judgment on its operation. However, it is noteworthy that the legislation emerged only after a lengthy period of consultation among industry groups, other affected parties, and governments such that the result was a highly consensual system for product approval.

Four additional measures, considered jointly as the "rational use of drugs" directives, sought to approximate member state regulation of advertising and promotion, the legal classification of drugs (i.e., prescription-only or over-the-counter), product labeling and information leaflets, and wholesale distribution. In some areas, the effort was successful, notably the labeling and leaflet directive, which resulted from extensive consultations among industry, consumer groups, and the Commission. However, in other areas, the differences among member states were too large to bridge. Because the classification given the same product in different member states varies widely, agreement could be reached only on general guidelines for making the determination. Similarly, in the case of advertising and promotion, which aroused the greatest popular interest, the differences among member state rules in several areas, such as the maximum number of prescription drug samples that could be given to doctors and the enforcement of controls over advertisements, were left essentially unchanged by the directive.

On the pricing side, the scope for EU legislative action is limited because the member states maintain competence over national budgets. In 1989, the pricing transparency directive was adopted, which required that the criteria on which member state authorities take action on pricing and reimbursement be objective and transparent and that no discrimination be made among companies. Although admirable in theory, the directive has proven of marginal use to companies because its effectiveness depends on companies' making complaints against government agencies, and they are understandably reluctant to criticize their best customers. Thus, in the eyes of the industry there has been no significant change in the ability of member states to engage in discriminatory action on pricing and reimbursement.

Another aspect of the pricing issue causes great concern to the pharmaceutical industry: parallel importing. The often wide differences in the prices of products among the member states is largely a function of administrative decisions taken by member state authorities rather than a reflection of economic factors. Until recently, these differences did not result in significant parallel trade flows. However, with the progressive removal of national barriers, the scope for such trade has expanded sharply, potentially accounting for losses to the manufacturers equaling industry's entire European research and development budget, according to industry's most extreme scenario. Although industry believes some form of protection would be appropriate to counter the distortion of competition arising from these noneconomic disparities, none is likely because that would run directly counter to the principles of the single market.

US industry represents a major component of the European pharmaceutical sector, accounting for about one-quarter of sales of medicinal products—some representing exports from the United States, but mostly products manufactured in the EU. Although not always the case in the member states, US industry has not faced discriminatory treatment arising from EU integration measures.

On the whole, the Commission has supported the pharmaceutical industry, including that portion of US origin, as one of Europe's premier high-technology sectors, while maintaining the policy goal of enhancing the health of EU citizens. The Commission (and ultimately the Council in 1992) accepted industry's arguments in favor of extending patent protection to offset part of the long lead-time for research and the approval process, and in 1994, it issued a non-binding industrial policy statement for the industry, calling for actions to reduce the impediments to the development of innovative drugs and to increase the sector's competitiveness.

Implications for Government-to-Government Relations

Having examined the implications of economic integration for US business, it is necessary to consider how it affects the US-EU relationship at the governmental level. It is, of course, difficult to identify that portion of the relationship that relates specifically to economic integration. The range of interaction between the United States and the EU is vast, and one cannot easily divide EU policies into integration and non-integration categories. Nonetheless, a number of general and specific considerations bear on the effects of integration efforts in the EU.

The starting point of this discussion—which is unrelated to the integration or non-integration nature of particular issues—must be recognition of the overall non-conflictual nature of economic relations between the United States and the EU. The two large, developed, and complementary economies interact, on the whole, under agreed rules of the game and with problems accounting for only a small share of the total level of economic activity, even though that may not always be apparent in the US-EU governmental relationship because problems require governments' attention, whereas "nonproblems" normally do not. This relatively benign situation is also a consequence of the conclusion of the Uruguay Round, which had been the locus of confrontation between the United States and the EU on a number of important issues. Even though several issues were left unresolved, in effect they receded from center stage on the international trade agenda.

Nonetheless, the relationship has had to contend with far more than minor, episodic problems. The US-EU economic agenda has always contained contentious issues, with some bilateral disputes festering for years, if not decades; often the temperature has risen sharply, even when the value of the economic interests at stake has been relatively small.

The most complete account of bilateral economic problems, or areas of concern, is contained in the annual reports of the US Trade Representative (USTR) and the European Commission on trade barriers. The USTR's *Foreign Trade Barriers*, required under US trade legislation, interprets "trade barriers" broadly to include import policies, standards-testing-labeling-certification, public procurement, export subsidies, inadequate intellectual property protection, service barriers, and investment barriers. Since the mid–1980s, in response to the USTR's report, the Commission has issued a *Report on US Barriers to Trade and Investment*, which covers a similarly wide range of areas, both "horizontal issues" (measures not specifically aimed at imports and foreign investment that nonetheless affect them, such as taxation and public procurement policy) and sectoral barriers and impediments.[14] However, the reports are more useful in cataloging the totality of existing and potential problems than in identifying the main outstanding issues.

Turning to the "integration" issues, the first on the list is clearly the CAP, one of the EU's basic integration measures and one that has adversely affected US agricultural interests since its inception in the early 1960s. Over the past three decades, the CAP has resulted in the disappearance in Europe of what had been a substantial market for US grain and in heightened competition in third markets by an aggressive export subsidy program. The United States agreed in the 1970s to cease attacking the CAP regime as illegal under the terms of the General Agreement on Tariffs and Trade (GATT). However, numerous trade disputes have erupted over specific EU agricultural policies, and the conflicts have often been heated. Although many issues will continue to require bilateral solutions, the Uruguay Round settlement on agriculture provides for multilateral discipline and reduction of subsidies. In addition, bilateral disputes will be limited until 2004 under the "peace clause," which provides for exemption from countervailing duty actions and other GATT/WTO challenges as long as Uruguay Round agricultural commitments are maintained.

The various present and potential problems arising from the single market measures or policies, described earlier in this chapter, are, of course, subjects that continue to occupy the US government, which has sought to influence the EU's decision-making process or otherwise bring about policies more favorable to US interests. In some cases, this means seeking to ensure that US business obtains the full benefits of market-opening measures, as it did in opposing the original reciprocity clause of the second banking directive. In other cases, it means seeking to prevent economic integration from resulting in restricted market access, as occurred when the EU's import regime for bananas raised the level of protection. In yet others, US business interests can be adversely affected, but it is difficult for the United States to influence the EU decision-making process, as in the case of decisions by the Commission on state aid to national airlines (which can distort the competitive situation in the air transport sector).

One aspect of integration in which the EU's import regime has invariably created a conflict with the United States is enlargement of the Union. Accession to the EU requires the new member state to adopt the EU's common external tariff and any other measures of protection imposed at the external border. As a result, some tariffs may be raised, while others are lowered. In those areas where US interests have been adversely affected by the imposition of the higher EU tariff on goods entering the acceding country, the United States has demanded compensation under the terms of the GATT.[15] Each time the EU has countered that compensation is required only to the extent that the trade damage from tariff increases is greater than the benefits derived from tariff decreases. The United States and EU have argued, often heatedly, over the interpretation of the relevant GATT article, most recently in the case of tariff increases, notably on semiconductors imported into Finland and Sweden (affecting several hundred million dollars in annual trade). Although the two sides have never agreed on the issue of principle, they have always reached a negotiated settlement.

In addition to these trade and investment issues, which account for the bulk of US-EU interaction on the governmental level, increasing attention is being paid to developing reciprocity and cooperation between regulatory authorities and systems. As the EU moves toward the harmonization of standards and technical regulations and the extension of its system of mutual recognition, both sides have recognized their interest in exploring possibilities for reducing the trade impediments resulting from the differences in their regulatory regimes.

However, this is a complex task. In many respects the concepts of regulation differ. For example, German safety standards for toys are designed to make the toys 100 percent danger-proof, whereas standards in the United States presuppose the consumer will exercise some caution. On the other hand, testing requirements for new pharmaceutical products are more onerous in the United States than in the EU member states. There are also differences in the role of government. In the United States, legislatively mandated technical regulations are tested and certified by government agencies (e.g., FDA for medical devices), while industry standards, which are voluntary, are maintained by the private sector (e.g., for pressure vessels). In the EU, the respective responsibilities of government and the private sector are often different, and in most cases, the private sector carries out the certification function.

As a result of these differences, reciprocity can be difficult to achieve, particularly when it is a question of a US agency accepting the action of a nongovernmental body in the EU. Furthermore, there are US legislative restrictions on the authority that regulatory agencies can delegate. Thus, for example, while the FDA may be willing to accept the inspection or test results regarding a medical device from a European body, it is legally prohibited from accepting its certification.

And finally, it is often difficult to persuade regulators to consider alternative principles and methods of regulation. There is bound to be some reluctance to move away from the existing substance or mechanics of regulation.

Nonetheless, some progress has been made in two directions: cooperation among regulatory authorities and mutual recognition of testing and certification. Regulatory cooperation is taking place largely through an intensified dialogue between officials and experts on both sides. One example is the periodic meetings held since 1989 between the FDA and Directorate-General III (Industrial Affairs) of the Commission on foodstuffs, pharmaceuticals, and medical devices. Another is meetings between the US Environmental Protection Agency (EPA) and Directorate-General VI (Agriculture) to discuss their respective regulation of pesticides with a view to avoiding or reducing trade disputes.

While it should be theoretically possible—and would be mutually beneficial—to harmonize regulatory practices on both sides of the Atlantic—and efforts will undoubtedly continue—it will be a long-term process under the best of circumstances because of differences in approach, often reflecting different scientific traditions and legal systems, as well as the inertia of the regulatory process. However, the emphasis is not on regulatory convergence but rather on exchanging information on regulatory procedures and developments, with a view to increasing the regulators' awareness of the trade implications of their activities and fostering a cooperative dialogue under which problems of incompatibility or enforcement can be mitigated or avoided. Of necessity, this is a voluntary, cooperative process, but it is one that can be expected, over time, to lead to a reduction in obstacles to trade.

The more direct line of approach—one potentially providing greater immediate benefits to manufacturers—has been the effort to negotiate the reciprocal recognition of testing and certification so that a product produced on one side of the Atlantic can be inspected and certified before export in the country of production. As indicated above, this would reduce the costs and uncertainty to the producer. The United States has entered into a number of such mutual recognition agreements with certain EU member states in specific regulatory areas (e.g., good manufacturing practice for cosmetics, medical devices, and pharmaceuticals). However, these are not sustainable under the single market, and thus they will eventually be phased out. On the other hand, negotiations have been under way since 1994 on a mutual recognition regime between the United States and the EU. Although twelve areas have been identified for consideration, work has proceeded slowly and on a more restricted list.

One success story predates this effort. After years of contention over different systems of meat inspection, which had interrupted transatlantic trade, the United States and the EU reached an agreement in 1992, under which the two sides recognized the equivalency of their two veterinary inspection systems and provided a mechanism for meat to be inspected by local inspectors in the country of origin, subject to periodic oversight by the inspection service of the importing country.

Of a rather different nature is the cooperation between competition authorities of the two sides—the US Department of Justice and Federal Trade Commission and the Commission's Directorate-General IV (Competition Policy)—which face common problems and occasionally overlapping jurisdictions. A significant step forward was a memorandum of understanding signed in 1991, which provided for an exchange of nonconfidential information on the implementation of competition rules and cases of mutual interest, cooperation, and coordination of actions by US and EU competition authorities, and a commitment by each side to take into account the important interests of the other in enforcing its competition rules. Although the European Court of Justice ruled in 1994 that the memorandum was void because it had been negotiated by the Commission without obtaining the Council's approval, the memorandum was reconfirmed by the EU (this time through the appropriate procedures) in 1995.

Looking to the future, US economic interests will necessarily be affected by two events looming in the EU's future. One is enlargement to the east. By definition, that will extend the area of the EU customs union, thereby providing companies in the EU—including, of course, US and other non-EU companies—with increased access to those markets. During the period leading up to accession, the EU will benefit from preferential trading arrangements with countries in Central and Eastern Europe, which will, of course, ultimately become permanent once these countries join the EU. Enlargement will also further extend the scope of EU legislation and regulation in ways that may or may not benefit US interests. On the other hand, enlargement will probably force changes in the CAP, the overall effect of which will be to reduce the level of subsidy to EU farmers, a development that would benefit US agricultural interests.

The second event—of greater potential significance to US interests—is economic and monetary union (EMU) and the single currency. The implications of the emergence of a new world currency will depend in part on whether demand for the single currency will be greater than that of the total demand for the currencies that will be merged into the single currency. In other words, will investors prefer to hold assets denominated in the EU single currency, and, if so, to what extent? If that takes place on a significant level, the relative importance of the dollar as an international currency will be reduced, with two consequences. First, it will diminish the influence of foreign demand on the value of the dollar, as a result of which the exchange rate would be a closer reflection of the US current account balance. In that case, the dollar's value would be more predictable, though probably lower than it is now because of the reduction in foreign demand for dollars. Second, it will reduce the flexibility available to US monetary authorities in setting monetary and fiscal policy because foreigners would be less prepared to participate in funding US deficits through purchases of dollars.

However, few experts believe the shift will be substantial, at least in the early years of the new currency. Market operators can be expected to follow a cautious policy as the European Central Bank establishes its credibility. In any event, it is unlikely that the United States will find it difficult to finance its current account deficit. Nevertheless, the single currency could contribute to the long-term decline of the dollar as a world currency, and that would have the consequences listed above, although over time.

Notes

1. See the discussion on implications of the single market for US business in Michael Calingaert, *The 1992 Challenge from Europe: Development of the European Community's Internal Market* (Washington: National Planning Association, 1988), Chapter 7. For a representative business view, see testimony by Lionel Ulmer, representing the US Chamber of Commerce, before the Subcommittee on Trade, Committee on Ways and Means, US House of Representatives, March 20, 1989.

2. The World Bank paper "EU Bananarama III," January 1995, asserted that the EU had chosen "some of the worst features of the earlier policies of a few of its member states and made them the general rule ... in creating the unified banana regime." As quoted in "World Bank Study Attacks EU Banana Regime," European Report, No. 2010, January 25, 1995.

3. "Companies or firms formed in accordance with the law of a Member State and having their registered office, central administration or principal place of business within the Community shall ... be treated in the same way as natural persons who are nationals of Member States" (Treaty of Rome, Article 58).

4. Nonetheless, it is argued by some that the language of Article 58 *is* ambiguous in two respects: first, that EU law applies only between member states and thus that while a member state cannot discriminate against firms of another member state, it can discriminate against a firm from outside the EU; and second (and contrarily), that the treaty does not place strictures on the Union, only on actions by member states, and thus that Union actions can discriminate against firms from non-EU countries.

5. There is no question about the importance of the film industry in Europe. The (US) Motion Picture Association estimates that the industry's earnings in Europe contribute about $3.5 billion annually to the US balance of payments. Less clear, however, is extent of earnings forgone as a result of restrictions in the EU.

6. For example, gas connectors and nonwoven fabrics, according to the US Department of Commerce, have opted out.

7. At the time the memorandum of understanding was under discussion, a debate took place over whether automobiles produced by Japanese manufacturers inside the EU should be included in the quota, with European manufacturers asserting that they should be included, while the Commission and the United Kingdom (where most Japanese investment has occurred) argued that the automobiles in question represent "European production." According to a senior Commission official responsible for this issue, public reports to the contrary not withstanding, the text made clear that transplants were not counted, and the issue was never raised in monitoring meetings with the Japanese.

8. A European Commission report documented differences in the price of the same model between member states as high as 56 percent. See "Car Prices Still Vary Hugely between Member States," *European Report*, No. 2061, July 26, 1995, p. III/5.

9. In 1995, the Commission initiated proceedings in the European Court of Justice against Spain for failure to notify what measures of transposition it had taken in regard to the third directives on life and nonlife insurance. At the same time, the Commission initiated proceedings against Belgium, Ireland, and Italy for failure to implement the 1991 directive on annual accounts and consolidated accounts of insurance companies.

10. The European Court of Justice ruled in the 1992 Bachmann case that member states could restrict tax relief on life insurance premiums to policies held with local insurers.

11. Health Industry Manufacturers Association, *The Global Medical Device Market Update: Markets for Medical Technology Products,* Report #94–1 (Washington, 1994), p. 26.

12. Ibid., pp. 7 and 80.

13. Ibid., p. 84.

14. The 1995 reports are *1995 National Trade Estimate Report on Foreign Trade Barriers*, United States Trade Representative (Washington, 1995), and *Report on United States Barriers to Trade and Investment 1995*, Services of the European Commission (Brussels, July 1995).

15. It should be noted that this applies only to tariffs that have been bound under the General Agreement on Tariffs and Trade (GATT).

9

US-EU International Interaction

Having considered the implications of the process of European integration for US economic interests, an issue essentially concerning the US-EU bilateral relationship, it is relevant to assess how the development of European integration will affect the interaction between the United States and the EU as two major players on the world's economic, political, and security stage. In other words, how will they deal with each other in the multilateral context, and how, in turn, will that affect multilateral consideration and resolution of issues?

Economic

As described in previous chapters, European integration has proceeded much further in the economic than in the political or security areas. To a far greater extent, the European Union acts, or at least speaks, with a single voice on economic issues. This is particularly the case with trade, where the Treaty of Rome empowers the European Commission to represent the European Community and now the EU. In the trade negotiations of the General Agreement on Tariffs and Trade (GATT) (and, subsequently, the World Trade Organization, WTO), for example, the Commission—operating, it should be emphasized, under a mandate given it by the Council (i.e., the member states)—represents the EU and negotiates on its behalf. The individual member states are observers of the process; however, they are the ultimate decision makers. As a result, tension is built into the EU, particularly when trade deals are being negotiated, as was the case in the final stages of the Uruguay Round, when France blocked the Blair House agreement, which was intended to resolve the thorny US-EU conflict over agriculture, and forced its modification. The role of the European Parliament is limited: it is excluded from the operational aspects of trade policy, it provides its opinion on trade

agreements requiring formal Council approval, and it must give its assent
(without the possibility of amendment) on major trade agreements, such
as the Uruguay Round.[1] Neither the Single European Act nor the Maastricht Treaty altered the competences for trade or the procedures for
dealing with trade issues, and there is no reason—or pressure—for the
Intergovernmental Conference (IGC) to change the existing relationship
among the Commission, the Council, and the Parliament.

However, a new element emerged as a result of the Uruguay Round. A
major breakthrough of the round was the extension of the scope of the
negotiations—and agreement—to "new issues," notably services and
intellectual property protection. Although the Commission contended
that the agreements in these areas should be approved under the existing
procedures for merchandise trade, member states objected. The case was
taken to the European Court of Justice, which ruled that the competences
varied according to the subject. In some areas (notably merchandise
trade) the Union, represented by the Commission, enjoys exclusive
authority, while in others (such as trade in services and intellectual property protection) the competence is shared between the Commission and
the Council. Thus, tensions will undoubtedly remain in the relationship
between the Commission and the member states, and the Commission
will continue to balance the interests and demands of the member states,
while seeking to guide the direction of trade policy.

The United States and the EU are without question the principal determinants of the structure and content of the world trading system. No
major changes take place unless they are in agreement. This was clearly in
evidence in the recently concluded Uruguay Round, which was largely a
bilateral US-EU negotiation, and it was the case (indeed, even more so) in
earlier rounds. Thus, changes in the US-EU trade relationship resulting
from European integration can affect the world trading system. To what
extent has or will that happen?

The change is the emergence of a European trading bloc, as an increasing number of countries have joined the EU or entered into closer economic relations with it through the establishment of the European
Economic Area (EEA) in 1994, the accession in 1995 of three new members, and the progressive movement of the Central and Eastern European
countries toward membership. Thus, there has been both an enlargement
of the EU and, more generally, an extension of its "sphere of influence"
over the other participants in the EEA and the prospective new members.
However, the implications for the United States are difficult to assess.
Member states' orientation on trade issues will continue to range from
liberal to protectionist. The liberal preponderance was modestly strengthened by the accessions of 1995. On the other hand, when further enlarge-

ment to the east takes place, it will probably add, also modestly, to the protectionist-leaning camp because of those countries' relatively weaker economies.

The numerical advantage of the EU may be felt in the WTO, where both the member states and the Commission are represented through bloc voting. However, few issues are decided by formal votes, and US-EU differences are normally resolved through negotiation rather than votes. Nonetheless, votes were the deciding factor in the acrimonious contest for Director-General of the WTO—Renato Ruggiero was elected to the position in 1995, due to the large number of EU-controlled votes (member states, prospective members, and developing-country recipients of EU aid)—an unfortunate precedent from the US perspective.

Although the EU has traditionally followed the US lead in the multi-lateral trade field, a possible harbinger of change in that situation was the EU's initiative in salvaging an interim multilateral financial services liber-alization agreement in the WTO in mid–1995 after the United States had withdrawn its support.[2] However, it remains to be seen whether that was an aberration, resulting from particular circumstances and personalities (in particular, the assertive EU commissioner, Sir Leon Brittan).

The counterpart trading bloc on the other side of the Atlantic is the North American Free Trade Agreement (NAFTA), covering the vast expanse from Canada to Mexico and potentially encompassing much of South America. While the development of these blocs has been accepted, on balance, with equanimity (or at least resignation), each side harbors concerns that the other bloc will result in greater protection against out-siders. Thus, the EU and the United States will continue to scrutinize the other bloc for signs of discrimination and protection. On the other hand, that situation could change if the two blocs were combined into a "super" free trade area, the subject of a growing debate (see Chapter 10).

In the other two principal international economic institutions of the monetary/development/trade triad—the International Monetary Fund (IMF) and the World Bank—there is no collective EU membership; rather, each member state belongs in its individual capacity. Although this reflects the fact that the establishment of these two institutions predated that of the EC, there has been no rationale, particularly in the case of the IMF, for the member states, each of which carries out its own economic and monetary policy, to subsume its membership under an EU umbrella. A single EU membership in the World Bank would be of marginal signifi-cance. However, that is not the case with the IMF.

At such time as the economic and monetary union (EMU) is formed, in particular when a single currency is introduced, it must be presumed, if not required, that the participants will merge their IMF memberships into a single membership for the group. The collective strength of this group of participating countries will equal the sum total of the votes of the member states in question because IMF voting is based on the size of quotas that reflect their gross domestic product (GDP). Thus, the establishment of the EMU will have two consequences that will potentially increase the EU's economic influence and power. First, as discussed in Chapter 8, the single currency may emerge as an alternative reserve currency to the dollar. Second, it may create a major voting bloc—by definition more cohesive than the individual member states—in the IMF, potentially larger than that of the United States (depending on which member states join the EMU). Although the United States will undoubtedly maintain its veto power in the IMF, it is possible, if not likely, that the EMU bloc will gain a similar prerogative.

With these developments in the offing, the present configuration of the Group of Seven (G–7) becomes increasingly anachronistic—leaving aside the question of its utility and appropriateness in the near 21st century. The G–7 has no formal status or powers, but rather operates as a sort of consensus-seeking forum for arriving at coordinated actions among what are (or were) deemed to be the world's major powers. As one observer put it, the G–7 is the *"de facto* steering committee for the world economy."[3] The EU member states that participate are France, Germany, Italy, and the United Kingdom (the other G–7 members being Canada, Japan, and the United States). Although initially resisted by the member state participants, the Commission has gradually become recognized as the "eighth member" of the G–7, although it does not participate in the work of the G–7 finance ministers. Along with the Council Presidency (when the member state in office at the time is not a G–7 member), the Commission represents the interests of the EU as a collectivity, in particular those of the smaller EU member states. However, it is, in fact, treated as the junior member of the group.

A major activity of the G–7 has been to seek (with little success of late) to enhance the coordination of economic policies, particularly monetary policy, among the leading powers. In Europe, monetary policy is largely set by Germany; the role of the other EU members, with the minor exception of the United Kingdom, has been minimal. However, once the EMU is formed, monetary policy will become the collective responsibility of the participating member states (although clearly led by Germany), and then it would be logical for the EU to alter its representation in the G–7, opting for either a single EU seat or at least a single seat for the member states participating in EMU.

However, unlike the situation in the IMF, there is no compelling reason for this to happen because the G–7 is not a formally constituted decision-making body, and its membership is not directly related to monetary strength or systems. Regardless of the rationale for a possible amalgamation of membership, the four member states that presently participate in the G–7 can be expected for reasons of power and prestige to insist on maintaining their individual membership. Their arguments will carry weight until such time as a far greater degree of political integration has been achieved in the EU, particularly as the G–7 shifts its focus increasingly to noneconomic issues. Furthermore, with Italy excluded as a founder member of the EMU and the United Kingdom a doubtful participant, a combination only of the French and German membership would simply exacerbate the imbalance between membership and influence in the G–7.

In any event, it is questionable whether the substitution of membership by the EU or EMU participants in the G–7 for that of the four present members will increase the influence of the EU in the G–7. On the contrary, it could be argued that the EU would lose from the reduction in its number of its seats at the table.

Finally, a word is in order concerning the EU's role as a provider of economic assistance. Aid programs form an important component of EU policies toward the developing world, although the bulk of aid from the EU is given by member states on a bilateral basis. However, the EU's aid program in Central and Eastern Europe is not only its largest, but also its most significant because the Commission chairs the Group of 24, the body established to coordinate the activities of the donors of aid to that area. The latter function has substantially increased the visibility and substantive input of the EU (represented by the Commission) in the aid field. In addition, it represents an important step in US-EU cooperation in that the EU undertook this activity at the recommendation of the United States. As a senior member state official put it, this event was a "watershed" in US-EU relations, where the United States for the first time said, in effect, to the EU: "This is your problem; please handle it."

A word is also in order concerning assistance to other parts of the world. In areas such as Haiti and Rwanda, where international aid efforts have been mounted to address urgent problems, the United States has carried on a dialogue with the EU (the Commission) in an effort to improve the coordination of operational policies. More generally, the United States and the EU have moved in the direction of greater cooperation in their development and humanitarian assistance programs. However, as the US aid appropriations continue to decline and those of the EU to increase, the United States tends to seek more actively to influence EU funding decisions, a situation that does not necessarily sit well with the EU.[4]

Political

As described earlier in Chapters 4 and 7, there is no question of the EU's developing a genuine common foreign policy, i.e., a single policy in which there is no scope for policies of the individual member states, until well into the next century, if then. However, the EU has moved gradually in the direction of policy coordination and, on occasion, common positions and joint actions. As the EU has edged into the foreign policy arena, the United States has shared some of the leadership it had hitherto exercised, in some cases willingly, in others less so.

In post-Cold War Central and Eastern Europe, where a sharp reversal of policy and a large commitment of resources were clearly called for, the United States encouraged and welcomed the EU's assumption of an active role. The ability and willingness of the United States to devote resources to the area were limited (relative to the magnitude of the requirements), and it deemed the EU to have a more direct interest—indeed, obligation—to assist the countries of Central and Eastern Europe in their economic and political transformation. In particular, the United States has pressed the EU to accelerate the process of economic and political integration of the countries of Central Europe into the EU.[5]

The case of ex-Yugoslavia, of course, is *sui generis*, although some of the same considerations apply for US policy there as with Central and Eastern Europe in general. Without going into detail, suffice it to say that the United States has looked to the EU to take the lead in resolving the civil war, while working together through various channels, particularly that of the contract group (see Chapter 4).

Conversely, in the Middle East peace process, there is some divergence between the United States and the EU. The United States wants to manage the process, as it has done from the outset, believing that it alone enjoys sufficient trust of the two sides (and the necessary power) to bring about an eventual settlement. Its main interest in EU involvement in the peace process—previously largely cosmetic—is that the EU contribute to any financial package, as it has already done in the case of the 1994 Israeli-Palestinian accord. However, the EU, or at least certain member states, would prefer to play a more active role. They want to protect and promote their economic and political interests—in some instances considerable—in the Middle East, vis-à-vis those of the United States, both at present and in a possibly peaceful future.

The United States has also consulted closely with the EC and the EU on foreign policy issues since the early 1970s, beginning with the European Political Cooperation (EPC) and continuing with the Common

Foreign and Security Policy (CFSP). Mutual policy briefings have become a matter of course, such that each side has become privy to the foreign policy thinking of the other in considerable depth (leading one US official to describe the United States and the EU, somewhat hyperbolically, as being "joined at the hip"). However, there has been a qualitative differ-ence between the EPC and the CFSP. While discussions under the EPC framework were limited to exchanges of information, an effort has been made since the inception of the CFSP to coordinate policies and actions in the pursuance of mutual interests. The United States and the EU worked together in bringing about the unlimited extension of the Nuclear Non-Proliferation Treaty and in persuading Russia to accept a role for the Organization for Security and Cooperation in Europe in Chechnya. In addition, they have looked to areas where they could coordinate their policies. In this regard, increasing attention has been placed on issues of development assistance, particularly as US resources have dwindled while its policy interests remain, thus enhancing the relative importance of the EU's role.

However, despite the increased activity in this area, the potential for cooperation between the United States and the EU is limited by two fac-tors. First, the relationship is unbalanced in that the United States carries out a foreign policy, whereas the EU does not as such. Although the EU can deal with certain long-term issues (e.g., forging a new relationship with the countries of Central Europe), it is poorly equipped to respond to crises requiring immediate attention (e.g., the tribal massacres in Rwanda). Second, there is no fixed interlocutor on the EU side (see Chapter 10). It is the troika, which changes every six months. Further-more, one or more of the troika members may have no interest in a partic-ular issue or, conversely, their interests may diverge.

These limitations are manifested in the experience with the three groups of US and EU experts established at the semiannual meeting among the presidents of the EU (i.e., the rotating Council Presidency), the European Commission, and the United States in July 1994 to study common problems: one to study ways and means by which joint US-EU action can strengthen democracy and economic cooperation with and between the countries of Central and Eastern Europe; a second to study ways and means of combating international organized crime and drug trafficking; and a third to study how joint efforts in international relations can be improved. Work has proceeded slowly, and on the issue of greatest immediacy and public concern—combating crime and drug trafficking— little tangible result is possible because EU competence lies with the EU member states under the third pillar.

Security

The nature and intensity of interaction between the EU and the United States on security issues was altered by the introduction of a security role for the EU in the Maastricht Treaty and the end of the Cold War. The constants of the Soviet threat, the clear-cut role of the North Atlantic Treaty Organization (NATO) as the defense bulwark, and a strong US military presence have given way to a weakened but potentially dangerous Russia, uncertainty as to NATO's mission, and a sharply reduced level of US forces in Europe. The questions raised by the changed circumstances—what is the nature of the security threat to Europe, what roles should be played by NATO and the Western European Union (WEU), how should the countries of Central Europe participate in European security arrangements, what can and should be the nature of an EU (or European in some other configuration) security identity, to what extent will the United States participate in European defense, inter alia—have been, and will continue to be, the subject of debate and deliberation.

Without any doubt, the United States will continue to be the predominant participant in European security, reflecting the breadth and intensity of its global interests and its economic and military prowess. However, as described in Chapters 4 and 7, a European voice is emerging on security issues, a development initially opposed by the United States, fearful of undermining the effectiveness of NATO, but later welcomed as a means of sharing more equitably the defense burden in Europe.

The development of such a European security role will produce costs and benefits for the United States. By definition, it will diminish the degree of influence and control over European security policy presently exercised by the United States. And it will carry the risk of duplicating or otherwise reducing the effectiveness of NATO. On the other hand, it should make it easier to arrange a European contribution to military action (as in the case of the Gulf War) and European military operations in which the United States does not wish to participate (through the WEU, although of necessity in cooperation with NATO). However, any such development—inevitable though it may be—can only take place over a relatively long period of time.

Notes

1. The language of Article 228(3) of the Treaty of Rome as amended by the Maastricht Treaty is ambiguous regarding the agreements on which the Parliament's assent is required. Not surprisingly, the Parliament has sought to exploit this ambiguity to expand its role.

2. After the United States withdrew its offer of most-favored-nation treatment in the face of inadequate offers of market access from a number of countries, the Commission (with Commissioner Leon Brittan orchestrating the effort) proposed a one-month extension of the negotiating deadline and then put pressure on a number of countries, particularly Asian, to improve their offers sufficiently to achieve a necessary "critical mass" for the agreement.

3. C. Fred Bergsten, "Like it or Not, a Lifeless G–7 Threatens the Livelihood of All," *International Herald Tribune,* June 13, 1995, p. 8.

4. This sentiment was reflected in the remark of EU Commissioner Bonino that "we will not pay their bill," as quoted in "EU and U.S. Link Aid Efforts," *International Herald Tribune,* September 28, 1995, p. 7.

5. Although not detracting from the wisdom of US policy, it should nonetheless be noted that integration presents greater problems of adjustment for the EU than for the United States, especially regarding the opening of its markets to Central European imports.

10

US Policy Response to European Integration

The US response to the evolving process of integration in the EU must be viewed from two perspectives: that of public policy and that of the business sector.

Public Policy

Goals and Objectives

The starting point for determining what policies and strategies are appropriate for the United States must be its goals and objectives. These, in turn, are based on a number of premises. In both the economic and political spheres, these premises, goals, and objectives are relatively non-controversial.

The basic premise is that the US-EU relationship covers a broad economic and political spectrum and that it is a positive relationship, in which there is a preponderant degree of mutual interest and common view of the world. As a recent report noted—indeed, understated—"what unites America and the European Union is more important than what has been driving them apart."[1] Each benefits from political stability and economic prosperity in the other; in the case of the United States, political stability in the EU means the absence of security threats, and economic prosperity means expanded opportunities for commercial interchange. The two unions operate in a multipolar world, in which, by working together, they can improve the possibilities for influencing developments in accordance with their shared objectives. Based on these premises, then, US goals and objectives in the EU are:

- Economically: (a) to ensure that the EU's market is open to all firms that wish to operate there on the basis of a transparent regulatory regime characterized by liberal rules and nondiscriminatory treatment toward non-EU firms; and (b) to obtain EU support in seeking to maximize the ability of companies to engage in trade, investment, and other crossborder commercial activities within the framework of acceptable multilateral rules.
- Politically: (a) that conflict be avoided among the nations of Europe, in particular through the successful transition of the countries formerly dominated by the Soviet Union into the Western democratic, free market system; and (b) to the extent that political integration takes place in the EU, that the EU play a positive participatory role—consonant with the role and objectives of the United States—in dealing with problems around the world. In the effort to achieve the latter objective, the United States seeks to maximize its access to the EU's foreign policy deliberations and its influence on the EU's thinking and actions.

Policy on Integration

It has been a constant of US foreign policy since the end of World War II to welcome and support integration measures in Europe. The rationale—indeed, the imperative—in the early postwar years was clear: to minimize the ability and inclination of the countries of Europe to wage war against each other and to facilitate the reconstruction of the European economy. That policy has remained unchanged. Despite early concerns that European economic integration would result in trade diversion rather than creation, it rapidly became apparent that integration facilitated economic activity and accelerated growth, thereby providing benefits to the people of Europe and, not incidentally, offering significant opportunities for US business. Political integration was supported essentially as an article of faith, reflecting more an extension of the earlier commitment to postwar cooperation and a general belief that Europe would benefit from emulation of the Union on the other side of the Atlantic than a well-considered view of the implications for the United States of such a development. In any event, the lack of progress in European political integration made this largely a theoretical proposition.

However, US policy in the second half of the 1990s must be based on the present, not the past. The rationale for supporting economic integration in the EU remains valid: the benefits to the world from the resulting higher level of economic activity and the opportunities offered to US business—advantages that more than offset the increased competition that US firms will face in Europe and third countries. At the same time, however, US support must continue to be premised on the EU's implementing integration in accordance with free market principles and in a transparent, nondiscriminatory manner. An additional rationale is that an integrated EU—hence an EU speaking with a single voice—is better able to work with the United States in bringing about a favorable economic climate around the world, particularly regarding opening markets and establishing effective rules governing economic interchange (e.g., dispute settlement mechanisms and investment agreements).

On the other hand, as the EU moves, albeit slowly, in the direction of political integration, US policy must be subjected to more careful scrutiny from the point of view of the two objectives listed above. First, it is necessary to reconsider the role of integration in preventing the recurrence of conflict among the nations of Europe. In the late twentieth century, it is impossible to conceive of an armed conflict among the member states of the EU, reflecting both the degree of economic and political intertwining that has taken place and the changed nature of war. Similarly, the likelihood of a serious falling-out among the member states in the foreseeable future is remote.

Nonetheless, such an eventuality should not be excluded in perpetuity. Unlikely though it may be, circumstances could arise under which, for example, Germany, over time, would consider its interests best served by downgrading its support of the EU and the leadership it provides, while, under a number of possible scenarios, France could decide to oppose rather than accommodate German predominance in the EU. In either case, the political stability of Europe could be severely weakened, and that would run counter to US interests. Thus, a long-term political rationale exists for continuing US support for European integration.

However, political (and economic) stability is much more directly and immediately affected by the transformation of the countries of Central Europe. The potential for instability and conflict in this area is obvious—possibilities that will be diminished to the extent these countries become linked into the economic and political system of Western Europe. For that reason, the highest priority of the United States as regards integration is for this linkage (eventually including membership) to take place as rapidly as possible, a priority that the EU shares, as described previously, and to which it is committed.

Regarding the more general issue of US support for EU political integration as a means of promoting US political objectives, that policy is based on three assumptions:

- that the United States and the EU share a common set of values (e.g., democratic government and free market economy) and general view of the world (e.g., concern over Islamic fundamentalism);
- that their policy prescriptions are largely convergent; and

- that the development of greater political cohesion will enable the EU to exercise a more active foreign relations role, thereby mitigating the burden on the United States of providing political leadership in the world.

The first assumption is unquestionably valid and does not require elaboration. The second is valid, but only when qualified by "largely." It is difficult to envisage the United States and the EU supporting substantially different policy approaches or prescriptions for a particular problem or set of issues. However, differences can nonetheless be sufficient to bring the United States and the EU into conflict. For example, the general approaches of the United States and the EU on the Middle East conflict during the years preceding the peace process initiated in the early 1990s by the Bush administration differed in the relative degree of support given to the Arab states and Israel, with the EU leaning more toward the positions of the former and the United States leaning in the opposite direction. More recently, there has been a tendency, at least among certain member states (and outside the realm of the Common Foreign and Security Policy, CFSP) to seek to improve relations with nations the United States believes should be kept firmly at arm's length (Iran in the case of Germany and Iraq in the case of France).

Thus, the third assumption also has to be qualified. As a general proposition, it is valid. If and as the process of EU political integration continues, the EU will become an increasingly active participant in world politics. Although that is not a zero-sum game, such a development will tend, on the whole, to reduce the relative influence and weight of the United States. The EU will then assume part of the burden presently borne by the United States, while adding to the effectiveness of the policy in question. Recent examples are EU efforts (although admittedly driven in large part by one or a small number of member states rather than by the EU collectively) to deal with problems in Algeria and Rwanda.

However, such burden-sharing will not necessarily promote US policy goals because, as just described, EU policies and actions will not always accord with those of the United States, even though US-EU concordance of views will undoubtedly outweigh the differences.

Consideration of what is the appropriate US attitude toward European integration must also take into account the fact that whatever the pace and form of integration in the EU, it will be determined very largely by the Europeans themselves. In the 1950s and 1960s, active US promotion of European integration contributed substantially to the launch and development of the European Community. Now, however, the relationship is essentially one of equals, and under the circumstances decisions on integration will be taken by the Europeans on the basis of their judgment of how their interests can be best served. The US role will be that of a friendly counselor rather than a rich uncle. Thus, US support for or opposition to either the concept of integration or particular aspects thereof will have only a limited effect on developments in the 1990s.

The US ability to influence the process of integration is probably stronger in a negative than a positive sense. In other words, urging that a particular line of action be followed will probably have less effect than seeking to prevent something from happening. Thus, for example, the EU will be less likely to heed US encouragement to adopt qualified majority voting on third pillar issues but more likely to hesitate before overriding US objections to a European security identity. In fact, the shift in US position from opposition to support of the latter was an important factor in determining the security provisions ultimately adopted in the Maastricht Treaty.

Nonetheless, the EU not only welcomes but expects US support for the concept of European integration, and that has been given. Every US post-World War II administration has voiced such support, and the Clinton administration is no exception. For example, at a joint press conference with the presidents of the Council and the European Commission, President Bill Clinton stated:

> ... the United States strongly supports the European Union. Throughout my entire administration I have advocated the cause of the European Union. I believe our best partner, as we look toward the 21st century for prosperity and for peace, is a Europe united in democracy, in free markets, in common security. We have supported that, and we will continue to support it.[2]

In the previous administration, President George Bush had given renewed importance to the EC and upgraded the bilateral relationship—symbolized by the conclusion of the Transatlantic Declaration in 1990 (see below)—and the Clinton administration has sought to build on that foundation.

In any event, it is inconceivable that the United States would overturn fifty years of policy by voicing opposition to European integration. Not only would it be interpreted by Europeans as an "unfriendly act," seeking to weaken Europe at the expense of the United States. Most important, it would run counter to US interests. European integration accords with US interests because, as analyzed above, the United States has more to gain economically and politically from an integrated than from a fragmented European Union. As President Clinton said in Brussels, "We will benefit more from a strong and equal partner than from a weak one,"[3] to which the US Ambassador to the EU added: "We support European integration ... because it is in our own, most fundamental interest. The solution to virtually every significant international problem ... requires us to work with ... the European Union."[4]

That has been and should continue to be US policy: the United States supports moves toward economic and political integration in the EU. However, the operative word is "supports," not "urges." The US position should be one of supporting a general concept, i.e., welcoming steps that have been taken—as long as they do not damage US interests—but not pressing the EU for or against any specific means of promoting integration. That will set the best tone for the US-EU relationship.

The United States should not seek to become a party to the developing debate in the EU. On the whole, the United States does not have a clear stake in any particular form of integration beyond the overall advantages to be gained from greater integration. In any event, US efforts, especially in public, to influence the course of the debate would risk producing the contrary result.

Potential for Conflict

As has been the case since the formation of the EC in the 1950s, the US-EU relationship encompasses both conflict and cooperation. To some extent, conflict is inevitable with two large unions: divergent interests and objectives will necessarily coexist with shared ones.

However, the new element of the 1990s has been the disappearance of the common security threat that provided the underpinning to the American-European relationship. In its absence, conflicts, which might previously have been resolved reasonably amicably, may prove more contentious because one or both participants no longer feel restrained by concern that conflict could damage the essential security relationship.

On the economic side, the breadth and depth of the relationship make it inevitable that disagreements and disputes will arise from integration measures. This requires the US government to engage in what is essentially a micro rather than a macro policy. In other words, it must monitor policies and actions under consideration and already taken in the EU, and it must press for changes that it deems appropriate. That is the traditional role of government, one the US government has carried out for the most part effectively in the past in its dealings with the EC and the EU, as it will undoubtedly continue to do in the coming years.

Although it is difficult to forecast the precise form in which problems will arise, US policy makers will need to scrutinize developments in the economic integration process, with particular attention on:

- Protection at the external border: will the EU seek protectionist solutions to harmonization problems (e.g., the banana import regime)?

- National treatment: will the EU seek to limit the legal protection and benefits of integration offered firms on bases other than the physical establishment of a company (an issue, as mentioned earlier, that is relevant in the United States as well)?
- Access: will the EU permit all participants in its marketplace, irrespective of their origin, equal access to the decision-making and regulatory process?

Although most of the economic conflicts between the United States and the EU have related, and will continue to relate, to bilateral trade, conflicts arise outside the borders of the two unions, and they may increase as a result of integration. One such area is voting procedures in international economic institutions, where the EU often holds a numerical advantage. The major instance was the fight over the appointment of Renato Ruggiero as Director-General of the World Trade Organization (WTO) (see Chapter 9). Although there have been few such instances, the potential exists for the EU to "gang up" on the United States by using its voting strength to block US desires in bodies where each member state has a vote (at times in addition to that of the European Commission). Although that will more likely happen in the case of appointments, conflicts may also arise over substantive issues, or at least the EU may adopt more assertive positions that will not necessarily correspond with US interests, e.g., its initiative on a multilateral financial services agreement (see Chapter 9).

In the political sphere, as indicated above, increasing involvement by the EU, as distinguished from the member states, in foreign policy is bound to produce some degree of conflict. In part that will reflect different perspectives on how to deal with situations in geographic proximity to the United States or the EU (e.g., the United States will view with greater concern than the EU what it perceives to be threats to security in the Caribbean). However, in a more general sense, the United States, reflecting its historical leadership role, will more likely favor stronger policy responses (e.g., on issues of state terrorism), while the EU will give greater priority to the economic implications of such action.

Potential for Cooperation

Fortunately, at the official level the US-EU relationship is characterized far more by cooperation than by conflict on bilateral, third-country, and multilateral issues. The potential for expanding the area of cooperation is considerable.

For example, in view of the inevitability of bilateral economic disputes, much thought has been given to possible methods of improving conflict resolution. Although the idea is not new, a recent effort has been made to institute an "early warning system." This is intended to give the two sides time to anticipate potential or impending problems, thereby, it is asserted, increasing the chances for a prompt and effective resolution of the problem rather than, as is often the case, waiting until it assumes a political character and becomes the subject of acrimony and mutual retaliation.

The concept is unobjectionable, and, indeed, tangible results can be expected over time. Nonetheless, the potential benefits from an early warning system should not be exaggerated. Disputes often reflect differing economic interests and philosophies, with resolution coming only at the end of a tough, often unpleasant bargaining process. That has certainly been the case with most of the agricultural disputes between the United States and the EU: the issues and differences were clear to all, but resolution, to the extent it has occurred, has proven difficult.

A new element that could affect the resolution of US-EU trade disputes is the dispute resolution mechanism introduced as a principal innovation of the WTO, and intended to correct one of the deficiencies of the procedures of the General Agreement on Tariffs and Trade (GATT). However, it remains to be seen how that mechanism will in fact affect US-EU disputes, particularly in view of the ambiguity on the US side between its desire for a strong legally based structure for dispute resolution that is not subject to political influence and its concern over the element of supranationality that could limit its freedom to undertake what it considers to be appropriate remedial action.

An important area for potential expansion of cooperation is the differences in the regulatory regimes of the EU and the United States (see Chapter 8), the source of many bilateral problems and obstacles to trade. This is an area of key importance to the US business community: at a widely attended meeting organized by the US Department of Commerce in mid–1995 to initiate a US-EU business dialogue, the US companies and trade associations identified as their highest priority fast action on establishing the mutual recognition of product standards, testing, and certification. As described in Chapter 8, for a variety of historical and other reasons, the systems of setting standards, testing products, and certifying conformity to standards often vary significantly between the two sides of the Atlantic; in addition, the United States and the EU use different administrative and legal systems. Hence, the task of reducing the impediments to trade arising from regulatory differences will be difficult. Nonetheless, it is in the economic interest of both sides—i.e., to facilitate the interchange of goods and services—that these differences be bridged in ways that standardize and speed up the respective procedures. This should remain an important objective of the US-EU dialogue.

Looking beyond regulatory cooperation, dialogues have been initiated between the United States and the EU in recent years on a variety of subjects where there is mutual interest in exchanging information and ideas. Although some of these subjects might be termed "traditional," such as customs procedures and training, many are issues with important implications for the future, on which governments are seeking to develop new policies, both domestically and internationally. For example, dialogues have been initiated in biotechnology, high technology, and the information superhighway; however, clearly there is room for more such activity.

Moving from the bilateral to the multilateral scene, there is a strong convergence of views between the United States and the EU on a number of international economic issues, and thus potential for cooperation in their mutual interest. This is clearly the case with respect to the opening of foreign markets. However, the situation in Japan illustrates the difficulties inherent in working together. Both the United States and the EU would benefit from improved access to the Japanese market. However, leaving aside the merits and demerits of any particular approach, the United States and the EU are to some extent in competition with each other over Japan, and each harbors a degree of suspicion about the other's motives. The EU fears that the United States seeks to conclude deals in which it is the main beneficiary, while the United States believes the EU prefers the US to perform the "heavy work" of negotiation while expecting an equal share in the results. In addition, the two sides disagree over tactics—the EU traditionally opts for "quiet diplomacy," while the United States is inclined to attack frontally—and it has proven difficult, if not impossible, to achieve a meeting of the minds.[5]

This suspicion was evident in the 1995 dispute between the United States and Japan over access to the latter's market for automobiles and parts. The EU concurred in the US portrayal of the problem but publicly decried US tactics; the United States alleged that the EU was aiding the Japanese by siding with them in questioning the legality of the US action and then (as a reward) obtaining a side arrangement from the Japanese on inspection.

The United States and the EU also share a common interest in broadening the scope of international economic activity that falls under international disciplines. Through joint US-EU efforts, that process began with the introduction of services and trade-related intellectual property and investment measures in the Uruguay Round agreement. It is important that these efforts continue, particularly in the field of investment where enormous economic interests are at stake that are essentially identical in the United States and the EU.

Just as political integration in the EU contains the seeds of conflict with the United States, it also contains the potential for cooperation. However, as mentioned above, the convergence of US and EU interests and objectives make cooperation, not conflict, the likeliest course. The range of issues for possible US-EU political cooperation is vast, although less specific and less subject to measurement of results than in the economic sphere. In a major speech on transatlantic relations in June 1995, US Secretary of State Warren Christopher stressed this theme, listing four areas where he urged US-EU cooperative efforts: halting the spread of weapons of mass destruction; fighting international crime and terrorism; coordinating humanitarian and development assistance; and cooperating in regions where the US-EU share interests and historical ties, such as in the Mediterranean and the Middle East.[6]

Multivoiced Union: Finding an Interlocutor

The ability of the United States and the EU to carry out their relationship, and thus the potential for working together on a broad range of issues, is diminished by the fact that the Union is not the equivalent of a sovereign government but rather is based on a unique mixture of powers ceded to the EU institutions (or decided upon by less than unanimity) and others left in the hands of the member states. Although some Americans yearn for an EU "speaking with one voice"—and, indeed, urge that the process of European integration advance so that that will be the case—in reality, the situation is ambiguous and will remain so for the foreseeable future. The United States must necessarily deal with (a) the Council (i.e., the member states), a collective decision-making body with a rotating leadership; (b) the Commission, the EU's executive arm that serves as de facto representative of the EU to third countries; and (c) the Parliament, which plays an increasingly important role in the legislative process, but a considerably lesser one in other areas. Clearly, the EU has no single voice—there is no single interlocutor.

This situation has been little affected by the integration process. What has changed is the broadened scope of activities undertaken at the EU, rather than member state, level and the increased potential for cooperative US-EU activities. Hence, the search by the United States for the most effective interaction with people or institutions acting on behalf of the EU.

Over the years, US government officials have debated the relative importance of the Commission and the member states as the focal point of US efforts to influence EU decision making and develop mutually supportive policies and programs. Some assert that the main interlocutor of the United States, hence the main focus of attention, should be the member states because, as representatives on the Council, they hold the ultimate decision-making power. Others counter that US efforts should be focused on the Commission because of its central role in all EU activities and because in so doing the United States enhances the position of the Commission, a development that accords with US interests. The premise of the latter assertion is that the Commission's interests and objectives on the whole coincide with those of the United States and that the Commission is often an "ally" of the United States in influencing the positions of the member states.

There is some truth to this claim. In a number of areas, the Commission not only subscribes to positions that accord with US interests but is able to influence EU policy in that direction. The most notable example is trade policy: the Commission has generally been a force for liberalization, contributing over time to a softening of the protectionist orientation of some of the member states. However, as described earlier, the Commission's room for maneuver is limited; it can negotiate only on the basis of a mandate from the member states. In addition, the Commission has often proven unable or unwilling to take firm action against member states not carrying out the terms of an agreement or exploiting areas of ambiguity in political commitments. Furthermore, the competence of the Commission, particularly in noneconomic matters, is limited. Thus, in areas where the United States would welcome closer cooperation—especially the third pillar—the Commission is a minor participant.

To a large extent, US dealings with the Council take place with the member states. The Council's secretariat does not fill the role of representative of the Council or channel of communication for nonmember countries in the same way as does the Commission, although contacts between the United States and the secretariat do take place (see below). In a formal, and for the most part practical, sense, the representative of the Council is the member state holding the Presidency at a particular time, and it is to that country that most US approaches are made.

Not surprisingly, there is a certain amount of rivalry between the Commission and Council, and thus the United States can be placed in an intriguing position when there is a tug-of-war between the Commission and member states regarding their respective roles. Often, each looks for "recognition" from the outside. Occasionally, both the Commission and the member states attend an international conference, at which the Commission seeks to speak on behalf of the EU, while the member states insist on speaking individually on their own behalf. In another manifestation of the same phenomenon, when the United States and Russia convened a meeting on the problem of ex-Yugoslavia in mid–1994, member states and EU institutions pressed the US State Department for invitations to attend as part of the European representation because they could not agree among themselves. Needless to say, the United States may be able to use the leverage presented it on such occasions to its advantage.

However, the issue of EU interlocutors for the United States should not be seen as an either-or proposition. Rather, the lines of communication between the United States and the EU must encompass the Commission, the Council/member states, and to an increasing extent the

Parliament. The relative degree of attention the United States needs to focus on one or the other institution will depend on the subject matter.

Insofar as EU legislation is concerned, the three main EU institutions (other than the European Court of Justice) are involved. The Commission plays a key role by initiating proposals; thus, it is important to seek to influence the contents of its proposals before they have been formally approved internally. Similarly, efforts should be made to influence the actions of the Parliament, at least in areas where the cooperation and, particularly, co-decision procedures apply. However, as the final arbiter of legislation, the Council is the most obvious point of contact, in other words, the member states, although occasionally the secretariat will be used as a channel for transmitting US views.

Often overlooked is the importance of timing. It would be wrong to assume that the member states do not become involved in the development of legislation until late in the process. Almost invariably, they are deeply involved from the moment the Commission initiates its internal consideration of a legislative proposal because the Commission wants at least some assurance that its draft legislation will ultimately gain member state acceptance.

On CFSP, the main interlocutor of the United States is the member state holding the Council Presidency, regardless of which one, or the three members of the troika. In addition, the United States works closely with the CFSP unit of the Council secretariat. On some foreign policy issues, notably ex-Yugoslavia, the United States works closely with members of the UN Security Council (France and the United Kingdom, plus any other member states that might hold a rotational seat). In any event, the United States maintains an intense dialogue on foreign policy issues (whether or not related to CFSP) with the major member states.

However, the US dialogue with the EU over foreign policy issues also includes the Commission. In addition to holding an unofficial "16th seat" at the Council table on CFSP, it is the source of funds to carry out whatever EU policies are decided upon (especially the granting of aid).

Not unlike the situation obtaining with CFSP, exchanges on matters pertaining to the third pillar include those with the relevant part of the Council secretariat, member states, and the Commission. In fact, on all issues where competence is shared between the Commission and Council, the United States maintains contacts with both institutions, including the Council secretariat.

None of these considerations should mask the weakness of the EU as a partner with which the United States can deal on an equal footing—one that can speak with authority on behalf of the EU and can deliver on undertakings. That weakness, of course, is inherent in the makeup of the

EU, a circumstance that may—or, more likely, not—be changed by the IGC.

A final consideration. Despite the effort to find valid EU interlocutors for the United States, the conclusion should not be drawn that US interests inevitably are best served by actions taken at the EU level rather than by the member states. Civil aviation negotiations is a case in point. The United States has pressed member state aviation authorities to agree to "open skies" agreements, under which all restrictions on destinations, fares, and frequencies are eliminated. Such agreements are attractive to European airlines desiring increased access to the US market. They also accord with the interest of US airlines, in particular because they can gain traffic rights for internal European travel by combining the rights obtained in bilateral agreements between the United States and individual member states. In 1995, the United States concluded such agreements with Austria, Belgium, Denmark, Finland, Luxembourg, and Sweden.

The Commission has sought to end this practice and assume responsibility for civil aviation negotiations on behalf of the EU on the grounds that the competitive threat from US airlines can be limited by the increased negotiating leverage that would be obtained through a single EU negotiator. However, it can gain such powers only if they are granted by the member states, which have, however, shown little enthusiasm for ceding these prerogatives to the Commission.

Facing the Twenty-First Century: A New Relationship?

As the twenty-first century approaches, the context of the US-EU relationship is changing: the US security umbrella no longer protects Europe from an unfriendly, if not hostile, power in the East; the boundaries of the EU now cover virtually all of Western Europe and will soon spread into much of Central Europe; however, concurrent with the EU's expansion, the strains among conflicting interests and objectives inside the Union have intensified, thus threatening the homogeneity of the EU, which will in any event be shattered when economic and monetary union (EMU) is established; meanwhile, the level of attention to and interest in European developments has shrunk in the United States.[7]

As extensively described in this book, the US-EU relationship remains a crucial one; if it is effectively managed, the United States and the EU will reap both the economic and political benefits. What, then, should be the form and content of that relationship?

A key element must be an active and extensive dialogue and consultation. Obviously, dialogue and consultation will not in themselves ensure that all problems will be resolved amicably, but they can contribute significantly to mutual understanding, thereby increasing the likelihood that ways will be found to work together in the economic and political spheres and that solutions to problems, or at least ways of containing them, will be found.

This has, in fact, been taking place, and at an accelerating pace, particularly as the scope of "domestic concerns" has increasingly impinged on relations among nations. Over an ever-broadening range of issues, officials of the United States and the EU discuss common issues, problems, and solutions. To some extent this dialogue has been structured—as in the periodic meetings between the US Food and Drug Administration (FDA) and counterpart officials at the Commission—but it is not always the case, nor need it be.

The overall US-EU relationship is covered by a formal consultative structure codified in the Transatlantic Declaration, entered into in 1990. In the Declaration, a bilateral statement of principles, the United States and the EU "reaffirm their determination further to strengthen their partnership." The Declaration provides, inter alia, for biannual meetings of the President of the United States with the Commission and Council presidents, the US Secretary of State with the member state foreign ministers and the president of the Commission, and US-EU cabinet-level meetings. The intention of the regularly scheduled meetings is to force the highest level of policy makers on both sides to focus on issues of common concern, as well as to give impetus to the process of broadening and deepening the bilateral dialogue, and this has been the result.

These meetings, with the exception of cabinet meetings, have taken place regularly. In place of the latter, periodic subcabinet meetings—i.e., senior officials from US agencies and the Commission—have been held. This has proven to be a very useful forum (more so than cabinet meetings would have been) for discussing issues and working toward their resolution.

While these developments have all contributed to US-EU cooperation, two caveats are in order. First, it is important that form not be mistaken, or substituted, for substance. The fact that periodic meetings take place does not in itself ensure a close, mutually beneficial relationship. Second, dialogue and consultations will not necessarily produce agreement, or even reduce the level of mutual ill-will—as the results of thirty-plus years of consultations and discussions on the Common Agricultural Policy (CAP) make clear. However, on balance, just as the development of the habit of consultation and working together among member state officials is leading to greater understanding and cooperation, so is it the case for the US-EU dialogue.

Nonetheless, in early 1995, proposals began to surface for the United States and the EU to enter into a closer, more formal relationship. The proponents argued as follows: The United States and the EU are in danger of drifting apart as each becomes more inward-looking (the EU concentrating on development of the Union, the United States on domestic concerns), each is turning its focus to another area of the world (the EU to Central and Eastern Europe, the United States to Asia), and the traditional security bonds are loosened (the common security threat from the Soviet Union has disappeared, and people with direct experience of the World War II and the early postwar era are dying). These developments run counter to the interests of the two sides. Both the EU and the United States will gain from a wider, deeper relationship.[8] The existing substance of and institutional arrangements for interaction are inadequate for taking advantage of the possibilities; hence, it is maintained, a new "glue" is required.

It should be noted that the impetus for "doing something" is greater on the European side than on the American, reflecting European concerns about the consequences of a perceived diminution in the US interest in and commitment to Europe. It is also motivated in part by concern over US efforts to engage in competitive liberalization of trade, i.e., working toward free trade areas in the Asia-Pacific area and in Latin America. In mid–1995 both the European Council and the incoming Spanish Presidency called for a strengthening of the transatlantic dialogue, and the Commission launched a study for presentation to the Council on substance and mechanisms for deepening the US-EU relationship.

Proposals fell into two categories. One took as its point of departure the Transatlantic Declaration, the other regional trading agreements. The declaration is viewed by some as a disappointment or missed opportunity in that it has entered the scene virtually unnoticed. Although it has served a useful purpose by establishing (or formalizing) the bilateral consultative process, it has not galvanized public interest and support for the relationship. The proposed remedy was to build on the declaration in some way, possibly through a further, more far-reaching statement of principles or specific obligations or perhaps even a US-EU treaty modeled, for example, on the Franco-German Treaty of 1963 (whose value is largely, but no less importantly, symbolic). Such an effort would be directed primarily to the United States; its purpose would be to "renew the contract," by directing public attention in the United States to the relationship and to increase the level of official US engagement in European affairs. In addition, it would presumably contain a security dimension.

The other proposal was to enter into a bilateral economic agreement, most frequently referred to as a Transatlantic Free Trade Agreement (TAFTA). Although proposed in one of its earliest versions by US labor union leader Lane Kirkland as an alternative to North American Free Trade Agreement (NAFTA)[9] and largely ignored at the time, the proposal took on new life through the convergence of views of those concerned with the future of US-EU relations and with the next steps in global trade liberalization. According to its proponents, TAFTA would remove the not insignificant bilateral tariffs that remain as well as move beyond those barriers to areas not presently or adequately covered under the WTO, such as investment and services.

A variation was a Transatlantic European Space, an economic umbrella encompassing a number of cooperative activities. Such a "Space" would presumably include a TAFTA plus a variety of other agreements—forming "building blocks" for the relationship—on issues that could range from competition policy to public procurement.

There are weaknesses in both of these approaches. Building on the Transatlantic Declaration would add little substance to the US-EU relationship; it is doubtful that in itself it would rekindle the spirit and actuality of cooperation. In any event, it does not conform to the normal framework of US relations with other countries and thus could cause perplexity and stir up opposition on procedural grounds that could be counterproductive.

Although TAFTA could advance trade liberalization for both the United States and the EU, the proposal gives rise to three legitimate concerns:

- that it would detract from important multilateral trade objectives by bringing the major share of world trade under a preferential arrangement;
- that because agricultural trade would not be included (unrestricted US-EU trade in agricultural products would be incompatible with the CAP), TAFTA would be neither politically nor legally feasible—politically in terms of acceptability to the US and legally in terms of conformity with the GATT (which requires that "substantially" all trade be covered); and
- that it is unrealistic to expect that greater liberalization in trade and related fields can be agreed upon between the United States and the EU than what was concluded in the Uruguay Round (where they were the main protagonists).

In essence, the two approaches merged as discussions proceeded during the year between the United States and the EU on redefining or relaunching the bilateral relationship. The result was the adoption at the US-EU summit meeting in Madrid in December of what was termed "the new transatlantic agenda," consisting of a statement of purpose and a joint US-EU action plan. The agenda takes the consultative mechanism of the Transatlantic Declaration as a point of departure, but moves into specific areas for common action. The statement of purpose lists four major goals: promoting peace and stability, democracy and development around the world; responding to global challenges; contributing to the expansion of world trade and closer economic relations; and building bridges across the Atlantic. The action plan consists of a lengthy, detailed enumeration of areas for common action. Although a few relate to specific immediate undertakings (e.g., the aim to conclude a bilateral customs cooperation and mutual assistance agreement by the end of 1996), the vast majority are hortatory or general: "we will work together," "we will cooperate closely," "we will endeavor to conclude," "we will explore." No mention was made of the proposed TAFTA; rather, it was agreed that a joint study would be undertaken on facilitating trade and further reducing or eliminating tariff and non-tariff barriers.

It is premature to pass judgement on the new transatlantic agenda. Without any doubt it establishes an ambitious, comprehensive framework for the United States and the EU to work together to achieve mutual goals in the coming years. As such, it represents a serious attempt to highlight the importance of the bilateral relationship and the potential for mutually advantageous common action. Whether it remains a wish list or serves as the basis for intensified, meaningful activities will depend on many factors, including political will on both sides, the ability to bridge genuine differences in approach and attitude, and the institutional ability (particularly on the EU side) to deliver results.

Whatever the outcome, the key consideration is that the bilateral relationship can and should be significantly improved—there is insufficient mutual understanding, exchange of facts and ideas, and combined efforts at problem-solving. Both sides would gain much from a stronger relationship.

However, there is no obvious way to achieve this objective, nor is it indisputable that an overarching structure or framework is required. Mature reflection is more likely to produce meaningful answers than a search for a political or psychological quick-fix—and in any event, the ability of the EU to move on many issues will be limited until the conclusion of the Intergovernmental Conference (IGC). In the last analysis, success in enhancing the relationship will be determined largely by the conscious effort of leaders and followers on both sides to work together, based on their recognition that it is in their mutual interest to do so. The process should be incremental: identifying economic, political, and "third pillar" areas where the two sides can move from consultation to joint action, undertaking such action, and building on the progress achieved.[10] Structural changes will supplement, but not replace, that process.

Private Sector

The types of concerns of the US private sector vary considerably depending on whether the firms in question have invested or are otherwise physically present in the Union or are exporters of goods or services from the outside. Although the interests of these two groups overlap in certain EU policies and actions, their perspectives are somewhat different. The first group seeks to be treated and to be able to participate in EU economic and political life on the same basis as European companies; the second is concerned with barriers to entry and access to decision making.

In either case the two critical elements are involved:

- Obtaining information relevant to company operations (bearing in mind that, in many cases, the definition of "relevant" must be interpreted broadly). That can be accomplished in various ways: through a company's own resources, through the services of representative organizations, by hiring consultant services, or a combination thereof.
- Establishing a mechanism or mechanisms for influencing decisionmakers. For companies established in the EU, an important component of that mechanism must be recognition as an EU enterprise. Such recognition will increase their credibility and the likelihood that they will be treated on the same basis as other EU firms, irrespective of the source of their capital or seat of control. Although this is partly a matter of law, it is also a matter of conduct and the resulting public perception. To some extent, companies, particularly larger ones, will prefer to undertake some activities on their own. However, virtually all companies will find it advantageous to work in groups: alliances with like-minded companies and as participants in representative organizations. Despite the inherent weakness in representative organizations—the necessity to forge a consensus among members' views, which frequently dilutes the effort—the latter are on the whole the most effective influencers of decision-makers in the EU.

In connection with these two elements, mention should be made of the unique role filled by the European Union Committee of the American Chamber of Commerce in Belgium. Representing the interests of companies of American parentage in Europe—and including a significant percentage of membership from among firms and individuals servicing such companies—the committee has carved out an important niche as a major repository of information relevant to US business and an influential and effective lobbying organization. In addition, at the initiative of the US Department of Commerce and the European Commission, a Transatlantic Business Dialogue was established in 1995 to bring together private sector leaders from both sides of the Atlantic to identify commercial issues of mutual interest which they believe merit the attention of and action by governments in the coming years. In their first meeting held in Seville in November 1995, chief executive officers of American and European companies called on political leaders in the United States and the EU to remove all obstacles and public policy impediments to the operation of the market on both sides of the Atlantic, and, more generally, to promote the transatlantic business relationship, work toward an open world trading system, and help develop a secure framework for international investment. The conference participants submitted specific recommendations in four areas—standards, certification, and regulatory policy; trade liberalization,; investment; and issues relating to third countries— and agreed to hold a follow-up meeting in 1996.

A final point is the important contribution of the US government in promoting the interests of the US private sector. Both with regard to company-specific problems and particularly to sectoral concerns, the US government has a proven record of assisting US companies in defending their legitimate interests, especially against discriminatory treatment. Among the long list of such instances, mention should be made of the US government's opposition to the original reciprocity provisions of the second banking directive, efforts to limit quotas on foreign broadcasting, and assistance to the US power-generating equipment industry in gaining access to member state public markets.

In any event, the potential for US business in the evolving European Union is great, and the advantage taken of it will depend in the first instance on the efforts of the US private sector, supplemented by the support given it by the US government.

Notes

1. Robin Gaster and Clyde V. Prestowitz, "Shrinking the Atlantic: Europe and the American Economy" (Washington: North Atlantic Research Inc. and Economic Strategy Institute, 1994), p. 1.

2. Berlin, July 13, 1994.

3. Speech to a multinational audience of future leaders of Europe, January 9, 1994.

4. Ambassador Stuart Eizenstat speech to British Conservative Association in Belgium, Brussels, July 5, 1994.

5. EU officials complain that the United States is not prepared to consider alternative strategies, viewing the relationship, in the words of one, as similar to that between the Lone Ranger (US) and Tonto (EU).

6. "Charting a Transatlantic Agenda for the 21st Century," Casa de America, Madrid, June 2, 1995.

7. One indication of the latter is reported in John E. Rielly, *American Public Opinion and U.S. Foreign Policy, 1995* (Chicago: Chicago Council on Foreign Relations, 1995), p. 24, which records a sharp drop between 1986 and 1994 in respondents considering that the United States has a vital interest in France, Germany, and the United Kingdom.

8. See, for example, Bruce Stokes, "How to set the transatlantic ball rolling," *Financial Times*, April 19, 1995.

9. Lane Kirkland, "A Trade Marriage Made in Heaven," *Washington Post*, May 19, 1993.

10. Such an approach, though limited to the economic relationship, was articulated by Robert B. Zoellick, formerly a senior official in the Bush administration, in "How to Achieve Trans-Atlantic Free Trade," *The Wall Street Journal Europe*, June 14, 1995.

Selected Bibliography

Andrews, John. "Family friction (A survey of the European Union)." *The Economist*, October 22, 1994.

Belmont European Policy Centre. *The New Treaty on European Union*, Volume 2: Legal and Political Analyses. Brussels, 1992.

Brittan, Leon. *Europe: The Europe We Need*. London: Hamish Hamilton, 1994.

Buigues, Pierre, and John Sheehy, "The Internal Market Program—The Impact on European Integration." Brussels: Doc. II/133/95. European Commission, 1995.

Cooney, Stephen. *American Industry and the New European Union*. Washington: National Association of Manufacturers, 1994.

Dinan, Desmond. *Ever Closer Union? An Introduction to the European Community*. Boulder: Lynne Rienner Publishers, 1994.

European Commission. "Completing the Internal Market," White Paper from the Commission to the European Council. COM(85) 310. Brussels, June 14, 1985.

———. "Growth, competitiveness, employment. The challenges and ways forward into the 21st century." *Bulletin of the European Communities*, Supplement 6/93. Luxembourg: Office for Official Publications of the European Communities, 1993.

———. "Making the most of the internal market: Strategic Programme," Communication from the Commission to the Council. COM(93) 632. Brussels, December 22, 1993.

———. "State of Community law concerning the internal market." Published semi-annually.

———. "The Community Internal Market: 1993 Report." COM(94) 55. Brussels, March 14, 1994.

———. "The Single Market in 1994." COM(95) 238. Brussels, June 15, 1995.

Grant, Charles. *Delors: Inside the House that Jacques Built*. London: Nicholas Brealey Publishing, 1994.

Hoeller, Peter, and Marie-Odile Louppe. "The EC's Internal Market: Implementation, Economic Consequences, Unfinished Business." Working Papers No. 147, OECD/GD(94)87. Paris: Organization for Economic Cooperation and Development, Economics Department, 1994.

Lipsius, Justus. "The 1996 Intergovernmental Conference." *European Law Review*. Vol. 20, No. 3, June 1995.

Ludlow, Peter. et al. *Preparing for 1996 and a Larger European Union: Principles and Priorities*. CEPS Special Report No. 6. Brussels: Centre for European Policy Studies, 1995.

Nugent, Neill, ed. *The European Union 1994: Annual Review of Activities.* Oxford: Blackwell Publishers, 1995.

Smith, Michael, and Stephen Woolcock. *The United States and the European Community in a Transformed World.* London: Royal Institute of International Affairs, Pinter Publishers, 1993.

US Chamber of Commerce, International Division. *Europe 1992: A Practical Guide for American Business* (Update #4). Washington: US Chamber of Comerce, 1993.

Index

About the Book and Author

In this fresh and timely account, Michael Calingaert explores the successes and failures of European economic and political integration, analyzes the factors that will determine its future course, and outlines the directions in which the European Union is moving as it approaches the twenty-first century. Assessing U.S. interests affected by European integration, Calingaert recommends policies for the United States to consider in the face of an increasingly integrated Europe. With its broad coverage and readable synthesis of a wealth of detailed information, this book will be of interest to students, scholars, and policymakers alike.

Specializing in economic and commercial affairs as a career diplomat, Michael Calingaert held a variety of senior positions at American embassies (Economic Minister in London and Rome) and at the State Department (Deputy Assistant Secretary in the Bureau of Economic Affairs). In 1989, Mr. Calingaert moved to the private sector. For four years, as the Pharmaceutical Manufacturers Association's Director of European Operations, he represented the interests of the U.S. research-based pharmaceutical industry in the European Community.

While a Visiting Senior Fellow at the National Planning Association in Washington, Mr. Calingaert wrote the first U.S. study of the EC's single market, the widely acclaimed *The 1992 Challenge from Europe: Development of the European Community's Internal Market* (1988).

Mr. Calingaert renewed his affiliation with the National Planning Association in 1993 as a Senior Fellow. In 1994 he was also appointed Research Fellow at the Institute of European Studies of the Free University of Brussels. In the same year he co-founded the Monnet-Madison Institute.

Today Mr. Calingaert is a consultant and author on European affairs and U.S.-European relations. He has written numerous articles for *Business Economics, California Management Review, The New York Times,* and various other publications.